# The God of Gods

# The God of Gods: A Canadian Play

by

CARROLL AIKINS

*A Critical Edition*
*Edited and with an Introduction by*
KAILIN WRIGHT

University of Ottawa Press | OTTAWA

uOttawa

EDITING MODERNISM in Canada

The University of Ottawa Press gratefully acknowledges the support extended to its publishing list by the Government of Canada and by the Canada Council for the Arts. This book has been published with the help of a grant from the Federation for the Humanities and Social Sciences, through the Awards to Scholarly Publications Program, using funds provided by the Social Sciences and Humanities Research Council of Canada.

Copy editing: Helen Guri
Proofreading: Robbie McCaw
Typesetting: CS
Cover design: Lisa Marie Smith
Cover image: *Cumshewa* by Emily Carr (detail), 1912. Watercolour over graphite on wove paper, mounted on cardboard, 52 x 75.5 cm. Reproduced with permission from the National Gallery of Ottawa. Photo © NGC.

**Library and Archives Canada Cataloguing in Publication**

Aikins, Carroll, 1888-1967, author
The god of gods : a Canadian play / Carroll Aikins ; edited by Kailin Wright. -- A critical edition.

Includes bibliographical references.
Issued in print and electronic formats.
ISBN 978-0-7766-2327-6 (paperback).--ISBN 978-0-7766-2329-0 (pdf).--
ISBN 978-0-7766-2328-3 (epub)

I. Wright, Kailin, editor II. Title.

PS8501.I45A17 2016 C812'.52 C2016-901977-2
C2016-901978-0

# Contents

# Table of Figures

# Acknowledgements

This project was generously funded by the Editing Modernism in Canada project in affiliation with the Social Sciences and Research Council of Canada, as well as by St. Francis Xavier University's Start-up Grant and University Council for Research Award. The University of Toronto also offered valuable support during this project's early stages. This book has been published with the help of a grant from the Federation for the Humanities and Social Sciences, through the Awards to Scholarly Publications Program, using funds provided by the Social Sciences and Humanities Research Council of Canada.

I am especially grateful to the estates of Carroll Aikins and Sir Barry Jackson for their assistance with this project and with copyright. I received essential resources—including theatre reviews, critical essays, and photographs—from interviews and correspondence with Alan Filewod (University of Guelph), James Hoffman (Thompson Rivers University), and Jerry Wasserman (University of Victoria). Craig Henderson, members of the Naramata Heritage Museum, Peter Ord at the Penticton Museum and Archives, and Naramata elders generously shared histories of Naramata and the Aikins family. Participants at the Editing Modernism in Canada Conference on Editorial Problems (University of Toronto, 2010) were integral to the shape of this project; the questions, discussions, and fellow panelists informed the theoretical scope of the critical introduction.

Many thanks are due to my colleagues and mentors at the University of Toronto and St. Francis Xavier University as well as to the members of the Editing Modernism in Canada project. For their expertise and assistance during the course of my research, I would like to offer my heartfelt thanks to Colin Hill (University of Toronto), Dean Irvine (Dalhousie University), and Mary Nyquist (University of Toronto). Colin Hill and Dean Irvine provided essential research and training opportunities in Canadian modernism as well as editing. My University of Toronto colleagues, Tony Fong, Jennifer McDermott, and Spencer Morrison, offered helpful comments on earlier drafts of the introduction. Laura Estill (Texas A&M), in particular, was a reader at every stage. I am also indebted to Melissa Dalgleish (York University), who served as a tireless and insightful research assistant on this project.

The editorial team at the University of Ottawa Press's Canadian Literature Collection—in particular Dean Irvine, Elizabeth Schwaiger, and Dominike Thomas—helped bring this book to press and I am very grateful for their editorial expertise.

Finally, I want to thank the librarians at the Thomas Fisher Rare Book Library, the Birmingham Library, the Victoria and Albert Museum, and the University of London Senate House Library for gently guiding me through the rough hollows of the archives.

# Introduction

Separated lovers, a tree-clad "Indian" reserve, and a woman who jumps to her death do not comprise a "new" (*Evening Despatch*) or "unusual" (*Stage*) play by today's standards, but early-twentieth-century reviewers clamoured for *The God of Gods*' (1918) "original" (E. C.) tale of "the North American Indian" (Johnston).[1] Written by Carroll Aikins, an avid promoter of Canadian theatre, *The God of Gods* has been performed in the United Kingdom more often than in Canada and found its first success during its premiere at the Birmingham Repertory Theatre, in 1919, when reviewers applauded the "rare artistic delicacy" (*Evening Despatch*) and heralded it as "the first drama written by a Canadian to be presented in England" ("A Reader's Notes" *Winnipeg*). As a result of its popularity, the play returned to the Birmingham Repertory Theatre for a second run, in 1920.[2] It was later mounted in Canada at Toronto's Hart House Theatre in 1922 and again in the United Kingdom at London's Everyman Theatre in 1931.[3]

Credited for "put[ting] Naramata on the map," Aikins (1888–1964) was born in Stanstead, Quebec; educated in Winnipeg, Manitoba; and later became a prominent community member of Naramata, British Columbia, where he operated one hundred acres of farmland and a fruit-packing business while also pursuing a productive career in the arts as a poet, playwright, director, and theatre founder (Berry 4). How a playwright, poet, and theatre practitioner came to own one hundred acres of farmland poses something of a mystery, but Aikins's father was a real-estate agent who invested in Naramata and convinced Aikins to move, presumably for health reasons. Aikins's health problem (a spot on his lung) had been an issue for some time, taking him to Europe (where he reportedly met theatrical modernists Gordon Craig and Adolphe Appia) and preventing him from enlisting in the ambulance corps (Berry 4).[4] Aikins's daughter, Carroll A. Beichman, recounts that Aikins met Craig in Paris before World War I during one of his trips abroad. The dry, warm weather of Naramata likely made it an ideal place for Aikins's health in Canada.

While in Naramata, Aikins wrote at least four plays: *The Destroyers: A Drama in Three Acts* (1915), *The Fullness of Life: A Play in Three Acts* (1917), *Real Estate: A Comedy in Three Acts* (1918), and *The God of Gods* (1918). *The Destroyers* critiques Canada's involvement in the war and characterizes the demands of patriotic duty as a form of slavery. This stringent anti-war sentiment likely explains why the play was never produced, and O'Neill suggests that "this may be the only Canadian play written during either of the world wars or the Korean conflict to espouse such anti-war sentiment during the actual warfare" (70). Both *The Fullness of Life* and *Real Estate* are rooted in British Columbia's history and dramatize the lives of Naramata citizens. *The Fullness of Life* takes place in the Cascade Mountains and contemplates socially sanctioned expressions of love, challenging the notion that marriage is love's fullest expression. The play's contemplation of societal definitions of love resonates with *The God of Gods* because Yellow Snake questions the divine expectation that Suiva remain a virgin. Aikins's Yellow Snake voices a progressive sexuality that does not demand virginity from women and that calls into question the devotion to fear above love in the name of spirituality. As the title *Real Estate* suggests, the main character of that play, Joseph West, is a real-estate agent. The role may have been inspired both by Aikins's father, John Somerset Aikins, who convinced Aikins to move to Naramata, and the town's founder, John Moore Robinson, who actively sold land. Called "the father of Peachland, Summerland and Naramata," Robinson travelled to the Okanagan to make his fortune in mining but ended up selling land (Salting 3). Robinson's daughter has the same name as Joseph West's daughter in the play, further linking these two real-estate peddlers (Henderson). Robinson is well-known in Naramata for promoting the area as the "California of the North" and for selling land with false promises of a year-long summer—humorous sales techniques that echo Joseph West's tall tales of the riches of British Columbia (Henderson). *The God of Gods* stands out as Aikins's only script with an all-aboriginal cast of characters, and, perhaps as a result, as his only play to reach the stage.

There are a number of elements—besides Aikins's contribution to the development of Canadian theatre and the play's international acclaim—that make *The God of Gods* a rich subject of inquiry and account for its successful production history. These include its aboriginal motifs, anti-materialist themes, theosophical philosophy, subtle anti-war politics, theatrical modernist techniques, and Nietzschean intertexts. Integrating the play's anti-materialist and theosophical messages, the aboriginal hero enshrines a highly expressionistic landscape as a metonym for a new social system founded on egalitarianism. While the play's political messages and modernist production techniques offer rich fields of study for scholars today, the early-twentieth-century theatre reviews, production images, and playbills concentrate on the entertaining allure of the aboriginal characters. Ultimately, these historical documents offer a look into how British and Canadian theatre audiences responded to primitivism, theatrical modernism, and theosophical tenets from the play's inception in 1918 to its final production in 1931.

Set in a mountainous landscape that closely resembles Naramata, Aikins's play warns against corrupt power and materialist greed by depicting the fall of an aboriginal community. The play concentrates on two lovers: Suiva and her beloved rebel suitor Yellow Snake, "the singer" (see fig. 1). Suiva, however, is the love interest of not one but two men: the community's outsider, Yellow Snake, and the chief's son, Mablo. Driven by romantic jealousy, Mablo gathers his men to kill the singer. The play ends when Suiva discovers her lover's death, realizes that the religious system is corrupt, and, echoing Friedrich Nietzsche, announces: "God is dead" (66). With the climactic final scene, Aikins erects the lover-artist figure Yellow Snake as the ultimate creator and true God. Reviewers praised this "dramatic, unexpected ending" (Johnston) and exclaimed that "the play ends on a note of real moving tragedy" (*Stage*). In the last moments of the play, Suiva throws herself into an onstage pool (see fig. 2) as the surrounding worshippers crouch in horror of her disobedience and in devotion to the idol.

FIGURE 1. SUIVA AND YELLOW SNAKE DISCUSS THEIR FUTURE IN ACT I OF THE 1919 BIRMINGHAM PRODUCTION. COURTESY OF THE BARRY JACKSON ESTATE.

FIGURE 2. SUIVA LOOKS INTO AN ONSTAGE POOL DURING THE 1919 BIRMINGHAM PRODUCTION. COURTESY OF THE BARRY JACKSON ESTATE.

## CANADIAN THEATRE HISTORY

Much of the play's historical significance lies in Aikins's vital role in Canadian theatre: he created the Home Theatre in 1920, which was built on the second floor of a fruit-packing and storage building in rural Naramata, British Columbia, and he was artistic director at Toronto's Hart House Theatre from 1927 to 1929. In 1921 and 1922, the media celebrated Aikins's Home Theatre as "the first national theatre," as "the first Canadian Little Theatre," and for producing the "first Passion play ever given in Canada" (qtd. in Hoffman 51).[5]

Aikins's wife, Katherine Aikins (see fig. 3), explains in an interview with James Hoffman, "My husband became very busy with plans for building a small theatre combined with a utilitarian packing house" ("Katherine" 13). The theatre was located on the second floor of a fruit-packing and storage building with a pitched roof and twelve rows of "mission style benches" (see fig. 3) that resembled a small rural church (Hoffman, "Katherine" 13). Opened on November 3, 1920, by Prime Minister Arthur Meighan, the Home Theatre was a rural "national theatre" with seating for one hundred viewers, touted for its not-for-profit approach to performance that elicited feedback from audience members (Hoffman, "Katherine" 13). Adding blank sheets to the programs, Aikins was invested in improving his artistry and requested that the audience's commentary on the

FIGURE 3. AIKINS'S HOME THEATRE, 1920–22 (HOFFMAN "KATHERINE" 13). COURTESY OF THE OKANAGAN ARCHIVE TRUST SOCIETY.

FIGURE 4. AN "ORIGINAL PERFORMANCE" FROM THE HOME THEATRE IN 1921 (HOFFMAN "KATHERINE" 14). COURTESY OF THE OKANAGAN ARCHIVE TRUST SOCIETY.

FIGURE 5. "KATHERINE AND CARROLL AT THE MANOR HOUSE ON REKADON RANCH, NARAMATA 1950" (HOFFMAN "KATHERINE" 12). COURTESY OF THE OKANAGAN ARCHIVE TRUST SOCIETY.

productions be returned to him. Based on photographs and an interview with Katherine, the Home Theatre's floor plan, atmosphere, and stage design has been reconstructed by Hoffman: "The stage was on floor level and extended from the first row of seats approximately thirty feet. The width of the acting area was about twenty feet. On the stage level, along the entire length of the back wall was the permanent plaster 'sky-dome' as it was then called. To one side of the stage was a small costume area" ("Katherine" 13). The lighting system, designed by Lee Simonson and manufactured in New York, has been described as "the most modern and complete in Canada" for its time ("Katherine" 13). While the Home Theatre has since been torn down, the building's ground-storey fruit-packing area remains and can be seen on the "Aikins Loop" street.

The theatre's location above a fruit-packing and storage room enabled actors and theatre students to work on local farms in order to pay for room and board. After the 1920 opening production of John Millington Synge's *The Tinker's Wedding*, with local actors, Aikins recruited students for this rare work-study opportunity. In June 1921, the Home Theatre's Canadian Players mounted student productions of Zona Gale's *The Neighbours* and Doris Halman's *Will-o-the-Wisp*. From September 1921 to the fall of 1922, the students performed Oliphant Down's *The Maker of Dreams*, a selection from Euripides's *The Trojan Women* (translated by Gilbert Murray), an original passion play entitled *Victory in Defeat:*

*A Study in Spiritual Progress in the Life of Christ*, Synge's *Riders to the Sea*, and Anatole France's *The Man Who Won a Dumb Wife*. Most notably, *Victory in Defeat* featured readings of Scripture that dramatized "The Consecration," "Mary of Bethany," "The Betrayal," "The Crucifixion," and "The Resurrection," among other scenes. The passion play, according to Hoffman, was "as close as the group ever came to an authentic, original 'art' production" as exemplified by "Craig and Appia" (64).

Reportedly, owing to the unforeseen drop in apple prices in the fall of 1922, the Home Theatre was unable to mount any future productions and closed.[6] The Home Theatre's history, for Hoffman, "like many others of the post–World War One era was a brief, but inspiring moment in the genesis of modern North American theatre" (14). In the theatre company's first program, Aikins leaves no doubt about his goals: the Home Theatre was built for "the giving of Canadian plays by Canadian actors" and "for a true expression of the Canadian spirit" (qtd. in Hoffman 56).[7] Aikins, then, was not only a playwright but was also deeply invested in defining what it meant to be a Canadian dramatist and to participate in a Canadian theatre tradition.

In the end, the theatre that Massey described as "the most significant [...] in Canada" (*Prospects* 203) never reached its full potential because of economic demands. An undated newspaper clipping in Aikins's scrapbook reveals the community's attempt to keep the Home Theatre in production through the creation of the Canadian Players' friendly Society. The society's primary objective was to raise enough money to help Mr. and Mrs. Aikins buy back their lighting equipment by inviting "contributions from all who believe with them that the closing of the Home Theatre would be a serious loss to the Canadian people" (qtd. in Hoffman 69). The community's pleas for financial help were not enough to save the theatre. With the sudden closure of the Home Theatre, Aikins's ambitions to tour and produce an all-Canadian play were never realized. Betty Clough laments that "an ironic fact was that so far as can be determined no Canadian plays were performed" at the Home Theatre (121). Likely unaware of the theatre's closure, *The Living Age* boasts of the Home Theatre's potential in 1923 and ironically dismisses the financial demands of such a project, exclaiming, "It is not, of course, a commercial undertaking. All the better! It is cram-full of promise—a daring experiment, and a fascinating one" (549).

Despite his contributions and dedication to Canadian theatre, Aikins and his work have gone relatively unacknowledged. Hoffman's "Carroll Aikins and the Home Theatre" (1986) argues for Aikins's inclusion in the Canadian theatre canon, but before this article "restored Aikins's profile to a higher level," as O'Neill surmises, "theatre historians had concurred in assigning Carroll Aikins's contributions to Canadian theatre a lesser rank than did his contemporaries"

(65). O'Neill adds to Hoffman's scholarship, offering a comprehensive overview of Aikins's otherwise forgotten plays, including those that have survived only in manuscript. O'Neill asserts that Aikins "must be acknowledged for introducing Canada to the Art Theatre movement through his playwriting and his experiments at the Home Theatre" (89). Aikins's work was influenced by modernists in Europe (Craig, Appia), the United States (the Little Theatre movement), and Canada (the Group of Seven painted the scenery for Hart House Theatre during Aikins's tenure as artistic director).

## THEATRICAL MODERNISM

Aikins was an instrumental figure in early-twentieth-century Canadian drama and in the promotion of Canadian dramatists, but his largely unpublished dramatic oeuvre still raises the question: why, in 1919, did the Birmingham Repertory Theatre decide to stage a work by a relatively unknown Canadian playwright? Still more perplexing, why did London's Everyman Theatre—that was struggling with wavering ticket sales and that was dedicated to promoting British artists—choose *The God of Gods* in 1931 as its first production under new management? Bache Matthews, in a history of the Birmingham Repertory Theatre, explains that *The God of Gods* "had never been played before, but was selected from the large number of plays offered to the theatre as showing unusual ability in its author" and that "its theatrical qualities called for stage presentations" (24). While Matthews's remarks help explain why the play was chosen for production, the reasons for *The God of Gods*' continued success abroad are open to conjecture. The Birmingham and Everyman theatres, and their audiences, may have been drawn to Aikins's play for one or more of several reasons: it had never been performed before, it critiques obedience to false religious and political figureheads, it uses what audiences would have deemed an exotic setting, and its aboriginal subject matter together with its spiritual moralizing lends itself to experimental staging.

*The God of Gods*' theatrical modernism promotes a self-reflexive aesthetic through an onstage artist-audience figure (Yellow Snake) who not only calls attention to the play's dramatic form, but also comments on social context. This commentary has a political, if not altogether radical, purpose: to critique materialism and religious idols. Modernism is, to borrow from T.S. Eliot, caught between "contemporaneity and antiquity" in its use of a myth to structure the "immense panorama of futility" that comprises modern values, such as materialism (177). James Joyce similarly uses Homer's *The Odyssey* to structure the meaninglessness of contemporary life in *Ulysses*. Whereas Eliot and Joyce import mythologies from elsewhere, Aikins is among the Canadian modernists who draw from aboriginal mythologies native to what is now called Canada.[8]

Like its European counterparts, *The God of Gods* participates in theatrical modernism. The Birmingham production fostered expressionistic lighting techniques and movement, which reinforced the play's self-reflexive awareness of drama as a genre that can encompass a variety of arts, such as dance, music, poetry, and painting. O'Neill argues that, owing in large part to Yellow Snake's singing and poetic descriptions of natural landscapes, *The God of Gods* is conducive to an expressionist directorial interpretation, a contention supported by Birmingham theatre reviewers who assert that the play "lends itself to picturesque stage treatment, which Mr. Filmer has made extremely effective (the lighting effects are noteworthy)" (*Stage*). Birmingham Repertory Theatre's first production incorporated Appia's modernist theatre techniques of projecting light onto a cyclorama—a curved wall or curtain at the back, and sometimes sides, of the stage, often used to depict a vast landscape—and of using coloured lighting as emotional expression (O'Neill). As O'Neill explains, the set was "filled with abstract trees" and "permit[ted] a variety of cyclorama lighting effects that included 'dawns, and sunsets and racing clouds,' which one reviewer found to be the best 'we have seen in Birmingham'" (85–86).[9] The set's "abstract trees" and emotive cyclorama lighting resonate with the abstraction of nature in the modernist visual arts and were popular techniques for theatrical modernists in the early twentieth century. In fact, Birmingham Repertory Theatre's artistic director, Barry Jackson, became known for his uses of expressionistic sets and lighting techniques (O'Neill).

The expressionistic lighting effects were not unique to Birmingham's productions and also align with the Home Theatre's aesthetics. The Home Theatre featured "lighting equipment capable of handling 10,000 watts of power to light a concave plaster wall at the back" in order to create cyclorama effects inspired by the Birmingham Repertory Theatre and by America's Little Theatres (O'Neill 87). In his pursuit of a theatre devoted to producing innovative Canadian plays, Aikins even consulted with Maurice Brown, who founded the Little Theatre in Chicago, and American theatre architect Lee Simonson.

Later productions of *The God of Gods* show an even deeper investment in expressionism, especially in photos of Birmingham's 1920 production (directed by Jackson). Although the Birmingham and Toronto productions were critiqued for their failure to portray a specific aboriginal tribe or geographic location, O'Neill argues that the 1920 Birmingham production's lack of particularity is a symptom of expressionism and that Paul Shelving's designs are one of the earliest examples of expressionistic drama. Shelving's costume and set designs were used for the 1920 Birmingham production (see fig. 7), and his costumes were retained for the Everyman Theatre's production in 1931. For O'Neill, Shelving's refusal "to realize any locality in its literal detail" exemplifies a move away from "photographic reality" and a "move towards a creative stagecraft in which essentials [actor's actions and speeches] are emphasized by eliminating non-essentials" (86). O'Neill asserts that "the universality of Shelving's setting transcended its particularity" of "the First Nations peoples in the mountains of British Columbia" (86). While theatre reviewers have criticized these later productions' lack of locality, O'Neill presents an alternative way to approach *The God of Gods*' set designs by embracing their universality as an innovative, expressionist choice.

In *Saturday Night* and the *Globe*'s coverage of the 1922 Hart House production, the reviewers also note the lack of geographic and ethnographic detail. "The atmosphere of the play," an anonymous reviewer for the *Globe* declares, "might be anything barbaric, but not Indian" (18). Hector Charlesworth's review in *Saturday Night* similarly extolls that the play "could be effectively laid in any part of the Western Hemisphere which includes both the Rockies and the Andes." The Canadian set designs, like their European counterparts, gesture towards an expressionist representation of the landscape that transcends national boundaries, much like Yellow Snake's Hidden Waters transcends notions of ownership or cultural differences.[10] *The God of Gods*, then, participated in the burgeoning expressionist movements in two nations.

*The God of Gods*' contribution to innovative theatre practices does not stop at Britain's border. While agitprop theatre (political, leftist theatre originating in 1920s Soviet Russia) and symphonic expressionism (coined by Herman Voaden as a blend of music, light, sound, dance, and lyrical speech) were novel theatrical forms in 1930s Canada, Aikins at once anticipates and integrates these two modernist forms by using an expressionistic landscape as political intervention.[11] In reaction to the play's commodity-driven religious system, the poet-figure Yellow Snake presents nature—trees, sun, water—as the embodiment of an alternative world that promotes egalitarianism and interconnectedness.

## THEOSOPHY

With its emphasis on spatial location, spirituality, and equality, *The God of Gods* also dramatizes theosophical beliefs promoted by some of Canada's art circles during the late nineteenth and early twentieth century.[12] Theosophy—which Helena Petrovna Blavatsky defines as "Divine Knowledge or Science" (Blavatsky 1) and others call "the Mother of the New Age" (Cranston 521)—was a cornerstone of

Canada's burgeoning arts in the 1920s.[13] When translated from its Greek roots, theosophy means "Wisdom of the Gods" (Blavatsky 1) and often encompasses tolerance of religious and racial differences, thereby emphasizing a culture of equality. Although the belief system dates back to Ammonius Saccas in the third century, the modern, international Theosophical Society aimed "to reconcile all religions, sects, and nations under a common system of ethics, based on eternal verities" (Blavatsky 3), and was formed in opposition to commercialism, materialism, and rationality (McCann). In theosophical writings, as in Yellow Snake's speeches, nature is an integral symbol and vehicle for the divine.

Founded in 1924, the Canadian Theosophical Association offers a widely used definition of theosophy that integrates Blavatsky's beliefs and that captures theosophical tenets prevalent in Canada when Aikins wrote the play:

> The Theosophical Society is composed of students, belonging to any religion in the world or to none, who are united by their approval of the Society's Objects, by their wish to remove religious antagonisms and to draw together men and women of goodwill whatsoever their religious opinions, and by their desire to study religious truths and to share the results of their studies with others.
>
> Their bond of union is not the profession of a common belief, but a common search and aspiration for Truth. They hold that Truth should be sought by study, by reflection, by purity of life, by devotion to high ideals, and they regard Truth as a prize to be striven for, not as dogma to be imposed by authority.
>
> They consider that belief should be the result of individual study or intuition, and not its antecedent, and should rest on knowledge, not on assertion. They extend tolerance to all, even to the intolerant, not as a privilege they bestow but as a duty they perform, and they seek to remove ignorance, not punish it.
>
> They see every religion as an expression of the Divine Wisdom and prefer its study to its condemnation, and its practice to proselytism. Peace is their watchword, as Truth is their aim. ("The Theosophical Society")

The Canadian Society's emphasis on "Truth" and "tolerance to all" engages with Blavatsky's seminal works and is in keeping with international writings on theosophy. *The God of Gods* dramatizes these key theosophical tenets: the play's central characters perform monologues on tolerance and discoveries of religious truths—or untruths, as the female protagonist (Suiva) realizes that the community's religious idol offers little more than stage tricks.

The play's critique of a false religious idol further echoes theosophy, which, as Blavatsky explains, "reject[s] the idea of a personal, or an extra-cosmic and anthropomorphic God" (42) and instead chooses "a Universal Divine Principle, the root of All, from which all proceeds, and within which all shall be absorbed at the end of the great cycle of Being" (43). Voicing these theosophical values, Yellow Snake rejects the reserve's organized religion and instead creates his own belief system based on equality and anti-capitalist values. In short, the play's hero, as Waning Moon explains, "has wild ways and does not fear the God" (7). *The God of Gods*' multifaceted political messages about religion, materialism, war, and art dramatize theosophical beliefs.

Like many Canadian artists of his day, Aikins was a theosophist and was involved with both Okanagan's Summerland Theosophical Society (Clough 121) and the Toronto Theosophical Society (Wagar 5).[14] Aikins's fellow Canadian theosophist artists include Roy Mitchell, Albert Smythe, and the Group of Seven's Lawren Harris, J. E. H. MacDonald, and Arthur Lismer. The Toronto Theosophical Society, as Gillian McCann explains, was after all "a hothouse for incubating artistic movements and included in its ranks members of the Toronto literati and artistic community" (5).[15] Canadian theosophists Mitchell and Harris founded the Arts and Letters Club (1908). Roy Mitchell (playwright, director) in particular serves as a pivotal example of the intersection of art and theosophy in Canada at the time. In his capacity as artistic director of the Arts and Letters Club's "Dramatic Corps," Mitchell staged modern playwrights and experimented with what reviewers of the time described as simplistic set designs and lighting effects (Usmiani). As O'Neill says, Mitchell's productions with the Arts and Letters Club in Toronto "subscribed to [a] new theatrical spirit [ . . . ] and launched its own brand of independent theatre" (O'Neill 68). This new "brand of independent theatre" was further realized with the creation of Hart House Theatre in 1919—commissioned by Vincent Massey and with Mitchell serving as its first artistic director—which was touted as one of the best-equipped and largest theatres in North America (Usmiani). Mitchell, then, was not only a key contributor to the Little Theatre movement in Canada, but was also a predecessor to Aikins's role as artistic director of Hart House Theatre (see Fred Jacob's "Monday Nighter at Large" in "Biographical Notes and Articles"). For Mitchell, as with Aikins, theatre was ultimately a medium for his theosophical beliefs and served as a venue for his critiques of materialism (Duchesne 229). "Mitchell's work," Renate Usmiani asserts, "is a constant reminder of the religious origin of all theatre; it also evokes parallels of Herman Voaden and Bertram Brooker in Canada, of Paul Claudel and August Strindberg, and of all those others who drew dramatic inspiration from the inner sources of mysticism, rather than the external ones of physical experience." As Mitchell and Aikins demonstrate, the membership of Toronto's Arts and Letters Club and the Toronto Theosophical Society often overlapped, as both were dedicated to promoting literature, architecture, music, painting, sculpture, and drama.

In response to the significance of theosophy in the development of Canadian literature, painting, and theatre, Michele Lacombe's "Theosophy and the Canadian Idealist Tradition: A Preliminary Exploration" (1982), Samuel Eldon Charles Wagar's *Theosophical Socialists in the 1920s Okanagan* (2002), and McCann's *Vanguard of the New Age* (2012) offer substantial studies of theosophy in Canada. Emphasizing theosophy's widespread impact on the arts, McCann credits the theosophical movement as a catalyst in the Irish Literary Renaissance, as a major contributor of India's Independence movement, and as a root of modernist Canadian artistic advancements and originality during the early twentieth century.[16] In his work on the connection between the theosophical movement and socialism in British Columbia, Wagar notes that Carroll and Katherine Aikins "were prominent members of the Summerland Theosophical Society branch in the 1920s" (5) as well as collaborators in a "series of political retreats co-sponsored by the Federated Labour Party and the Theosophical Society" (iii). In fact, Wagar argues that British Columbia—where Aikins built and developed a theatre in the 1920s—was the "socialist 'heartland' of Canada in the early twentieth century" because of the strong beliefs in and influence of theosophy (iii).[17]

While *The God of Gods* resonates with the belief systems of Naramata and Toronto's theosophical societies, the play's modernist theatrical techniques and aboriginal subject matter seem to be more of a draw for the British theatres. Canadian reviews, by comparison, mainly concentrate on the play's representation of a Canadian locale and of aboriginal culture.

## PERFORMING ETHNOGRAPHY AND PRIMITIVISM

Although Aikins highlights a crisis of *religious* authenticity, his script, together with the Birmingham, Toronto, and London productions, unintentionally performs a crisis of *cultural* authenticity through ambiguous set designs, costumes, and reductive portrayals of aboriginal characters. The Birmingham Repertory Theatre's 1919 production, for instance, did not fully execute all of Aikins's costume and prop notes: "Since the war had caused shortages of cloth and since Jackson's costume shop would not open until 1920," as O'Neill explains, Birmingham's "costumes for the first production were standard off-the-rack Indian dress supplied by J. Burkenshaw & Sons of Liverpool, which made the minor characters 'comic in appearance' and defied the [perceived] authenticity of Aikins's detailed descriptions" (82).[18] Comparatively, Everyman Theatre's 1931 playbill notes the use of a "Red Indian Mask" supplied by the "Hamley Bros.," but it is unclear how the mask was used. The singular noun "Mask" suggests that it might have been used for the statue rather than for the group of aboriginal characters, which would have required more than one mask. Aikins takes care to detail Yellow Snake's "cougar skin tunic" (7) and the old chief's "black otter skins" with an "ornamented hatchet in his girdle" (22), but the play's costumes and depiction of North American aboriginal peoples who speak in broken English remain reductive both in the script and in its realizations onstage.

Aikins's accounts of the religious idol, to be fair, are also quite different from the staged realizations. Commenting on the Birmingham Repertory Theatre's production photos (see fig. 6), O'Neill explains that "*The God of Gods* statue does appear to have been pulled from stock scenery and is more reminiscent of an Aztec or African idol than of something created in British Columbia" (82). A reviewer for the *Birmingham Gazette* similarly complains that "the god was rather too palpably sawdust stuffed" (E. C., 10 November 1919). How, then, do we reconcile Aikins's progressive arguments for a unifying acceptance of all people and living things with the stock Aztec idol? Or, as Gordon Lester asks, "How, then, do we reconcile the progressive social commentary with the play's racist language (Kotwi, Suiva's mother, is described as a 'fat squaw' [7]) [. . .] and bizarre faux-native dialogue ('How should we eat if the fire died?' [8])?"

For theatre reviewers at the time, Aikins's portrayal of aboriginal culture served a political purpose: *The God of Gods*, as Charlesworth explains, "is a Voltairean fable designed to expose the methods by which (in the view of the author) established religion has maintained its hold over the ignorant masses everywhere and in all ages. He has made his story of the tribal god of a small mountain people a symbolical picture of this 'system'." O'Neill similarly asserts that "Aikins's work, like those of Lord Dunsany, Shaw, and other new dramatists of the time, set about to question the near-absolutist assumptions about truth, morality, and acceptable subject matter that had undergirded artistic practices during earlier centuries" (84). Ultimately, the artificiality of the play's formal features—the broken dialogue, painted background flats, stereotypical costumes—gestures towards the artificiality and theatricality of the audience's own culture, which is played out by aboriginal stock figures and the villagers. It is the audience and not the aboriginal tribe that is the real target of Aikins's religious and cultural critique.

There are a number of textual details that suggest that Aikins may have based his play on the Okanagan First Nations, or the Syilx people. His characters refer to a place named Grey Mountain, which can be found in the area, and the play depicts practices that resemble some key beliefs of Syilx people. For instance, the Okanagan First Nations measure time by moon cycles, just as the play uses the moon to signal the priestess's age (Waning Moon). Aikins's use of a stone idol also finds an ethnographic correlative with Okanagan First Nations, because in Syilx culture rocks are believed to be the oldest living forms and the preservers of memory. It is therefore fitting that Aikins uses a stone idol as a symbol of the reserve's all-knowing deity. Yellow Snake's spiritual connection to the water and to a place called Hidden Waters gestures towards the Syilx belief that water is sacred and the most important part of creation. The Okanagan First Peoples project, managed by a Syilx institution, explains that water is central to one of their people's lessons on humility, as water flows through the lowest levels and refuses to look down on others.[19] Yellow Snake's overarching message about the holistic nature of all living things (trees, birds, people) not only reflects Aikins's theosophical beliefs, but also expresses the Syilx's two important teachings on the elements: first, that the earth and all of its inhabitants are a singular living entity, and, second, that the coming together of all the elements and inhabitants is what sustains us and creates life (*Okanagan*). Finally, Mablo's gluttony can be seen as a corruption of the Syilx people's profound gratitude for food as well as their cultural values of sharing and of avoiding over-consumption (*Okanagan*). While critics aptly question the productions' authenticity, taken together, the stone god, the use of the moon, and the teachings about the unity of all living things suggest that the Okanagan First Nations could have inspired Aikins's aboriginal content.[20]

Despite the ethnographic correlatives with the Okanagan people, the productions' realization of the setting and aboriginal reserve lacked cultural specificity as was in keeping with theatrical modernism. The geographically vague set designs are especially germane to a work of theatrical modernism because, as Eric Aronoff argues, "in the modernist period, anthropologists like Edward Sapir counter definitions of culture as universal, diachronic narrative of progressive refinement or technological improvement with conceptions of culture as synchronic or spatial wholes, whose unit is the geographic region" (94). The modernist movement, then, coincided with a shift in anthropology that redefined culture in terms of specific geographic contexts. As if dramatizing this modernist anthropological practice, *The God of Gods* treats geographical location, art, and culture as not merely mutually constitutive but as synonymous: for Aikins's hero, Yellow Snake, the place Hidden Waters is at once poetry and a cultural unit. In presenting spatial form—in this case the imagined landscape of Hidden Waters—as culture and art, Aikins participates in what Joseph Frank describes as a larger modernist treatment of narrative "spatially, in a moment of time, rather than as a sequence" (46). Potentially responding to the play's emphasis on natural environment and space, Hart House director Bertram Forsyth sought the "assistance of archaeological experts like Prof. [Charles Trick] Currelly," who was director of the Royal Ontario Museum (Charlesworth).[21] Despite this effort at geographical specificity, reviewers criticized the Hart House production for its non-descript mountainous background and universality.

The productions' lack of geographical or cultural particularity illustrates the "scattered traditions" (3) and the "feeling of lost authenticity, of 'modernity' ruining some essence or source," which as James Clifford argues, is a defining element of primitivist modernism in the early-twentieth-century literature (4).[22] In short, the vagueness of the geographical setting and cultural tradition goes hand-in-hand with primitivist modernism's aestheticisation of the aboriginal other and of a prehistoric culture. Productions of *The God of Gods* dramatize the community's scattered traditions by recalling various elements of the Christian tradition (self-flagellation, call and response), Aztec culture (Aztec statue, sacrifices), and Andean religious beliefs (virgin priesthood, worship of sun and moon) from what Charlesworth can only describe as a "pre-historic period." With reference to the 1931 London production, one reviewer similarly notes in vague terms the balance of "modern" production techniques and ancient setting: "The note struck is 'modern.' It is also some thousands of years old. And it sounds to-day as amusingly from the other side of the Atlantic as it once sounded in the theatres of Athens [ . . . . ] The admirably staged production was well received by a crowded house" (W., H. M.). Although reviewers agree that there is a palpable mix of "modern" and "pre-historic" elements, they cannot seem to agree on the exact origin of the aboriginal culture, whether it be Aztec, Andean, or Greek—a confusion due, on the one hand, to the set design's universality and, on the other, to the script's unnamed sources of aboriginal traditional knowledge.

Despite the premiere's limited representation of aboriginal garb and culture, the Birmingham production was generally received as a realistic account of the "Red Indian" ("Feathers"). After all, the dramatizations of Aikins's play reflect the audiences' fascination with and reductive understanding of aboriginal peoples at the time. Reviewers of the first Birmingham production describe the performance as an accurate illustration of "Indian faith" (Bendell) and exclaim, "there is nothing impossible about this play" ("The God of Gods," *Stage*). The *Birmingham Gazette* foregrounds *The God of Gods* as "a play of unusual interest" ("Magic at the Empire") while the *Stage* celebrates "the story [as] an unusual kind" ("The God of Gods"). For Birmingham reviewers, the "Indian" characters and reserve were at once "unusual" (*Gazette*, *Stage*) and "new" (*Evening Despatch*),

FIGURE 6. THE 1919 BIRMINGHAM PRODUCTION USES AN AZTEC STATUE FOR THE ABORIGINAL RESERVE'S RELIGIOUS IDOL. COURTESY OF THE BARRY JACKSON ESTATE.

exemplifying a primitivist exoticism of even the most general representation of aboriginal culture. The *Birmingham Gazette* explains that the play is "quite different to anything that has been seen on the Repertory stage," in large part because "all the characters are American Indians" ("Magic"). The *Birmingham Evening Despatch* similarly highlights the aboriginal content as saleable and original: "Aikins's play [ . . . ] animates 'something new,' [ . . . ] not in the story, which is as old as anything else under the sun, but in the people concerned—a Red Indian tribe—and in their manner of dealing with some of the problems of life ('The God of Gods')." In 1919 Birmingham, Aikins's nationality and status as a playwright "from British Columbia" seem to lend the production all the authenticity it needs to be considered a true depiction of aboriginal life ("Magic at the Empire").

Even the addition of a melodramatic musical score and orchestra were not enough to derail the play's so-called realism. Although the 1919 playbill fails to spell Aikins's name correctly—which is likely why many of the theatre reviewers incorrectly attribute *The God of Gods* to "Aitkins"—it offers a list of the songs arranged and performed for the Birmingham production.[23] Aikins's manuscript and the published Hart House version do not provide a musical score, but Yellow Snake's role as "the singer" lends itself to musical accompaniment. Harold Mills conducted the musical numbers in the first production under the direction of

A. E. Filmer and with Jackson as set designer. The songs offer a typical primitivist syncretism of distinct cultural sources, such as Pawnee, Cherokee, and Dakota:

| | |
|---|---|
| "Pawnee War Song and Dance".................. | Collected by Theodore Baker |
| "Canadian Indian Airs".............................. | From Crotch's Specimens[24] |
| "Cherokee Cradle Song" ............................ | Collected by Theodore Baker |
| "Chiquito Indian Tune"[25] .......................... | |
| "Dakota Scalp Dance" ............................... | Collected by Theodore Baker |
| "Omaha Tribal Melodies" .......................... | Collected by A.C. Fletcher<br>Arranged by C.W. Cadman |
| "Dakota Serenade".................................... | Collected by Theodore Baker |

The songs' disparate aboriginal nations would seem to undermine the play's cultural accuracy; and these orchestral accompaniments, as O'Neill argues, would seem to elevate the play's melodrama. Yet a reviewer for the *Birmingham Post and Journal* maintains "[t]here is nothing in *The God of Gods* which cannot be believed—it might have happened, and if it happened it must have happened in this way" (qtd. in Brigg 33). Similarly, a reviewer for the *Stage* highlights the play's "reasonableness" despite, or perhaps because of, the "quaint and weird tribal music" ("The God of Gods"). For these reviewers of the Birmingham production, the play participates in ethnographic modernity to the extent that it laments the loss of an ideal artist figure whose poetry and imagined utopian society personifies the essence of aboriginal artistic creation.

Reviewers of the Hart House production complicate the play's participation in ethnographic modernity because both the play script and the production elements convey a loss of authenticity to reviewers. Toronto theatre reviewer Charlesworth bemoans the community's scattered national, cultural, and ethnographic references because "Though [Aikins's] story is laid in the Rocky Mountains of a pre-historic period," the play "could be as effectively laid in any part of the great spine of the Western Hemisphere which includes both the Rockies and the Andes." Charlesworth goes on to assert that Aikins's "red aborigines derive from races of the older world" because they participate in sacrificial rites and a worship of the sun and the moon that could derive from "legends of the Andean tribes" but "have at one time or another been practised by religious cults in every part of the earth." For Toronto audiences, or at least for this theatre reviewer, the reserve's spiritual practices and the set's mountainous backdrop dramatize a lack of spiritual and cultural realism, respectively.

While the 1919 and 1920 Birmingham reviewers believed that the play was an authentic representation of North American aboriginals, the 1922

Canadian reviewers did not. Hart House reviewers, in particular, argued that the production failed to capture a markedly Canadian setting. Commenting on the first Birmingham production, O'Neill asserts that the first act "failed to suggest British Columbian scenery" (85). In reviewing Hart House's version, Charlesworth similarly remarked, "it would perhaps be stretching a point to claim that this play is essentially Canadian in atmosphere." The sets leave something to be desired in their flat representation of the Canadian West through painted backdrops of mountains and trees: Birmingham's set design shows forests in the background (see figs. 1 and 7), and Hart House's backdrop includes generic images of mountains (see fig. 8).[26] The productions' differing subtitles help to explain the variants in set design: the Birmingham Repertory Theatre's absence of a mountain-clad set reflects their billing of *The God of Gods* as an "American-Indian" play, while Hart House's set exemplifies the designer's attempt to depict what the subtitle advertised as "A Canadian Play." The subtitles of the Birmingham's and Hart House's productions—"An American-Indian Play" and "A Canadian Play"—diverge from the original manuscript's functional subtitle, "A Play in Three Acts," thereby illustrating their respective investment in "Indian" and "Canadian" content as well as Hart House's limited portrayal of a uniquely Canadian landscape. Everyman Theatre's playbill (1931) refers to the play's subtitle as both "A Drama in Three Acts" and simply "A Drama," and

FIGURE 7. THE 1920 BIRMINGHAM PRODUCTION SET DESIGN BY PAUL SHELVING. COURTESY OF THE BARRY JACKSON ESTATE.

FIGURE 8. THE 1922 HART HOUSE SET WITH MOUNTAIN RANGES IN THE BACKGROUND. COURTESY OF THE HART HOUSE ARCHIVES.

FIGURE 9. DETAIL: WANING MOON IN THE 1922 HART HOUSE PRODUCTION. COURTESY OF THE HART HOUSE ARCHIVES.

some of the theatre's promotional material advertises *The God of Gods* as "A New Play." Everyman Theatre's subtitles and the musical accompaniment, with songs such as "God save the King" and "A Chorus of Woodland Birds," suggest that the final production stripped Aikins's play of its "Canadian" or "American-Indian" resonances and invested in a more European tradition.

Birmingham's and Hart House's variants in production design—as illustrated by costumes, stage make-up, and set—resulted in two different conceptions of the aboriginal "savage." Filed under the 1921–22 season, the Hart House Theatre archives contain five photos from Birmingham's 1919 production and only one from its own. Even though Hart House was in dialogue with Birmingham, as their archives suggest, they staged very different versions of Aikins's aboriginal community. Whereas Birmingham's serene forest and beautified Suiva produce a romantic version of a "primitive" culture, Hart House's toothless Indians (in what appears to be darkened face paint; see fig. 9) and mountainous backdrop present a more savage vision of an aboriginal reserve in what looks to be British Columbia. Like its Birmingham counterpart, the Hart House production pulled stock costumes and face-paint designs from local costumiers such as Malabar (see fig. 10).[27] The Hart House archives contain several images, filed under the

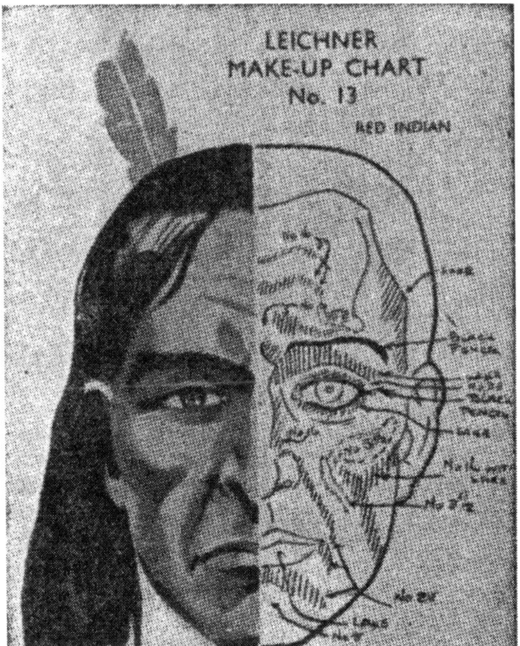


FIGURE 10. A HART HOUSE THEATRE GUIDE TO PERFORMANCE MAKE-UP. COURTESY OF THE HART HOUSE ARCHIVES.

years 1919–28, of stock aboriginal costumes with buckskin garb, feathers, and braided wigs. As evidenced by the make-up and costumes, Birmingham and Hart House relied on actors in redface and reinforced popular misconceptions of aboriginal peoples.

Over a decade after the Birmingham premiere, London reviewers of the 1931 Everyman Theatre production were not so eager to lap up the novelty and "realism" of Aikins's "drama of redskin life" (*Star* qtd. in Johnston). The Everyman Theatre reused Paul Shelving's costume designs from the 1920 Birmingham production, but reviews of the London mounting and its representations of aboriginal culture were mixed at best. One article describes the play as "sufficiently interesting," but the reviewer seems more pleased with the fact that "one can obtain . . . chops and steaks" than with the "story . . . [that] starts rather slowly, with everybody talking far too much" (P. P.). An anonymous article, entitled "Red Indian Drama," offers the most laudatory review, labelling the 1931 London production as "novel," "well-told and well-written" while also noting the play's "unusualness" that "partly, no doubt, account[s] for the favourable reception which it received." The "unusualness" likely refers to the "Red Indian" subjects and possibly to the playwright's status as a "Canadian author" ("Red Indian Drama"), both of which the reviewer takes care to note. Similarly, Ivor Brown praises some of the production elements: "Ritual in fine feathers has always spectacular possibilities, and Mr. Filmer [producer], with the aid of Mr. Paul Shelving [costumes] and Mr. Michael Weight [set designer], succeeded in revealing at the close the statuesque and colourful elements of idolatrous prostrations."

These positive excerpts, however, are the exception, for most of the media was skeptical of the performed "ritual in fine feathers" (Brown). Brown goes on to critique "the effect of a *charade* in which palefaces were masquerading in copper skins" (emphasis added). Another reviewer similarly describes "an air of *charade* about this business of the stone god" (E. L.; emphasis added). Overall, the 1931 British critics reacted differently from those who penned the 1919 and 1920 Birmingham reviews, which embrace the play's representation of aboriginal culture.

In addition to critiquing the 1931 performance of "stamping, grunting, and spitting" aboriginals, Brown bemoans the script's use of "prairie metaphor[s] about the fat deer and leaping trout." In fact, Brown twice describes the "prairie" setting, which implies that there may not have been a mountainous backdrop to the 1931 production. Taken together, the reviews of the 1931 production gesture towards a set design that is even less recognizable than its predecessor's as British Columbian: Brown notes a prairie setting; the reviewer P. P. stands out as one of the few to introduce Aikins as a "Canadian dramatist"; and reviewer E. L. seems to believe that *The God of Gods* was written by a British playwright, or that it ought to have been, given the Everyman Theatre's mandate to produce "new works by the most modern of British dramatists." "We wish," E. L. laments, "that the author had chosen a subject nearer home."[28] The confusion over Aikins's nationality and the reviewer's failure to attribute *The God of Gods* to a Canadian playwright may be symptoms of the production's subtitle. Whereas the Birmingham and Hart House productions highlight the play's "American-Indian" and "Canadian" subject matter, respectively, Everyman's subtitles, "A Drama in Three Acts" (page 1 of program) and "A Drama" (page 2 of program), provide little insight into the geography or ethnography.

Out of all four productions (1919, 1920, 1922, and 1931), Everyman's subtitles are the closest to Aikins's original, "A Play in Three Acts." Despite this fidelity to the original title, the 1931 reviews and playbill suggest that the Everyman production is the least faithful to Aikins's portrayal of a Canadian setting and aboriginal culture. The London playbill makes no mention of Aikins's Canadian nationality, nor does it include the descriptors "Indian" and "Canadian" anywhere in the program. For instance, Everyman Theatre's "Programme of Music"—composed by Anton Rubinstein and Richard Wagner—is much less "primitive" than the Birmingham score (see full program in dossier section):

| | | |
|---|---|---|
| Prelude | "Kamennoi-Ostrow" | Rubinstein |
| Overture | "A Chorus of Woodland Birds" | |
| Entr'acte 1 | "The Rhinegold" | Wagner |
| Entr'acte 1 | "Parsifal" | Wagner |
| Entr'acte 2 | "Parsifal" Finale | Wagner |
| Entr'acte 2 | "Twilight of the Gods" | Wagner |
| | "God Save the King" | |

Everyman's "The Rhinegold" and "Parsifal," in contrast with Birmingham's "Canadian Indian Airs," help to account for the 1931 reviewers' lack of discussion about the play's Canadian content and their incredulity when confronted with a "charade" of "copper skins" (Brown).

Like the 1922 Canadian reviewers before him, the *Province*'s Lukin Johnston asserts that the 1931 production "did not suffice to conjure up a convincing picture of the child-like mentality of the primitive savage, or to make realistic his faith in the power of the hideous stone image which spoke only through the mouth of a drunken, rapacious old priestess" ("Canadian Playwright"). In trying to take into account the British reviewers' contradictory mention of appreciative audiences and Indian charade, Johnston argues that "the hardest thing in stage-craft is to capture the atmosphere of barbaric romance, poetic imagery and simple, childlike innocence of the North American Indian" ("Canadian Playwright"); this challenge, according to Johnston, is compounded by the fact that a modern audience's "only conception of what an Indian looks like has been gained from story books" ("Canadian Playwright"). Stereotypes of the Indian's "childlike innocence" (Johnston) and "unusualness" (*Morning Post* qtd. in Johnston) are still strong in 1931, but reviewers are not as eager to celebrate a "barbaric" spectacle as a realistic triumph.

Johnston and fellow London reviewers also flocked to critique Martin Walker's "burlesque" (Johnston) portrayal of the chief's devious son Mablo, which pushed "the comedy element . . . much more to the fore than might be thought" (*Evening Standard* qtd. in Johnston). Brown admonishes Martin Walker for "treating his part with scant regard, as though he had no interest whatever in the prairie or its problems," and goes on to say, "Actors cannot always enjoy their parts; but, once they have taken them up, they should at least disguise their feelings." In these reviews, the productions' inauthentic staging of Canadian geography and aboriginal culture overwhelm the onstage performance of falsified religious idols and figureheads, thereby undermining the play's larger critique of organized religion.

From 1919 to 1931 *The God of Gods*' reviews become progressively more critical of onstage representations of aboriginal culture. A comparison of the 1919–20 Birmingham reviews and the 1922 Canadian reviews seems at first to suggest that British theatre goers were more willing to accept a stereotypical portrayal of aboriginal culture. The Canadian reviewers' scepticism, however, is not necessarily a sign of national differences, but may be owing to the fact that the Canadian production was later—albeit only by a little over one year—than the Birmingham shows. When comparing the four productions' reviews, the Canadian (1922 and 1931) and London (1931) reviewers are the most dismissive of the redface performances. It is important to note, however, that the 1931 reviewers retain an overt racial bias in their equation of aboriginal culture with "barbaric romance" and a "simple" mindset (Johnston).

Primitivism, while a sign of Aikins's time and theatrical modernism, is the axis upon which the play's political messages turn.[29] As Christopher Innes explains, primitivism "is one of the characteristic lines in theatrical Modernism, stretching from Wyndham Lewis, through Antonin Artaud in the 1930s, to the Living Theatre and the American avant-garde in the late 1960s" (140). Aikins dramatizes two opposing functions of the primitive—as a mirror for a dystopian present and as a symbol for a utopian past—in order to expose the false idols of an anthropomorphic God and of material goods.[30] In their blind adherence to a corrupt state based on fear and materialism, the primitive "Indian" worshippers function as an allegory for Western culture. By contrast, while Yellow Snake represents an idealized primitive, communal past, he is not a stereotypical character that represents all aboriginal peoples. Rather, he represents a philosophy of art, religion, and egalitarian politics. Modern materialist society, it seems, is the truly savage culture in this play. This message was not lost on reviewers of the time, who heralded the play as "an allegory to be interpreted—a whetstone for the wits" (*Birmingham Gazette*). In this way, the play's performance of "Indianness" operates as a vehicle for the larger political message.

In *The God of Gods*' capitalist-driven community, God is at once violent and vengeful. Variations of the phrase "I fear the God" (9), repeated throughout the play by Suiva, Kotwi, and the worshippers, function as a refrain. In the first act, Yellow Snake fulfills the community's desire for a punishing deity when he tells Suiva what he would do if he were God: he would "take trees for arrows and shoot them at the sun" and "bathe" Suiva's feet in "a gourd of blood," prompting "the priestess, Waning Moon, [to declare that] the God is angry" (15). Yellow Snake's mockery, however, quickly shifts to a more sincere tone when Suiva asks, "If you were God where would you live?" (14). In response to this question, he uses poetry to paint another world that he names "Hidden Waters," a name that is especially poignant considering that Suiva later escapes the corrupt society by throwing herself into the onstage pool. As a reviewer for the *Stage* suggests, "there is undoubted originality and imagination about Mr. Aikins' work, which is mainly in prose, though the first act has a leavening of poetry" (November 13, 1919). Using markedly poetic language, Yellow Snake reimagines the fear-driven, hierarchical religious system as one founded on egalitarian interconnectedness and embodied by the dreamscape Hidden Waters.

A gift economy, or non-market model of exchange and hierarchy, drives the characters, with the exception of Yellow Snake and Suiva, to obey the divine. Theories of gift economies in primitive culture are often attributed to Bronislaw Malinowski's anthropological research of Kula rings in the Trobriand Islands during World War I, as well as to Marcel Mauss's foundational text *The Gift*, wherein he theorizes the complexities of gift exchange in societies around the world. For Mauss there is no such thing as a free gift because reciprocation is always expected. The priestess Waning Moon's negotiation with Kotwi, as well as the community's sacrificial acts to the God, exemplify this tenet of gift economy as a system of exchange and social hierarchy. The play's rhetoric of gift giving veils the underlying mode of what Mauss would call reciprocation. For the tribe as a whole, the payments of animals, furs, wine, and other goods help to ensure that the God will not punish the community or its individual members. The play immediately establishes the community's non-market value system when, in the opening scene, Kotwi tries to trade her daughter Suiva for economic and social gain. Kotwi and Waning Moon negotiate an exchange of Suiva for goods, but they frame this exchange as a selfless gift in honour of the God when Kotwi says, "What is there more that I can *give* than my own child, my Suiva? [ . . . . ] And yet I *give* her" (9; emphasis added). Kotwi and Waning Moon repeat the verb "give," but there is the underlying expectation of capital return (in the form of cows and social standing): Kotwi only gifts her daughter because Kotwi will directly profit from Suiva's position as priestess. This scene supports Mauss's suppositions that aboriginal peoples participate in economies, and that gifts are contractual acts of exchange. In *The God of Gods*, it is not God but rather the commercial exchange of goods—Suiva for food—that ensures "full bellies" (7).

Much like Nietzsche, who denounces organized religions for losing sight of "nature" and the "essential" spirituality, Aikins performs a critique of religion and religious idols as tools for materialist greed. In short, *The God of Gods* was seen as an "allegory" or "fable" of materialism by theatre reviewers writing for the *Birmingham Gazette* (1919), the *Stage* (1919), the *Post* (1919), and *Saturday Night* (1922). The aboriginal peoples, whom reviewers describe as having innate "child-like innocence" (Johnston), are corrupted by greed and manipulated by Mablo, the stock, fat-capitalist character. It seems a fitting irony that Aikins would choose aboriginal characters to represent an unnatural state of monotheistic religion and idolatry because the "Indians" were associated with polytheism and nature. This expectation of aboriginal people's values would render the community's materialism and belief in a single, fearsome God unnatural in the eyes of the play's early-twentieth-century viewers.

Despite the play's overt allegory of and relationship to modern society, *The God of Gods* offers an alternative to materialist values and helps to distance the audience from their history of colonial conquest by aligning them with Yellow Snake. Throughout the play, Kotwi's critique of Yellow Snake's work ethic and Suiva's insistence that she will only "mate" with Mablo if "Yellow Snake has not made me a house by the young moon" (20) further underscore the characters' value of ownership in contrast with the ideal artist's inability to procure material goods. Yellow Snake builds Suiva an imagined home in Hidden Waters, but Suiva's pragmatism gets the best of her when she insists on an actual structure. The lovers come to a compromise as they create a model home with sticks, thereby realizing the house as a sculptural object or art piece. Yellow Snake, then, is the voice of critique and reason when it comes to the community's investment in both material objects and a false religious idol.

Shari H. Huhndorf explains that, in prompting the audience to identify with a "savage," authors enable viewers "to distance themselves from the conquest of Native America" (3). In short, viewers "go Native" in order to perform empathy for the "savage" and thereby disassociate from the role of the colonizers. For instance, Yellow Snake's vision of the alternative world called Hidden Waters contains repeated warnings against violence and colonial possession. Yellow Snake also inserts a lesson against material and perhaps even colonial conquest: "you must never . . . rob their nests" (16). And Yellow Snake's religious system denies an individualistic sense of ownership and conquest. Everyone, according to Yellow Snake, owns and bears responsibility for nature. As Suiva exclaims, "It's no more yours than mine or any other's" (17). There is a levelling of ownership as opposed to a mere reversal (in which the land would belong to aboriginal peoples and not to colonialists, to Yellow Snake and not to Mablo). In the imagined egalitarian world, "you hate no man and none hates you" (29).

Yellow Snake's notion of equality is so encompassing that it reveals the very notion of possession to be an illusion: because everyone owns, no one owns. When Yellow Snake speaks of "my house" (17) he does not, as Suiva at first believes, refer to a physical structure but rather to the "songs and plumage of all birds that nest and all the colours of all fish that swim" (17). In presenting the "songs and plumage" as "my house" (17), Yellow Snake further does away with colonial notions of personal property, instead accepting nature as his home. When faced with Mablo's marriage proposal, however, Suiva gives Yellow Snake an ultimatum that challenges his disavowal of personal property: "When Mablo asks me, I'll say this to him: If Yellow Snake has not made me a house by the young moon, then I will mate with you" (20). While Yellow Snake is the voice of artistry and anti-materialism, Suiva is a mediating voice that at once appreciates nature as artistry and advocates practical artistry. Suiva encourages Yellow Snake to build a house by working hard. She wants him to be a productive partner who is part of the workforce. The artist, then, is not exempt from physical labor and quantifiable productivity. Yellow Snake must create a house, and it cannot be made by poetry alone.

In addition to challenging materialism, Yellow Snake's imagined alternative "house" pointedly embraces "all birds," "all fish," and "all the colours," echoing theosophy in its emphatically intercultural society (17). Despite *The God of Gods'* faux-native dialogue and reductive character portrayals, the play engages in a subtle critique of racial hierarchy that is in keeping with theosophical values. Blavatsky goes so far as to assert that theosophy's primary objective is "[t]o form the nucleus of a Universal Brotherhood of Humanity without distinction of race, colour, sex, caste, or creed" (24). Yellow Snake's egalitarianism, then, rejects the hierarchies of racial "colours" and capitalist possession that consume the other members of the aboriginal tribe.

While the performance of "Indianness" is undeniably reductive, the aboriginal tribe's blind obedience to a corrupt God and capitalist system serves as an analogy for the audience's own subservience to a punishing deity, whether that be an anthropomorphic God or capitalism itself. If we approach *The God of Gods* as a political piece, Yellow Snake and Suiva's climactic deaths do not evoke a cathartic mourning for a lost past. Rather, Yellow Snake's heroism, art, and new religion based on nature model change for the audience: the alternative religion in large part emblematizes the writings of Nietzsche and theosophists on racial equality, the value of nature, and the importance of the arts. In this way, *The God of Gods* participates in the burgeoning political theatre of the 1920s–40s, often attributed to agitprop theatre, and promotes Nietzschean and theosophical philosophy.

## ADAPTING NIETZSCHE

Lester describes *The God of Gods* as a "loose adaptation" of *Romeo and Juliet*, while the *Canadian Adaptations of Shakespeare Project* (headed by Daniel Fischlin) cites *The God of Gods* because Aikins's play shares narrative elements with *Romeo and Juliet*. These elements speak to Aikins's Shakespearean literary influences (that is, both plays feature separated lovers and critique a divided community). Furthermore, *The God of Gods* offers a relatively rare example of an early-twentieth-century Shakespeare adaptation, and it is written by a playwright who grew up among scores of Shakespeare adaptors.[31] However, another possible approach to the play is to view it as an adaptation of Nietzschean philosophy. Although Aikins's ties to Shakespeare are no doubt significant and a rich subject for further inquiry, *The God of Gods* also dramatizes Nietzschean philosophy by exhibiting the reification of art as a new religion and model for society. *The God of Gods* engages with Nietzsche's concept of art in *The Birth of Tragedy* and his discussion of God in *The Gay Science*. Just as Nietzsche's "essential being" takes "eternal pleasure as the creator and spectator of that comedy of art" (*Birth* 33), Aikins's Yellow Snake voices a new religion modeled on art. Yellow Snake is, in Nietzsche's words, the "original artist of the world" (*Birth* 33). Like his modernist contemporaries—such as Bernard Shaw, who used Nietzschean philosophy for a socialist agenda in *Man and Superman* (1903)—Aikins adapts Nietzsche's *The Birth of Tragedy* in order to promote anti-materialist values.

Owing to Nietzsche's reputation as an originator of expressionism, it may come as no surprise that an expressionist play voices Nietzschean philosophy.

What is surprising, however, is that Aikins adapts Nietzschean philosophy—which outwardly rejects socialism, promotes hierarchy, and was popular among the Fascist regime—for an egalitarian agenda. "Nietzsche," as Steven E. Aschheim explains, "was the anti-egalitarian 'philosopher of advanced capitalism'" who had an "elitist contempt for levelling and despotic socialism" (164). Despite Nietzsche's anti-socialist elitism, his works have been used to support both the left and the right.[32] *The God of Gods*, which culminates with Suiva's realization that "God is dead" (61), adapts Nietzsche's concept of art and God to promote an alternative religion based on art, love, and egalitarianism.

*The God of Gods*' use of *The Birth of Tragedy* and *The Gay Science* at once places it in a field of literary modernism while also complicating the play's controversial, nebulous depiction of aboriginal peoples and their spirituality. Both *The Gay Science* and *The Birth of Tragedy* value an idealized ancient culture as a redemptive escape from the modern world. For Nietzsche, the ancient Greek tragedies are the best representation of communal art that unites its spectators through the common identification with archetypal figures. Whereas Nietzsche uses the ancient Greeks, Aikins uses an aboriginal character to represent a synthesis of the arts that, together, can replace religion: Yellow Snake is at once poet, singer, actor, and audience.

Aikins's engagement of theatre as a medium for social critique and change further echoes the tenets of Nietzsche's *The Gay Science*, which asserts theatre's ability to provoke self-recognition. As Nietzsche says, theatre in particular offers "the art of 'putting oneself on stage' before oneself" (*Gay* 79). David Kornhaber explains that "this self-recognition is possible for Nietzsche because the theatre is profoundly and uniquely capable of being at once experienced and understood, and through this duality proffers insights that no other single artistic form can attempt" (30). While the uniqueness of theatre's ability to critique and reflect society remains debatable, there is little room for interpretation when it comes to *The God of Gods*' celebration of art as an antidote for social, religious, and capitalist corruption.

By dramatizing many different genres (music, poetry, sculpture, theatre) and by elevating art to divine status, *The God of Gods* functions as a manifesto for the unique ability of theatre to present a collaborative synthesis of the arts or the Wagnerian *Gesamtkunstwerk* (total work of art). At the time of the 1922 Canadian production, groups such as Toronto's Hart House Theatre and the Arts and Letters Club were celebrating the synthesis of the arts. While Hart House Theatre brought together visual artists, architects, musicians, writers, and dramatists to mount plays, the Arts and Letters Club reinforced the significance of the five arts through its in-house periodical, *Lamps* (1910–39 and distinct from the *Lamp* journal), which is an acronym for literature, architecture, music, painting, and stage. In short, the play presents aboriginal culture through the filters of European and Canadian theatrical traditions and artistic ideals. Aikins builds on Nietzsche's theorization of art, which was itself inspired by Wagner, by emphasizing a particularly Wagnerian use of theatre that can provide spiritual and political redemption. In fact, Wagner used a theatre building—the *Festspielhaus*—to model egalitarianism (Geuss xvi). While the Wagnerian notion of *Gesamtkunstwerk* is in keeping with Nietzsche's idealization of collaborative arts, Wagner and Aikins's respective visions for an egalitarian society contradict Nietzsche's ideas of *Rangordnung* (rank ordering). In this way, Aikins revises Nietzschean philosophy to propose a theatre of inclusivity and equality.

Aikins does not use poetic language merely to carve out a relationship between nature and people; he presents an idealized art—a total work of art that includes multiple media—as a new form of religion. As Yellow Snake seeks a replacement for the chiselled stone idol, this highly aestheticized nature, wherein the birds are at once birds and sculptures of birds with "carved limbs and faces" (16), is the basis for an alternative religious system. Yellow Snake works to overthrow the vengeful hierarchical God through art and nature, thereby enacting Nietzsche's contention that "the terrible is tamed by artistic means" (*Birth* 40). In describing Hidden Waters, Yellow Snake realizes Nietzsche's Wagnerian ideal of a total work of art by incorporating poetry, music ("some are only voices"), sculpture ("some are made of stone"), and painting ("some are pictures made with blood") within the overarching medium of drama (*God* 13).

Yellow Snake is an artist of many forms in the narrative of the play. Though his role as the singer and poet are more overt, the first time we see Yellow Snake he is an onstage audience member. Yellow Snake "*climbs a nearby tree and hides in the foliage*" (7) for the duration of the first scene (see fig. 11); while watching Kotwi and Waning Moon, Yellow Snake "*follows the various turns of their conversation with interested but restrained pantomime*" (10; all italics in original). In this way, Aikins immediately presents Yellow Snake in the roles of spectator (he watches from the trees) and actor (he enacts pantomime). Aikins, then, includes the viewer in this ideal artistic realm, synthesizing artist and audience.

Nietzsche's, and in turn Aikins's, idealization of the *Gesamtkunstwerk* presents a highly collaborative vision of the arts (one that involves multiple arts as well as the audience), and, more specifically, endows a multidisciplinary artist with the godlike properties of the "original artist of the world" (*Birth* 33). According to Nietzsche, to be "one and identical with the essential being" is to be at "one and the same time subject and object, simultaneously poet, actor, and spectator" (*Birth* 33). *The God of Gods* adheres to this definition of God as artistry: Yellow Snake

FIGURE 11. YELLOW SNAKE FIRST APPEARS IN THE BOUGHS OF A TREE AS HE WATCHES THE PLAY'S OPENING SCENE BETWEEN SUIVA AND HER MOTHER, KOTWI, DURING THE 1919 BIRMINGHAM PRODUCTION. COURTESY OF THE BARRY JACKSON ESTATE.

is at once an artistic subject (poet, singer, actor), object (character to be viewed by the real audience), as well as a spectator (onstage audience). For Nietzsche, this complex artistic role can only be held by a godlike figure or "essential being" (*Birth* 33), which explains why Suiva calls Yellow Snake the true God during the play's final scene. In keeping with his divine role, Yellow Snake first speaks as a godlike voice in response to Suiva's prayer to the "Great God of Gods!" (13). Communicating with Suiva as only a voice from the treetops (see fig. 11), he defines himself in connection with the landscape as the "red berries and white blossoms" and the "singer of the glory in the morning!" (14). Later descriptions of Hidden Waters only serve to solidify this first intertwining of Yellow Snake, divinity, and the landscape.

In the wake of World War I, Aikins's engagement with Nietzschean philosophy elevates the pacifist Yellow Snake to a godlike hero. Suiva's ceremonial speech to commemorate Yellow Snake's death reads, as Lester suggests, "like a memorial to a fallen soldier" when Suiva declares, "You were a fighter but you'll fight no more. You were a hunter but you'll hunt no more" (59). As a fighter, Yellow Snake stands in for the many casualties of World War I, but he is a "fighter" only in a pacifist and figurative sense, in that he fights for the value of art. Yellow Snake battles against Mablo and his men most effectively by not engaging in armed combat, thereby rendering Mablo a "groundhog coward" (53). Even Amburi, the chief and father of Mablo, reprimands his son for shooting Yellow Snake in the back: "The man you killed broke the God's law, but he was not a coward. And for a son, I'd rather have him dead than you alive" (53).

Despite Suiva's initial reference to violence ("you'll fight no more") and the allusion to military funerals, Suiva honours Yellow Snake fittingly not as a soldier but as a "singer" and "dancer" (53). A difference between the original manuscript and the Hart House script gestures towards Aikins's initial emphasis on the loss of Yellow Snake as an artist more than a lover. The Hart House version ends Suiva's funeral rites with a description of Yellow Snake as a "lover": "You were a singer but you'll sing no more. You were a dancer but you'll dance no more. You were a lover but you'll love no more. You'll toss no more your dark hair to the sky!" (59). In the original manuscript, by contrast, Suiva's speech culminates with the loss of Yellow Snake the "dancer": "You were a singer but you'll sing no more. You were a lover but you'll love no more. You were a dancer but you'll dance no more! You'll toss no more your dark hair to the sky!" (48). In the earlier version, then, Yellow Snake's role as the tragic lover is flanked by his role as a singer-dancer. Ultimately, in both versions, Yellow Snake's role as artist—at once "singer" and "dancer"—is more pronounced than Yellow Snake the "lover" or the "fighter."

*The God of Gods* brings together many art forms in staging Yellow Snake as the "essential creator" who is at once lover as well as "poet, actor, and spectator" (*Birth* 33). The play's different art forms, in turn, exemplify the Nietzschean dichotomy of the Apolline (structured, ordered, epitomized by sculpture) and the Dionysiac (chaotic, intoxicated, epitomized by structureless music) artistic drives. In fact, the play's main dramatic tension, between the corrupt religious community and the poet-singer Yellow Snake, can also be described in Nietzschean terms as a tension between Apolline and Dionysiac forces: an Apolline rock sculpture represents the community's God, whereas the Dionysiac "art of music" characterizes Yellow Snake. Aikins also demonstrates art's potential deceptiveness when the worshippers fail to perceive the sculpture of God as an artistic rendering and instead mistake it for the real thing. With Apolline art, as Nietzsche warns, "in the worst case, the semblance would deceive us as if it were crude reality" (16). In spite of the tribe's religious leaders (Waning Moon, Amburi), who enforce strict rules characteristic of Apolline structure,

Yellow Snake engages in a world of Dionysiac "oneness" (*Birth* 19) where nature and people are interconnected. Nietzsche even celebrates the "magic of the Dionysiac" as the catalyst for the "reconciliation" of "nature [ . . . ] with her lost son, humankind" (*Birth* 18)—a reconciliation that resonates with Yellow Snake's drive to better integrate his community with a poeticized landscape. By simultaneously incorporating both "artistic powers" (*Birth* 18)—the Apolline and Dionysiac—Aikins participates in Nietzsche's "continuous evolution of art" (*Birth* 14) and showcases theatre's multi-disciplinary art forms.

"There can be little doubt," theatre critic Charlesworth wrote, that Aikins "intended his fable to serve as a criticism of anthromorphic conceptions of the deity generally; and that his ideas have a philosophic application." While Charlesworth adeptly highlights the play's religious critique, he underestimates *The God of Gods*' romanticization of aboriginal peoples when he suggests that Aikins's philosophical applications are "entirely unrelated to the romance of the North American Indians." It is precisely the aboriginal characters' idealized connection to the past and to nature that dramatizes Aikins's theosophical message that art and love are the keys to spirituality.

*The God of Gods* ultimately enacts a manifesto for the theatre that fuses Nietzschean philosophy with theosophy's belief in "the great cycle of Being" (Blavatsky 43) and a non-hierarchical "universal brotherhood" (Davy 118). Theosophy, like Suiva and Yellow Snake, rejects a singular anthropomorphic God and instead celebrates spiritual connection as epitomized by recurring terms like "love" and "light" (Blavatsky). When Suiva realizes that her lover has been killed, she laments not only her romantic loss, but also the loss of a godlike figure who personifies spiritual "love": "His name was love [ . . . ] He was God" (61). Responding to the play's didactic emphasis on love, the *Birmingham Evening Despatch* asserts that "Love, after all, is revealed as the god of gods" and the *Era* explains that "the God of Gods is Love."[33]

Integrating Nietzsche's concept of the "essential being" with theosophical tenets, Aikins stresses the significance of love as an overlooked element of Nietzsche's Superman. *The God of Gods*' integration of love and Nietzschean philosophy dramatizes the argument from the last printed article of *Lamp* (September 15, 1900), a Toronto theosophical journal from the late nineteenth and early twentieth century edited by Albert E.S. Smythe. Responding to the death of Nietzsche and the value of his works, Smythe argues that the "Over-man" needs "Love" in order to be "greatest" and the "servant of all": "Love, the inspiration of life, must be added to genius, before even the greatest can willingly, ay joyfully, take up the burdens which weigh down his weaker fellows. Without Love, the 'Over-man' may be a monster. With Love, the 'Over-man' becomes a Man of

God" (*Lamp* 223). In dramatizing Yellow Snake's death as the death of love, art, and God, Aikins weaves together the Nietzschean contention that "God is dead" with the theosophical pronouncement that a "Man of God" is a man of "Love." If *The God of Gods'* pronouncement of the artist-lover as the true God of Gods sounds like a New Age message, that is because it is: the play rearticulates the theosophical belief system of Aikins's day, which "prefigures the modern movements referred to collectively as 'New Age'" (McCann 6).

While Yellow Snake holds forth a new religious and social system for the audience to behold, *The God of Gods* offers a prismatic artifact of theatrical modernism, primitivism, theosophy, Nietzschean philosophy, postwar contexts, and early-twentieth-century Canadian drama. With its range of intertexts, political messages, and transatlantic production history, *The God of Gods* is indeed still as "unusual" (*Stage*) a play as the first reviewers claimed.

NOTES

1. For the full reviews, see the write-ups in the *Stage* and the *Evening Despatch* of the 1919 Birmingham production of *The God of Gods*, both entitled "The God of Gods," in the dossier section. E. C.'s "Feathers and Faith" (1919) as well as Johnston's "Canadian Playwright Meets with London Stage Success" (1931) can also be found in the dossier under "Reviews."
2. One of the British directors of *The God of Gods* has received as much, if not more, attention than the playwright himself, to the extent that the Birmingham Repertory Theatre archives record *The God of Gods* as a work by Sir Barry Jackson, who founded the theatre, created the set for the 1919 premier production, and directed the play's second run in 1920.
3. See Patrick O'Neill's "Carroll Aikins: Experiments in Playwriting" and related theatre reviews (dossier section) for further discussions of the play's reception in Britain.
4. As European modernist theatre practitioners, Craig (British) and Appia (Swiss) developed theories that integrated music, set, and movement (O'Neill 67). While Craig is best known for his *On the Art of the Theatre*, Appia is famous for his set designs for Wagner's operas.
5. See James Hoffman's "Carroll Aikins and the Home Theatre" (1986) for more information on the theatre house's design, mandates, and productions.
6. There are some inconsistencies in the date of the Home Theatre's closure. O'Neill writes that the theatre opened in the fall of 1920 and closed "after barely two years in operation" (65), suggesting that 1922 was the final season. Hoffman similarly concludes that the Home Theatre closed in 1922. Betty Clough, a family friend of the Aikins's family (Henderson), contradicts O'Neill and Hoffman when she reports that the Home Theatre produced plays in 1923, including *Victory in Defeat* (a passion play with excerpts from the Bible), Synge's *Riders to the Sea*, and a dance drama directed by Florence Levine (a dance and movement instructor from the Neighborhood Playhouse

in New York). Clough was a close family friend who had intimate access to Katherine Aikins's journals (that are reportedly lost now), a fact that gives credit to her account and warrants further inquiry; unfortunately, she does not give the bibliographic information of any newspaper articles that would substantiate her claim. Furthermore, as Hoffman suggests, the newspaper articles are unreliable at times and report the future potential of the Home Theatre long after both O'Neill and Clough date its closure. In 1924, for instance, the *Christian Science Monitor* declares that Aikins's Home Theatre "is a matter of great interest to Canadians" and that their players may "also be seen in several cities of the United States" ("The Canadian Players" 6). I date the closure of the Home Theatre as the fall of 1922 in keeping with the reports of O'Neill and Hoffman, and because Massey dates *Victory in Defeat* as 1922 in his biographical sketch of Aikins from *Canadian Plays from Hart House Theatre*.

7. The Home Theatre's dedication to promoting Canadian theatre is similar to the alternative theatre movement (1970s) that saw the creation of theatres across Canada devoted to producing Canadian art.
8. Dean Irvine argues for the prevalence of primitivist narratives in what he calls Canada's "salvage modernisms." Marius Barbeau, Douglas LePan, and Sheila Watson produced examples of Canadian modernist literature that engage with aboriginal mythologies. In *The Downfall of Temlaham* (1928), for instance, Barbeau integrates ethnographic findings and original stories from his research in the Skeena River's Gitxsan community. Marc Fortin (Université de Sherbrooke) is currently researching the history and multiple origins of this novel.
9. For the full review of *The God of Gods*, see the *Birmingham Post and Journal*, 10 November 1919.
10. See below for an extended discussion of Yellow Snake's imagined utopia Hidden Waters as well as the productions' primitivist representation of so-called "barbaric mysticism" (*Globe* April 1922) with no cultural particularity.
11. During the 1930s, Voaden's "symphonic expressionism" was, as Anton Wagner explains, "one of the few stylistic alternatives to the prevailing realism in Canadian theatre" (*A Vision of Canada* 12). By contrast, the agitprop drama of the leftist Worker's Theatre was documentary in style and politically reactionary; an exemplary production was Oscar Ryan, Edward Cecil-Smith, Frank Love, and Mildred Goldberg's collectively written play *Eight Men Speak* (1933). For further resources on agitprop theatre in Canada, see Alan Filewod's *Committing Theatre* (2011) as well as his scholarly edition of *Eight Men Speak* (2013).
12. Blavatsky's *Key to Theosophy* offers a comprehensive overview of the tenets of theosophy; see also Gillian McCann's *Vanguard of the New Age* for theosophy's contribution to a uniquely Canadian art scene and for a historical study of the Toronto Theosophical Society.
13. *Canadian Theosophist* (1920–2007), edited by Albert Smythe, was launched in March 1920 as a successor to *Lamp* (1894–1900). Both magazines contained Smythe's theosophical writings, thereby helping to popularize and articulate a wide range of theosophical beliefs.

14. Later in his life, Aikins turned to Buddhism, which shares many tenets with theosophy.
15. Smythe was the Toronto Theosophical Society's first president.
16. William Butler Yeats and A. E. (George Russell) were at once key figures of the Irish Literary Renaissance and of the Theosophical Society.
17. See Wagar's Master's thesis, *Theosophical Socialists in the 1920s Okanagan: Jack Logie's Social Issues Summer Camps* (2002), for further discussion of the intersection of theosophy and socialism in British Columbia.
18. The 1919 playbill lists the address of J. Burkenshaw & Sons as "28 & 29, Colquett St., Liverpool."
19. The Okanagan Indian Education Resources Society (OIERS), which operates under the name En'owkin Centre, owns and manages the Okanagan First Peoples project.
20. For more information on the Okanagan Syilx people, see *We Get Our Living Like Milk from the Land* (1994) edited by Lee Maracle, Jeannett C. Armstrong, Delphine Derickson, and Greg Young-Ing.
21. The Royal Ontario Museum was part of the University of Toronto from 1914 to 1946.
22. Illustrating the predicament of ethnographic modernity in relationship to a William Carlos Williams poem about a female "Indian" servant, Clifford explains that it is "ethnographic because Williams finds himself off center among scattered traditions" and it is modern because "the condition of root-lessness and mobility he confronts is an increasingly common fate" (3).
23. One of the road signs for the Aikins Loop in Naramata misspells his name as "Aikens."
24. See three volumes of William Crotch's *Specimens of Various Styles of Music Referred to in a Course of Lectures Read at Oxford and London* (1808–09) as well as Howard Irving's analysis of Crotch's score anthology in "Empiricism, Ideology and William Crotch's *Specimens*."
25. The "Chiquito Indian Tune" is unattributed to any source in the playbill.
26. Kenneth Noxon, "a young university student," created Hart House Theatre's set and backdrop for *The God of Gods* (Charlesworth).
27. The Hart House archives include a catalogue of theatrical costumes from Toronto's Malabar.
28. Although the reviewer clearly equates "home" with Britain, the suggestion that "the author [should have] chosen a subject nearer home" is vague because it lacks a clear possessive subject: it could refer to either the reviewer's home (which would leave open the possibility that E. L. knew that Aikins was Canadian) or Aikins's home (which would imply that E. L. thought that Aikins was British).
29. See Gina M. Rossetti's *Imagining the Primitive in Naturalist and Modernist Literature* (2006) for a critical focus "not on traditional period definitions but on the era's fears, fascinations, and preoccupations with the primitive and examine how and for what purposes naturalism and modernism came to rely on the primitive" (7).
30. Glenn Willmott's *Modernist Goods: Primitivism, the Market, and the Gift* offers an ethnographic study of the gift and of gift-giving culture. In examining the tension between gift culture and commodity culture, Willmott defines two types of modernism: imperialist modernism and aboriginal modernism.

31. According to Lester, Aikins inherited an interest in Shakespeare adaptations because he "was connected through class and family to an upper-class group that was adapting Shakespeare in the last decades of the eighteenth century and the first decades of the nineteenth century": Aikins's uncle, Charles W. Colby, was colleagues with Charles Moyse, who published *Shakespeare's Skull and Falstaff's Nose* (1889), and Andrew Macphail, who published *The Land* (1914), while Aikins's grandfathers "would have known" Nicholas Flood David, author of *The Fair Grit* (1876). For Lester, "these relationships clearly indicate the ways in which Shakespearean adaptations in Canada in this period were associated with certain class and educational privileges (if not a reinforcement of these)." Although *The God of Gods* appears to be only thematically connected to *Romeo and Juliet* through its emphasis on separated lovers who die by a crypt, Aikins's participation in an elite group of Shakespearean adaptors warrants further consideration.
32. See Aschheim's *The Nietzsche Legacy in Germany, 1890–1990* for an examination of "Nietzsche-socialism."
33. The *Era*'s ambiguous description of Suiva "denouncing the idol and crying out that the God of Gods is Love" suggests that the 1919 Birmingham production included the line "the God of Gods is Love" and thereby differs from Aikins's original manuscript and the Hart House version, which contain only the lines "He was the singer of the joy of life. His name was love. You killed him" (61); alternatively, the reviewer could be paraphrasing these very same lines.

# The God of Gods

# The God of Gods: A Canadian Play

CHARACTERS

YELLOW SNAKE, a singer.
AMBURI, Chief of the Seven Feathers.
MABLO, his son.
LERII, a mad old man.
SUIVA, a girl of the tribe.
KOTWI, her mother.
WANING MOON, Priestess of the God of Gods.
OLD MEN, worshippers.
OLD WOMEN, worshippers.

CASTS AND PRODUCTION CREW

*The God of Gods* was first produced at the Birmingham (England) Repertory Theatre on Saturday 8 November 1919 for two weeks with the following cast and crew:

| | |
|---|---|
| Yellow Snake, A Singer | E. STUART VINDEN |
| Amburi, Chief of the Seven Feathers | FRANK MOORE |
| Mablo, His Son | MELVILLE COOPER |
| Lerii, a Mad Old Man | ERIC H. MESSITER |
| Suiva, a Girl of the Tribe | SUSAN RICHMOND |
| Kotwi, Her Mother | ISABEL THORNTON |
| Waning Moon, Priestess to the God of Gods | MARGARET CHATWIN |
| Old Women | MAUD GILL |
| | SYDNEY LEON |
| | PHYLLIS SHAND |
| | MURIEL MACKENZIE |
| | WINIFRED HARE |

| | |
|---|---|
| Old Men | ARNOLD RIDLEY |
| | REGINALD GATTY |
| | F.G. SRAWLEY |
| | J.L.F. ROWLAND |
| | E.S. DANE |
| | W.N. CRYER |
| | E.W. BLADWELL |
| | C. OTTEWELL |
| | H.H. DAVIES |
| Producer | A. E. FILMER |
| Costumes | J. BURKENSHAW & SONS |
| Set Design | BARRY JACKSON |
| Conductor | HAROLD MILLS |

The play was produced at Toronto's Hart House Theatre, 18th-22nd April 1922, with the following cast and crew:

| | |
|---|---|
| Yellow Snake | R. DE R. ACKLOM |
| Amburi | E. A. DALE |
| Mablo | G. F. MCFARLAND |
| Lerii | WILFRID MAVOR |
| Suiva | LORNA MCLEAN |
| Kotwi | GRACE WEBSTER |
| Waning Moon | DORA MCMILLAN |
| Worshippers | MARIE BAYNON |
| | LOUISE BROWN |
| | JANE HINDS |
| | GERTRUDE MCKEON |
| | EDITH MCLAREN |
| | HELEN RYAN, MARY SMITH |
| | HELEN TEMPLETON |
| | MADELEINE GALBRAITH |
| | BETTY WEDD |
| | ROBERT HACKBORN |
| | A. C. CHELEW |
| | GILPIN BROWN |
| | WALLACE HOUSE |
| | KENNETH KETCHUM |
| | JOHN MCLEAN |
| | EDGAR STONE |

Director . . . . . . . . . . . . . . . . . . . . . . . . . . . . . . BERTRAM FORSYTH
Costumes . . . . . . . . . . . . . . . . . . . . . . . . . . . . MABEL LETCHFORD AND THE HART HOUSE THEATRE WORKSHOPS
Set Design . . . . . . . . . . . . . . . . . . . . . . . . . . . . KENNETH NOXON
Director of Music . . . . . . . . . . . . . . . . . . . . . . . . DR. HEALEY WILLAN

The God of Gods was performed at the London (England) Everyman Theatre in August 1931 with the following cast and crew:

Yellow Snake . . . . . . . . . . . . . . . . . . . . . . . . . . . ARNOLD RICHES
Amburi . . . . . . . . . . . . . . . . . . . . . . . . . . . . . . LEWIN MANNERING
Mablo . . . . . . . . . . . . . . . . . . . . . . . . . . . . . . . MARTIN WALKER
Lerii . . . . . . . . . . . . . . . . . . . . . . . . . . . . . . . . NORMAN SHELLEY
Suiva . . . . . . . . . . . . . . . . . . . . . . . . . . . . . . . . DOROTHY BARNES
Kotwi . . . . . . . . . . . . . . . . . . . . . . . . . . . . . . . . MARIE AULT
Waning Moon . . . . . . . . . . . . . . . . . . . . . . . . . . . RENÉE DE VAUX
Old Men and Women Producer . . . . . . . . . . . . . A. E. FILMER
Costumes . . . . . . . . . . . . . . . . . . . . . . . . . . . . PAUL SHELVING
Set Design . . . . . . . . . . . . . . . . . . . . . . . . . . . . MICHAEL WEIGHT
Dances . . . . . . . . . . . . . . . . . . . . . . . . . . . . . . ANTON DOLIN

# The God of Gods

## ACT I

*The scene represents the edge of a grassy, pine-clad plateau overlooking a lake and a range of mountains. To the left is a small circular tepee of weatherstained birch bark. To the extreme right is a large rock. The right entrances are before and behind this rock. The left entrance is well forward, screened by trees. Near the tepee is a cooking oven of blackened stones, and beside it, an earthenware water pot. At right-centre is a fallen log, and above it an old pine with heavy foliage.*

*The time is before sunrise of a June morning.*

*As the curtain rises* YELLOW SNAKE, *a young Indian, steals in from the right. He wears a cougar skin tunic and carries a small bouquet of red berries and white blossoms. He approaches the tepee cautiously and is about to lay his offering at the entrance when he is startled by a loud sneeze from within. He withdraws in a panic and, as the sneeze is followed by some further commotion, climbs a nearby tree and hides in the foliage.*

KOTWI, *a fat squaw, dressed in a gaudy blanket, backs out of the tepee and looks about her suspiciously.*

KOTWI: Who's there? (*She goes about grunting, looking behind rocks and trees.* WANING MOON *enters from the left. She is a thin old hag of a squaw and wears a ceremonial white garment ornamented with a silver crescent-moon.* KOTWI *turns and sees her.*) Oh! it's you, is it? I thought it was a hill dog.

WANING MOON (*stonily*): Have you forgotten what I am?

KOTWI *comes forward apologetically, inclines her head, and clasps her hands behind it.*

KOTWI: The God is great. He giveth us full bellies.

WANING MOON: The God is good to them that love his priestess.

KOTWI: I love you well.

WANING MOON: The God will hear me when I pray for you. And he will fill your belly.

KOTWI (*raising her head*): The God is great. He is the God of Gods.

*(Their tones, which have been ritualistic, return to normal.)*

WANING MOON *(seating herself on a log)*: He gets no older. It's not so with us. My legs are like the willows.

KOTWI: Aie! We're getting on. And soon they'll grind our meat between two stones. Shall I call Suiva? Have you eaten yet?

WANING MOON: Yes, I have eaten. Leave the girl to sleep.

KOTWI: You're up early and far from the God's altar. Is there evil word?

WANING MOON: No word at all. The God is drunk and happy in his dreams. But I wake early, and I'm glad to wake. My days are not so many as they were.

KOTWI: You needn't fear. The God will guide you to his Yellow Tent.

WANING MOON: I'm not afraid. But there must be a girl to take my place. Or do you want the holy fire to die?

KOTWI: No! How should we eat if the fire died? And the God angry? Ask him to make haste!

WANING MOON: I'm not dead yet. You keep your tongue tied up!

KOTWI: I meant no harm. Who is it he will choose? Is it Water Plume or old Coyote's daughter?

WANING MOON: She must be virgin.

KOTWI: Aie! Then they won't do!

WANING MOON: I thought that Water Plume . . .

KOTWI: She! You might as well believe the world is round like a sheep's bladder! She, a virgin! Pouf!

WANING MOON: The God will know.

KOTWI: He has sharp eyes, then. She is a sly one—ough! I won't let Suiva fish in the same stream. When will he choose the girl?

WANING MOON: The God is drunk. He bids me choose the girl.

KOTWI: And you've come here! Is it my Suiva that you want? *(Eagerly)* Eh? Is it Suiva? *(Calling)* Suiva!

WANING MOON: Not so fast! You're like the other mothers. They all want their girls to be the Young Moon. Why is that?

KOTWI: I can't speak for the others. For myself, I fear the God, and I will give my daughter.

WANING MOON (*knowingly*): Aie!

KOTWI: Why do you say "Aie"? What is there more that I can give than my own child, my Suiva? The God is great but he is old, and lives in the deep pool. No man has seen him; only his stone image. He is great, but she is young and like the doe in springtime. It is not sweet to live without a man! And yet I give her.

WANING MOON: Aie! You give her!

KOTWI: Well?

WANING MOON: When the fat deer are brought, and the bears' hearts, and the wild ducks and turtles, and burnt upon the altar, what does the God get of them?

KOTWI: He gets the smell.

WANING MOON: And who gets the meat?

KOTWI: Who should get it, if not the God's own priestess?

WANING MOON: And what does she do with it?

KOTWI: She eats it.

WANING MOON: And what she cannot eat!

KOTWI: She gives to the old and sick, and those who cannot see.

WANING MOON: And maybe, her own people? Her own mother, eh?

KOTWI: Maybe. It's not of that I think.

WANING MOON: Old Coyote offered me five cows if I would choose his daughter.

KOTWI: He is a liar, and his cows are sick. I'll give you five good cows.

WANING MOON: I am the daughter of the God.

KOTWI: I meant no harm.

WANING MOON: I must have ten cows.

KOTWI: Ten! Aie! But you are the daughter of the God! What do you want of ten cows?

WANING MOON: I want them for my nephew, Shiny Bird.

KOTWI: Your nephew?

WANING MOON: For ten cows, he will keep me till I die.

KOTWI (*Indignantly*): That won't be long. And now you don't eat much. Ten cows! Bah! He's a tight-skinned groundhog, Shiny Bird! He wants his meat all fat!

WANING MOON: He won't take less.

KOTWI: Give me but seven and I'll keep you!

WANING MOON: He has a house with stones for a big fire. The stones are warm in winter.

KOTWI: We have dry cedar brought and many deerskins. You would be happy with us, Waning Moon.

WANING MOON: I like to sleep with warm stones in my bed.

KOTWI: You shall have warm stones here.

WANING MOON: No, it's more fitting that I should die with my own people.

KOTWI: Aie! That's so. Well, I have asked you. Remember that I have asked you.

WANING MOON: The God will thank you. But, as I can't come here, how would you like your girl to take my place?

KOTWI: Where shall I find ten cows?

WANING MOON: You! You have five times ten!

KOTWI: I had when my man died. But now the most are stolen.

WANING MOON: Is that truth? I hadn't heard it.

KOTWI: Stolen, or died of the mouth sickness. It's hard to be a widow!

WANING MOON: That's so. That's so. Well, if you haven't ten cows . . . (*She rises painfully.*) Anyway, I doubt that Suiva would have pleased the God. The girl must be a virgin.

KOTWI: She is that! If any gabbing squaw has told you that she's not, she lies! She lies!

WANING MOON (*sardonically*): Aie! Aie!

KOTWI: There's never a man has touched her ankle-ring!

WANING MOON: Not Yellow Snake, the singer?

KOTWI: Not he, nor any other. I watch her like the mother grouse, her chick.

YELLOW SNAKE *follows the various turns of their conversation with interested but restrained pantomime.*

WANING MOON: How old is she?

KOTWI: The fingers of four hands.

WANING MOON: And has not tried her wings?

KOTWI: I swear she has not! You should not listen to such evil tongues.

WANING MOON: They swim together by the salmon traps.

KOTWI: Maybe they do. Cannot a virgin swim?

WANING MOON: Not with Yellow Snake. He has wild ways and does not fear the God.

KOTWI: Aie! But she fears the God. Every day she prays to him when the sun comes and goes. She fears him so, I'd rather die than tell her all that we've been saying. Your ten calls and all! It's a hard life for widows. (*She begins to sniffle.*)

WANING MOON: You're a good woman, Kotwi. And now I'll tell you something that you'll like to hear.

KOTWI: What's that?

WANING MOON: You know the Chief's son, Mablo . . .

KOTWI (*sharply*): Aie!

WANING MOON: He wants your Suiva for his woman.

KOTWI: How do you know?

WANING MOON: He told me so himself.

KOTWI: The God be praised! You're a good woman, Waning Moon. I hope you get your ten cows. Mablo! There's a man! With his own house and cattle! You don't catch Mablo swimming by the traps. And when Amburi dies, he'll be the Chief. Chief of the Seven Feathers! He'll smoke the silver pipe, and wear the yellow on his cheeks! And Suiva, my little Suiva, will be his woman! The God be praised!

WANING MOON: Yes, if she'll have him.

KOTWI: Have him? Of course, she'll have him! There's not a girl in all the world who wouldn't have him. When is he going to ask her?

WANING MOON: Pretty soon. He's afraid that Yellow Snake will get her.

KOTWI: I'll see to that!

WANING MOON: Don't tell her what I've told you.

KOTWI: Why not?

WANING MOON: I promised Mablo that I wouldn't tell. Good-bye.

KOTWI: You've made me happy like the jumping trout! (WANING MOON *eyes her stonily.* KOTWI *bends her head and clasps her hands behind her.*) The God is great. He giveth us full bellies.

WANING MOON: The God is good to them that love his priestess.

KOTWI: I love you well.

WANING MOON: The God will hear me when I pray for you. And he will fill your belly.

KOTWI (*with fervour*): The God is great! He is the God of Gods! (*She raises her head.* WANING MOON *turns and goes out to the left, walking with ceremonious dignity.* KOTWI, *highly delighted, goes to the tepee and calls*) Suiva! Oh, Suiva!

SUIVA (*off, sleepily*): Yes?

KOTWI: Wake up! Wake up! A great girl like you!

SUIVA: Is it the prayer hour?

KOTWI: Soon. The hills are bright. The sun is on the second ridge. Be quick!

SUIVA: I am putting on my tunic . . . Your voice is happy. Have you snared a grouse?

KOTWI: Maybe.

SUIVA: A big one?

KOTWI: Aie! Maybe a very big one!

SUIVA: A blue grouse?

KOTWI: A grouse with yellow on his cheeks. Di-di, di-di!

SUIVA (*calmly*): There is no grouse with yellow on his cheeks. You snared a meadowlark.

KOTWI: That smokes a silver pipe.

SUIVA: Just now I dreamt that I heard voices.

KOTWI: It was so. But hurry! Quick! The sun will soon be up!

SUIVA: I'm coming! Who was here?

KOTWI: Old Waning Moon.

SUIVA: The Holy One!

KOTWI (*chuckling*): The Holy One! Aie! Aie!

SUIVA: What did she want?

KOTWI: To talk of cows!

SUIVA: The moon is on you. Which way did she go?

KOTWI: The hill way—to the lake.

SUIVA: Was she alone?

KOTWI: You think the path is steep?

SUIVA (*reproachfully*): You know the path is steep. I'll go and help her.

KOTWI: No! I'll go! I'll go! She's a good woman!

SUIVA (*emerging on hands and knees*): Good! She's the God's daughter!

KOTWI (*going left*): So she is! Get water from the spring and build the fire. But, first, your prayers. *Both* prayers.

SUIVA: You needn't tell me that! (KOTWI *goes out.* SUIVA *rises to her feet. She is a very beautiful Indian girl, barefoot, with loose hair, and wears a single fawn-skin garment which leaves one shoulder bare and does not fall below the knees. She goes to the centre of the scene, turns, and with arms outstretched, addresses the sun, which has half risen above the mountain.*) Give thanks, torchbearer, to the God of Gods! And fear him, lest he crush the hollow reed that gives the breath beneath the great blue water! Fear him, torch bearer! (*She turns, comes forward, and kneels.*)

Great God of Gods, I am thy slave. I fear thee. Slay me not with tongue of fire in the crash of falling mountains.

Renew the springs, that I may drink. Renew the sweat upon the maize fields. Break thou the knees of the fat deer that I may eat, I and my people.

Make sharp and swift the arrows of my people. Make blunt the daggers of our foes and break their bow-strings. Withhold thy torch from them and fill their mouths with poison.

Give me to mate a strong man in my season, and bind him to me with the twisted vine. As with sweet balsam and sweet secret oil ease thou the labour of my child-bearing.

Or, choose me to thy service. Lay on my breast the face of the young moon and bid me be thy virgin. I will tend thy fire, and shear the foeman's hair to fill thy nose with incense.

Great God of Gods! I am thy slave. I fear thee! (*As she rises,* YELLOW SNAKE *throws the bouquet at her feet. She laughs, darts to it, picks it up, and peers about her to discover the thrower.*) Who are you?

YELLOW SNAKE (*mockingly*): I am thy slave. I fear thee.

SUIVA (*reprovingly*): Yellow Snake! Where are you?

YELLOW SNAKE: There, in your hand, red berries and white blossoms.

SUIVA: Come to me!

YELLOW SNAKE: I will not.

SUIVA (*peering in the long grass*): Are you a field-mouse?

YELLOW SNAKE (*laughing*): No.

SUIVA: A squirrel.

YELLOW SNAKE: No.

SUIVA: What are you, then?

YELLOW SNAKE: Your lover.

SUIVA (*seeing him, and clapping her hands*): Yes!

YELLOW SNAKE: And singer of the glory in the morning!

(*He swings down from the tree and takes her in his arms.*)

SUIVA: Yellow Snake! (*He kisses her ardently. She struggles to free herself.*) No! No! You mustn't!

YELLOW SNAKE (*laughing and continuing his embrace*): Why?

SUIVA (*in a low voice*): Take care!

YELLOW SNAKE (*releasing her hastily*): Your mother!

SUIVA (*laughing, half serious*): No. The God might see.

YELLOW SNAKE (*disgustedly*): The God! The God! That poor old man! There's too much water in his eyes. He can't see anything.

SUIVA (*frightened*): Take care! Take care!

YELLOW SNAKE: If I were God I wouldn't live in this dark pool. (*Approaching her*) Your hair is like the thunder-clouds! Your breath is like crushed lilies!

SUIVA (*to divert him*): No, don't! If you were God where would you live?

YELLOW SNAKE: I'd ride that cloud. I'd take the trees for arrows and shoot them at the sun.

SUIVA: You'd kill the sun!

YELLOW SNAKE: I'd wound him, so he'd limp and give us light after the birds are in their nests.

SUIVA: If you did that, we'd swim no more by moonlight.

*(She fixes the bouquet in her dress.)*

YELLOW SNAKE: Yes, we should. Because the moon's his mate and when she hears him cry she'll come to bathe his wounds with sweet spring water, but before she comes I'll catch a gourd of blood in my two hands and bring it down to you and bathe your feet.

SUIVA: With blood?

YELLOW SNAKE: With his blood, and I'll bathe mine too, and then, at night, we'll go and dance upon the mountain. And when our people see the light they'll think the God has struck some dead tree with his tongue. And that old hag, the priestess, Waning Moon will say the God is angry, and she'll make Amburi give her a fat deer to burn upon the altar, *(mockingly)* to fill his nose with incense. *(Angrily)* To fill her wrinkled belly!

SUIVA: Hush!

YELLOW SNAKE: And then I'll take you to the Hidden Water!

SUIVA: That's a dream! There is no Hidden Water!

YELLOW SNAKE: No?

SUIVA: Where is it?

YELLOW SNAKE: You'll find it with the sun's fire on your feet.

SUIVA: But you've not been there.

YELLOW SNAKE: I go when I will.

SUIVA: Where is it?

YELLOW SNAKE: Over there behind Grey Mountain.

SUIVA: The blue sea lies there.

YELLOW SNAKE: It's two days' journey higher than the sea.

SUIVA: Above the tree line?

YELLOW SNAKE: Many trees are there.

SUIVA: And birds?

YELLOW SNAKE: Aie! Trees and birds, but both are strange.

SUIVA (*lying down and resting her cheek on her hand*): Tell me! How are they strange?

YELLOW SNAKE (*seating himself, cross-legged*): It's the white truth I tell you.

SUIVA: Are the trees of gold? And the birds like little men?

YELLOW SNAKE: The birds look like these birds but they are really dreams that choose the trees they love and nest in them. They mate like thrushes but their young are not like birds at all. Some are of stone and have carved limbs and faces, rubbed and smoothed with sand, and some are pictures made with blood on birch-bark, and some are only voices. But when they sing it is like quick water under the white moon. And you must never hurt those birds or rob their nests.

SUIVA: Why not?

YELLOW SNAKE: Because, if you hurt them, you hurt the trees. If you kill them, you kill the trees; and if you kill the trees, you have no shelter from the sun and storm; and though you live, life will be dull as sleep is without dreams; and you'll be glad to die.

SUIVA: What else is there?

YELLOW SNAKE: There is grass—like this grass, and flowers, and berry-bushes; but they have juices red as your own blood. And when they are hurt they cry as children do. And when the wind runs through them and they're glad, you hear their laughter rippling up the hills. And there's a deep lake, deeper than the sky, with water whiter than a young deer's teeth. And when you swim in it you're strong as the black otter and swift as the clean trout and sweet as the white lilies. And when you drink of it your heart is friendly and you hate no man and none hates you. And when you look on it your eyes are stars, your hair is waving grass, your arms have bark like fir trees, and your legs are like polished stones in the creek bottom—you don't know what you are. The bees and birds come to you, the shy deer, the trees, the flowers, even the stones and fishes. You talk to them and they to you. And so the quick day passes; days and days.

SUIVA: Has any man gone with you?

YELLOW SNAKE: Not with me; but Lerii knows the way.

SUIVA: Mad Lerii!

YELLOW SNAKE: Aie!

SUIVA: That's strange.

YELLOW SNAKE: I have a house there.

SUIVA: Yellow Snake! You've made a house for us! By Hidden Water!

YELLOW SNAKE: If you will come.

SUIVA: A two days' journey? There, behind Grey Mountain?

YELLOW SNAKE: Maybe not so far.

SUIVA: One day?

YELLOW SNAKE: Maybe not one day.

SUIVA: How far? Where is it?

YELLOW SNAKE: How far can the heart leap when the dawn birds sing?

SUIVA: You haven't made a house!

YELLOW SNAKE (*with a wide gesture*): This is my house!

SUIVA: I thought you meant it!

YELLOW SNAKE: This is my house.

SUIVA: It's no more yours than mine or any other's.

YELLOW SNAKE: A man must have no fear in his own house. He must walk straight and know the way of it. He must know the songs and plumage of all birds that nest and all the colours of all fish that swim and all the words and ways of all the beasts. He must have no fear of any beast, or man, or God. If he's afraid, then this is not his house.

SUIVA: If you won't fear the God, then I shan't love you.

YELLOW SNAKE: Why should I fear him?

SUIVA: Yellow Snake!

YELLOW SNAKE: Why should I?

SUIVA: Why? Because he's God! He gives you the sun's heat and the moon's whiteness. He drives the salmon to your traps and curves your arrow to the quick deer's heart. He puts good magic in the roots of plants and hangs red berries on the bushes. And if you fear him he will prosper you. But if you fear him not, he will strike you dead. The hills will fall on you, or he'll put poison in your mouth so that your bones will rot like fallen trees. But if you pray to him and bring him gifts and do his bidding as the priestess tells, you will be rich and warm and happy and well fed, and you will live to see the ptarmigan turn white ten times the counted fingers of both hands. Oh, you must fear him! Fear him, Yellow Snake!

YELLOW SNAKE: I can't fear him. I can't fear anything.

SUIVA: Only the God.

YELLOW SNAKE: Fat Mablo fears the God. Will you love him?

SUIVA (*slightly diverted*): Mablo?

YELLOW SNAKE: Aie! He wants you for his woman.

SUIVA: What!

YELLOW SNAKE: I heard the priestess tell your mother so. That's why she was so happy. He's the grouse that smokes a silver pipe, and has the yellow on his cheeks.

SUIVA: The Great Chief's son! And he wants me!

YELLOW SNAKE (*superbly*): I also want you.

SUIVA: Chief of the Seven Feathers! Are you sure?

YELLOW SNAKE (*uneasily*): But you don't want him. You want me.

SUIVA (*teasingly*): It's no small thing to be the Great Chief's woman.

YELLOW SNAKE: Rather than mate with him I'd pick a three-years' skunk up by the tail.

SUIVA: He's not so very fat.

YELLOW SNAKE: The groundhog is a pine needle beside him.

SUIVA: Every day he prays at the God's altar.

YELLOW SNAKE: He doesn't pray. He eats the sacred meat after the God has smelt it.

SUIVA: That's a lie.

YELLOW SNAKE: I've seen him eat it.

SUIVA: How could you see him? Only the old men go within the gates—they and the Chief's son. You tell too many lies.

YELLOW SNAKE: It's not a lie. I've seen him from the top of the flat rock.

SUIVA: But that's within the gate!

YELLOW SNAKE (*sulkily*): What of it?

SUIVA: How do you get there?

YELLOW SNAKE: There's a deep crevice in the canyon wall. A cow could climb it.

SUIVA: They'll kill you if they catch you! They'll cut your hair off and throw it in the pool. (*Pleadingly*) No! No! You're lying to me! Tell me you've not been there.

YELLOW SNAKE: I say that Mablo eats the God's meat. He's a sly groundhog with an oily tongue. He only loves his belly.

SUIVA: You've not been there at all. You say these things because you're jealous of him.

YELLOW SNAKE: Jealous? No, I'm not!

SUIVA: You're only a singer, but he's the Great Chief's son.

YELLOW SNAKE: I don't care if he is.

SUIVA: He has a fine house, too, and lots of cattle.

YELLOW SNAKE: I don't care if he has.

SUIVA (*with a purpose*): I do!

YELLOW SNAKE (*startled*): Eh?

SUIVA (*defiantly*): I say I care.

YELLOW SNAKE: You wouldn't marry him?

SUIVA (*rising*): Maybe not.

YELLOW SNAKE: Maybe! You couldn't marry him!

SUIVA: My mother's old and we are poor. The winter's coming, we must have a house; and we must live.

YELLOW SNAKE (*springing up*): Then, you will be his woman? You! Suiva, it's not so? Tell me it's not so!

SUIVA: It will be if I choose.

YELLOW SNAKE: I'll kill you first!

SUIVA: Mablo's a man! He won't let you kill me!

YELLOW SNAKE: He's not a man! He's a round pot of bear's grease! And if you mate with him I'll kill you both! (*In agony*) You wouldn't mate with him!

SUIVA: When Mablo asks me, I'll say this to him: If Yellow Snake has not made me a house by the young moon, then I will mate with you.

YELLOW SNAKE (*wildly*): How can I make a house by the young moon?

SUIVA: By working hard, you will make it.

YELLOW SNAKE: The moon is half way here!

SUIVA: Get Shiny Bird and Blue Fox to help you.

YELLOW SNAKE: Yes! Yes, and while they work I'll sing to them.

SUIVA: You must work, too.

YELLOW SNAKE (*cunningly*): I know a place in the thick cedar woods where the close branches are like sloping walls. The ground's so thick with moss it springs like a muskeg. There's a place to sleep! Why must we have a house?

SUIVA (*gently*): When the birds mate, why do they build them nests?

YELLOW SNAKE (*after a pause*): That's so.

SUIVA (*drawing him down*): Sit down beside me and we'll make the plan.

YELLOW SNAKE: But tell me first you wouldn't mate with him.

SUIVA: I'll tell you nothing till the young moon comes. Give me that stick there! (*He hands her a dry stick which she tries vainly to break, then returns it to him.*) You break it in four pieces; two long, like that; and two short, like this. (*He does so, returns them to her, and gradually becomes interested as she arranges them on the sandy ground. She hands him back one of the smaller pieces.*) Now, break this one again, and we'll make the door. (*He breaks it, hands her the pieces, and sits down beside her. She arranges the fourth wall.*) The door must face the sunrise.

YELLOW SNAKE: We'll build it on the night side of the stream.

SUIVA: I know a hollow where the ground is smooth.

YELLOW SNAKE: So do I.

SUIVA: Below the traps?

YELLOW SNAKE: Not far. There's a young juniper with one arm in the stream.

SUIVA: And three flat stones to step on?

YELLOW SNAKE: Aie!

SUIVA (*clapping her hands*): That's my place, too!

YELLOW SNAKE: I thought so. Now, let's make the walls.

SUIVA: The inside first. Where shall we have the fire?

YELLOW SNAKE: Here, in this corner.

SUIVA (*nodding*): Yes.

YELLOW SNAKE: We'll lay the fire-stones.

(*They arrange some small stones in the form of an oven.*)

SUIVA: Where shall we sleep?

YELLOW SNAKE: On this side, with our feet this way, so we can see the stars.

(SUIVA *lays some grass in the place indicated.*)

SUIVA: Here are the cedar boughs.

(YELLOW SNAKE *adds some leaves.*)

YELLOW SNAKE: And here are the deerskins. Now, we'll make the walls.

(*They build a framework of dry sticks.*)

SUIVA: These are white birches.

YELLOW SNAKE: Yes. They gleam like silver. The light on them is like the moon on water.

SUIVA: And they are strong. They don't rot like pine saplings do.

YELLOW SNAKE: We'll chink them with grey moss that's warm in winter.

(*The corner posts of the house are forked, and in these forks they set the joists. Across the joists they lay rafters, and cover the house with a litter of leaves and pine needles.*)

SUIVA: We'll thatch the roof with rushes from the black swamp.

YELLOW SNAKE: And bind the rushes with thin willow boughs.

(*They add a few finishing touches.*)

SUIVA: And there's our home.

YELLOW SNAKE (*his hand on hers*): With sunlight in the door.

SUIVA (*rather shyly, taking his hand*): In our own house it will be well with us. (*The cracking of a branch is heard. They spring up.* SUIVA *laughs.*) It's mother!

YELLOW SNAKE (*preparing to clear out*): I fear no man, nor beast, nor God; but I fear her!

SUIVA: Quick! Where's the water pot! (*He picks up an earthenware pot.*) She hasn't seen us! Quick! Down to the spring!

(*Hand in hand, they run off to the right.* KOTWI *comes in from the left, grunting. She glances at the cold fire stones, looks in vain for the pot, and then calls, angrily.*)

KOTWI: Suiva! Suiva! (*There is no reply. She catches sight of the toy house and inspects it closely with growing indignation. There is the sound of approaching steps from the right. She turns to scold her daughter but discovers* AMBURI, *the old Chief, and his son,* MABLO. *They enter.* AMBURI *is a dignified, courtly, old man, accustomed to grant favours and command respect. He is dressed in black otter skins and carries an ornamented hatchet in his girdle. He wears moccasins and deerskin leggings.* MABLO *is a fat unctuous youth in brown bearskins.* KOTWI, *her expression changed to one of gratified surprise, goes forward to meet them.*) The Great Chief and his son, Mablo, do me much honour.

AMBURI (*graciously*): Your man was a good man, and we respect you.

MABLO (*wiping his hands on his costume*): There is no woman whom we honour more.

KOTWI: Will the Great Chief be seated?

AMBURI: Aie!

KOTWI: And the Chief's son?

AMBURI (*calmly*): The Chief's son will stand. Stand over there . . . What think you of him, Kotwi?

KOTWI: He is most handsome. His legs are like great tree trunks. He has the courage of a mother-bear, and yet his ways are gentle.

MABLO: That is so.

AMBURI (*sharply*): Let be!

KOTWI: He fears the God and doesn't run with fast girls.

AMBURI: It's true he fears the God.

MABLO (*unctuously*): The God is good to them that fear him.

AMBURI: Say on, my son. Tell Kotwi why we've come.

MABLO: You tell her, father.

AMBURI: My son has found your daughter to his liking.

KOTWI: My Suiva?

AMBURI: Aie! And he asks your leave to marry her.

KOTWI: So great an honour I'd not dared to dream of!

AMBURI: You say well.

KOTWI: She is a good girl, though, and fit to mate him.

AMBURI: Fears she the God?

KOTWI: Like thunder on the mountain. And I have taught her many things besides. She can sew double stitch with strong deer tendons and weave a blanket soft and white as snow. She can make baskets, too, that hold spring water, and smooth an arrow like stream-polished stones. And she is cunning to set snares for rabbits; and in the smoking sheds and at the traps no girl works harder.

MABLO: Can she cook?

KOTWI: Cook! When you eat deer meat as she cooks it, you'll think you never ate deer meat before. And a bear's heart! Or a blue grouse! Or a young trout! When she grills young trout I wonder that the God comes not from heaven to eat them!

MABLO: Does she wrap parsley round the fat bear's heart? Or does she cook it with wild spinach leaves?

KOTWI: She studs it with fine pellets of burnt grain and steeps it over night in berry wine, and wraps wet leaves round it, and cooks it in the ashes of green wood. For that alone a man might marry her!

AMBURI (*to* MABLO): Your belly will be glad, but life's not all big eating. (*To* KOTWI) Where is your girl? Is she not up yet?

KOTWI: She said her sun-prayer ere the sun was up!

AMBURI: Where is she, then?

KOTWI: She must have gone to the far spring for water. I'll call her to come quickly. (*Calling*) Oh, Suiva! Suiva! Come you here! I want you!

AMBURI (*rising*): Now that he has your leave he'll speak to her. Find your tongue, my son.

MABLO: Yes, father.

KOTWI: My girl will take you in her arms. Don't be too backward, Mablo.

AMBURI: Remember you're the Great Chief's son, and we have many cattle.

KOTWI: Think of the fat bear's heart!

MABLO: I needn't think of those things. I want Suiva.

KOTWI: She'll be the proud girl, or she's not my daughter!

AMBURI: We'll leave him to the asking. But I doubt not she'll have him.

KOTWI: She'll be his clinging vine or I'm a liar.

AMBURI: I have some things to say to you.

KOTWI: Great Chief!

AMBURI: We'll go along the lake path. (*They go towards the left,* AMBURI *leading.*) I hear your cattle have been stolen?

KOTWI: Aie! Most are gone! Now that my man is dead!

AMBURI: I know who stole them. He shall be killed, and you shall have his herd to graze with yours. He was a fool to steal the cattle of the Chief's grandchildren.

KOTWI: The God is great. He giveth us full bellies!

(*They go out left.* MABLO *makes some slight adjustments in his costume, slicks his hair, etc., and strolls over to the fore-right of the scene.* SUIVA *runs in from the rear right and, for a moment, fails to see him.*)

SUIVA: Here I am, mother! What made you call so loud? (*She pauses for an answer, then turns and discovers* MABLO.) Oh!

MABLO: Good morning, Suiva!

SUIVA (*dimpling*): Good morning, Mablo. I didn't know you were here!

MABLO: I came with father.

SUIVA (*encouragingly*): Yes?

MABLO: He's gone with your mother to walk along the lake path.

SUIVA: What gets you up so early?

MABLO: I never miss the sun-prayer. Afterwards I sleep. Did you make this little house?

(*He makes as if to stir it with his foot.*)

SUIVA (*swiftly*): Yes, but please don't touch it!

MABLO: You should have a fence around it to keep out the cattle.

SUIVA: We don't need a fence. We have no cattle.

MABLO: That's what your mother said. It's not so with us. We have more cattle than three men can count.

SUIVA (*baiting him*): It must be wonderful to be so rich. Always to know that you can kill a beast and have fresh meat.

MABLO: And one-tenth part of all the game that's caught and all the fish.

SUIVA: And a big house!

MABLO: With two doors and a cooking spit that turns a whole great haunch of deer.

SUIVA: And haven't you a grizzly skin to lie on, with brown-grey hair that's deeper than the bunch of grass?

MABLO (*nodding*): And I have anklets for the girl I marry.

SUIVA: How many anklets have you?

MABLO: They would go, all gold and silver, to your knee, and be some over for the other leg!

SUIVA: Imagine having anklets to your knees! She'll be a lucky girl, the one you marry!

MABLO: Aie! And pretty soon I'll choose her.

SUIVA: Does she know?

MABLO: Not yet.

SUIVA: When will you tell her?

MABLO: Do you think she'd like to know?

SUIVA: I'm sure she would.

MABLO: I'll tell her then. It's you!

SUIVA: I?

MABLO: I am not joking. You're the girl.

SUIVA: Oh, Mablo!

MABLO: And you will love me?

SUIVA: Mablo . . . Mablo . . . you tell me this so quickly. You have not courted me. I would blush to tell you so soon that I will love you.

MABLO (*coyly*): I won't look at you when you say it.

SUIVA: I would feel shame to tell you quite so soon! (*She stoops quickly and picks up a leafy branch about six feet in length.*) But I'll show you, Mablo. If you catch me before I strip this branch, then I shall love you well and be your woman.

MABLO: That's a child's game! I'd rather have you tell me.

SUIVA: Two leaves are gone!

MABLO: Don't be too quick. I have had no breakfast yet.

(*He runs at her and she pokes the end of the branch in his face. He stops abruptly, and she strips off a few more leaves.*)

SUIVA: You should run lightly for not having eaten. (*He makes a sudden dive for her. She eludes him lightly.*) If I were a fat cow, then you'd have caught me! (*She strips off a few more leaves.*)

MABLO: If I don't catch you then, maybe to-morrow you will tell me?

SUIVA: If you don't catch me I won't mate with you.

MABLO: You don't mean that.

SUIVA: As sure as these leaves fall.

(*He sets about the pursuit in earnest, but without success. They go in and out between the trees.*)

MABLO: There are other girls.

SUIVA: Then why chase me, and lose your breath?

MABLO: I want you. I will have you!

SUIVA: If you could run like Yellow Snake you'd catch me! (*He doubles at her around a tree.*) Oh, no, you don't! You are not cunning either! The leaves are falling fast. You must make haste! Be more like Yellow Snake; he'd catch me ere the falling of one leaf!

MABLO: He has no cattle!

SUIVA: He'll make a song of how the groundhog chased the squirrel.

MABLO: He has no house.

SUIVA: He'll have one by the coming of the moon! And I'll go mate with him unless you catch me! So catch me quick, my Mablo! Catch me! Catch me! (*She whips his legs. He yells and pursues. In his course, he comes near to destroying the toy house.*) Be careful! That's the little house we made! And Yellow Snake will make a big one like it! And I'll live there with him until I die! (*She has stripped all the leaves from the branch save a few at the top; these, she breaks off and throws in his face.)* And you can eat your anklets, you fat Mablo. *(She whips him soundly about the legs.)* Or hang them on the horns of an old cow! *(She whips him again.* MABLO *squeals.)* For Yellow Snake's my mate, you sleepy Mablo! So, don't come here again to make me laugh!

*(She throws the whip at him and runs out to the right. He is in a state of smarting fury and impotent shame. First, he starts after her, then, hesitates, turns, and catching sight of the toy house, runs at it, and kicks it with all his might. His bare toes go through the edifice but encounter the firestones. With a howl of pain he clutches the bruised foot and dances on the other.* WANING MOON *enters from the right.* MABLO *dances up to her.)*

MABLO: What think you, Waning Moon! She will not have me! She beat my legs with a young birch tree! And she's run off to mate with Yellow Snake.

WANING MOON: She will not have you!

MABLO: And she will mate with him.

WANING MOON: The God has made her mad. She is no woman for the Great Chief's son. Go ask old Coyote's girl. She is more proper and she has many cattle.

MABLO: I don't want his cattle or his daughter. I want Suiva.

WANING MOON: And she wants Yellow Snake. What can you do?

MABLO: He shall not have her!

WANING MOON: You must kill him then! But he is strong and cunning as the cougar! Aie! Stronger! For he stripped the yellow beast to get the skin he wears. And if you tackle him he'll kill you, Mablo.

MABLO: I didn't say I'd kill him.

WANING MOON: If you kill her the tribe will have your blood. You dare not do it!

MABLO: I don't want her dead. I want her living.

WANING MOON: Then you must poison him. I'll tell you how. Dip a sharp cactus in a boiling of snakes' tongues and hide it in his bed. When the thorns prick him he will die and none shall know who killed him. If any man suspect, I'll say that the God did it because he would not fear him.

MABLO: It will be worse for him to live and not to have her.

WANING MOON: How can that be? If he's alive he'll have her.

MABLO: She fears the God. Make her his virgin priestess. And if he goes within the gate the tribe will kill him.

WANING MOON: How will that help you?

MABLO: The Chief's son goes within the gate.

WANING MOON: Sly fox! Give me ten cows and I will choose her!

MABLO: I will give you five.

WANING MOON: Ten!

MABLO: Seven!

WANING MOON: Remember how she whipped you!

MABLO: Eight! Eight, and no more!

WANING MOON: Listen, Mablo. When your father dies you will be the Chief and it is known that the Great Chief has power over the priestess. If you want her then, no man can stop you. Give me ten cows!

MABLO: When will you choose her?

WANING MOON: Now. I hear her coming! (*In a whisper*) Promise me. Ten cows!

MABLO: Aie! You shall have them, but there's someone with her. Come this way! We'll watch them.

(*They take shelter behind the rock to the right where they are visible to the audience but hidden from* SUIVA *and* YELLOW SNAKE, *who enter from the rear-right, carrying between them a pot of water.*)

YELLOW SNAKE: I wish I'd seen you whip him with the birch tree.

SUIVA: He danced like a fat bear and squealed like a stuck rabbit.

(*They put down the water pot.* YELLOW SNAKE *discovers the remains of the toy house and indicates it to* SUIVA.)

YELLOW SNAKE: Look!

SUIVA: Our house!

YELLOW SNAKE: It's all in ruins!

SUIVA: He did it out of spite. It doesn't matter. It will be well with us in our own house.

(*She takes his hand rather shyly.*)

YELLOW SNAKE (*with a repetition of his previous wide gesture*): Aie! And in my house it will be well with us. If I live like the robin in his nest will you not go with me as white gulls go?

SUIVA (*nodding*): To the high mountains where the great bears are.

YELLOW SNAKE: And to the Hidden Water?

SUIVA: When you have put the sun's fire on my feet.

YELLOW SNAKE: And you'll not harm the birds or rob their nests?

SUIVA: If I should hurt your dreams, then I'd hurt you. If I should kill your dreams, then I'd kill you. And I love you.

(*They draw closer together.*)

YELLOW SNAKE: As I love you, as the white moon looks down on her own face.

SUIVA: In the deep lake that's whiter than a young deer's teeth.

YELLOW SNAKE: We shall swim there together and be strong.

SUIVA: And drink of it, so that we hate no man, and none hates us.

YELLOW SNAKE: I'll start today to cut the thin birch saplings.

SUIVA: And when the young moon comes . . .

YELLOW SNAKE: And when it comes . . .

(WANING MOON, *directed by* MABLO, *has unpinned the silver moon from her vestment. Holding it behind her, she goes to meet the lovers who are about to embrace.*)

WANING MOON: Suiva!

(*They spring apart. She advances.*)

SUIVA: Holy One! What brings you here?

WANING MOON: I have a gift for you.

SUIVA: A gift?

WANING MOON: Come nearer. Kneel. The God has spoken. The young moon is yours.

(*With a deft movement she fixes the silver moon on* SUIVA'S *tunic, then turns swiftly to encounter* YELLOW SNAKE, *who has sprung forward. He pauses before her outstretched arms.* MABLO *grins from his hiding place as the curtain falls.*)

## ACT II

*The scene represents a rocky canyon and is divided from left to right by a deep chasm at the bottom of which is a swift stream. The chasm is spanned by a huge, hideous stone image of the God of Gods. At the feet of the image, in an iron basket is a fire of pine bark. Beside the fire are a pot of meat scraps, a cup of wine and a sacrificial knife. The altar is approached by three stone steps; below, the torrent thrashes into the deep pool; beside it, at the right, is a pile of pine bark.*

*To the left, well forward, is a high, flat-topped rock which is reached by descending a natural crevice of the cliff behind it. To the right is a sheer cliff, pierced by a cavern with a door-like opening. The background shows only the scarred face of a cliff tufted with ferns and stunted pine trees.*

*The right and left entrances are around the forward ends of the cliffs.*

*It is sunset of the same day. As the curtain rises,* WANING MOON *is discovered grilling a chop over the sacred fire;* MABLO, *resembling a fat poodle, sits on the altar step waiting for it to be finished;* LERII, *a mad old beggar, dressed in disreputable rabbit skins, is squatting on the ground to the right of the altar, and peering into the deep pool.*

MABLO: I'm hungry, Waning Moon.

WANING MOON (*exhibiting the chop*): It's almost done.

MABLO: Don't burn it.

WANING MOON: Huh! You'll get no meat from Suiva, red or black.

MABLO: By and by, I will.

WANING MOON (*indicating* LERII): If you go mad like Lerii! She says she will feed no other with the God's meat.

MABLO: Wait and see. (*He lowers his voice and glances towards the cavern.*) She can't hear us, can she?

WANING MOON: No. She's at the farther end putting on her white dress.

MABLO (*grinning*): We didn't lose much time.

WANING MOON: Even her mother hasn't seen her since.

MABLO: Or Yellow Snake!

WANING MOON: He's standing by the gate.

MABLO: He'll come no further. This is her house and mine.

WANING MOON: Don't be too rash. Your father is a just man, Mablo.

MABLO: I said nothing.

WANING MOON: He'd strike you quickly as he would a stranger.

MABLO: But I said nothing. Isn't the meat done?

WANING MOON (*inspecting the chop*): Aie! It's as he likes it. (*She holds it under the nose of the image and intones in a whining voice.*) Great God, this is the five-pronged buck you sent; this is his body. Shiny Bird killed him with a flinty spear and sends you his body to devour that you may send more deer to Shiny Bird. He fears you, God. Set more deer in his path!

(*This formality over, she is about to hand the chop to* MABLO *when* LERII *suddenly demands it.*)

LERII: Meat!

WANING MOON: You've had a bone, mad Lerii.

MABLO (*impatiently*): It's getting cold. Don't mind him.

(*She hands* MABLO *the chop which he devours gluttonously.*)

LERII: I want meat.

WANING MOON: Don't bother me. Go back and look for pictures.

LERII: I've watched the pool all day. I am tired of watching the pool, and now the shadow's on it.

WANING MOON: It was almost dark when you saw Pantherhead fall from the pointed rock.

MABLO (*with his mouth full*): And three days later he did fall.

LERII: Of course, he fell. I saw him. His face was torn and all his bones were broken.

MABLO: How did he come to fall?

LERII: He put his whole weight on a rotten tree. When you found him there was a dead branch in his hand.

MABLO: Who told you that?

LERII: I saw it in the pool.

MABLO (*to* WANING MOON): There was a dead branch in his hand.

LERII: He held so tight, you had to twist it from his hand . . . like this!

MABLO (*gasping*): That's so.

LERII: And then you gathered up his arrows and put them in your belt. The bow was broken but you took the bow-string.

MABLO (*uncomfortably*): I gave them to his woman.

LERII: That may be. I only saw what happened at the rock.

MABLO (*to* WANING MOON): Do you think he does see pictures in the pool?

WANING MOON (*non-committally*): Who knows? The God has touched him.

MABLO: He tried to show me one the other day. I couldn't see it.

LERII (*turning*): It was there.

MABLO: I couldn't see it.

LERII (*shrugging*): The belly has no eyes.

(MABLO *is put out of countenance;* WANING MOON *is shocked at this affront to the Chief's son.*)

WANING MOON (*sharply*): Go to your place, mad Lerii!

(LERII, *completely shattered by her tone, slinks to the edge of the pool and sits down.*)

MABLO: Where's the wine?

(WANING MOON *passes him the wine-cup.*)

WANING MOON: Don't let her see you!

(*He glances at the cavern, turns his back to it, and drinks.*)

MABLO (*returning the cup*): It's a good wine. Who made it?

WANING MOON: Coyote's girl. (*She inspects the contents.*) You don't leave much. No matter. I'll have to fill it for the rites.

MABLO: Does Suiva drink it at the rites?

WANING MOON: Not likely. At the rites, she wets the God's lips with it.

MABLO: Does the tribe know she will take the vows tonight?

WANING MOON: Aie! They know! Already they show me less respect. As I came in, more than a score were gathered at the gate and many did not greet me. But you will see them fawn to Suiva's hand! Until she gives her place up to another. It's the God's priestess, not the maid, they care for! Filthy dogs!

MABLO: You've had a good life, Old Moon.

WANING MOON: Well, that's true. In all these years I have never once been hungry and never once gone sober to my bed.

MABLO: You've got no cause to grumble. (*He gets up, and hands her the bone.*) Here's the bone. The God might like it.

WANING MOON (*taking it*): Aie! He's fond of bones. (*She lays it deftly among the flames of the brazier.*) The fire is low; give me some pine bark. (MABLO *gives her some bark which she lays on the fire.*) Now, take the cup. I'll fill it from the goatskin.

MABLO: Can't I stay?

WANING MOON (*coming down from the altar*): You'll come in with the others.

MABLO: I'd like to see her now.

WANING MOON: You had better wait. You'll see her at the rites and afterwards as often as you like. (*They go towards the left entrance.* WANING MOON *turns and calls.*) Oh, Suiva!

SUIVA (*off*): Yes?

WANING MOON: Your mother's at the gate. I'll send her in. (*In a lower tone*) Come, Mablo!

(MABLO, *who has been trying to peer into the cavern, shakes himself, and follows her out to the left. As they disappear,* SUIVA *comes from the cavern. She wears a long white vestment, and, at her breast, a silver moon. She goes to the altar, makes obeisance to the image, and then, after a hesitating pause, directs her attention to the flat-topped rock, the place which* YELLOW SNAKE *professed to have visited.* LERII, *whom she had not seen, gets up and approaches her from behind. He watches her a moment before speaking.*)

LERII: He isn't there.

SUIVA (*startled*): Mad Lerii! You frightened me! I . . . I thought I saw an eagle.

LERII: You saw no eagle for his wing is broken. He'll flap his wings no more in the sun's face. (*He indicates the image.*) He is the happy one. He has no wings.

SUIVA: Poor Lerii!

LERII: He has a stone heart. He will live forever.

SUIVA: When you fell into the pool it was his hand that saved you.

LERII (*going to the edge of the pool*): When I fell in the pool I looked for him. I looked in the green cavern. I looked in the white tent. He wasn't there.

SUIVA (*joining him by the pool*): And while you looked he had you by the hair. He pulled you from the whirlpool and threw you on the sandbar.

LERII: It was a log I held to.

SUIVA: Poor Lerii.

LERII (*spitting in the pool*): Bah!

SUIVA: You mustn't do that!

LERII (*suddenly*): Look!

SUIVA: What?

LERII (*pointing in the pool*): A picture!

SUIVA: Where?

LERII: By the black rock. No, no! Don't look!

SUIVA: I see no picture.

LERII: Now it's gone.

SUIVA: What was it, Lerii?

LERII: Nothing.

SUIVA: What?

LERII: The God is hungry.

SUIVA: I'll feed him by and by.

LERII: Aie! You'll feed him by and by.

SUIVA (*vaguely disturbed*): What was the picture?

LERII: Never mind, you'll see. (*A slight pause*) But you'd do better if you ran away. (KOTWI *enters from the left and overhears this speech.*)

KOTWI: What's that you are saying!

(SUIVA *runs to her and takes her in her arms.* LERII *gets up and grins idiotically.*)

SUIVA: Mother!

KOTWI (*importantly*): I've come to see my daughter, the new priestess. You go away, mad Lerii.

LERII: Ask me the question first.

KOTWI: Not here, at the God's altar!

LERII: Then, I won't go.

KOTWI: If I ask it once, then will you go?

LERII: Ask and find out.

SUIVA: Yes, ask it, mother. There's no harm.

KOTWI: What does the God know, Lerii?

LERII: The God knows nothing, even less than you know. (*Chuckling insanely, he goes out right.*)

SUIVA: Poor Lerii!

KOTWI: When he fell in the pool he saw the God, and those who see the God go surely mad.

SUIVA: He says he didn't see the God.

KOTWI: That proves he's mad. And if he's mad he must have seen the God. Now, let me look at you!

SUIVA: Do you like my new dress?

KOTWI: Stand off a little. (SUIVA *does so.*) Now, turn around. (SUIVA *turns slowly.*) It's not quite even. Let me catch it up. (*She takes a fishbone from her own costume and adjusts the skirt to her liking, then stands off and inspects her again.*) There! It's beautiful. When the girls see you they'll turn inside out! (*She approaches her again.*) May I lay my hand on the young moon?

SUIVA: I'll ask the Holy One.

KOTWI: Tut, child, I'm your own mother! (*She fingers the silver crescent.*) Aie! It's cold and heavy. But they say to touch it cures the belly ache.

SUIVA: Have you the belly ache?

KOTWI: No. And it's not much belly ache I'll have with no big girl to catch me grouse and rabbits. Didn't Mablo want you for his woman?

SUIVA: Yes.

KOTWI: And you wouldn't have him?

SUIVA: No.

KOTWI: Why not?

SUIVA: I couldn't, mother, I love Yellow Snake.

KOTWI: That's a poor reason to refuse the Great Chief's son.

SUIVA: Have you seen Yellow Snake since I came here?

KOTWI: He's standing by the gate with his long bow and arrow. All the old women are laughing at him. They bid him sing you out of the God's temple. They call him lazy lie-a-bed.

SUIVA: What does he say to them?

KOTWI: He says no word.

SUIVA: Why is he armed?

KOTWI (*shrugging*): To shoot the sun, maybe.

SUIVA: Did he say that?

KOTWI: I said it.

SUIVA: So did he. He said he'd shoot the sun and catch a gourd of blood in his two hands and bring it down to me and bathe my feet.

KOTWI: He is a worthless singer of mad songs.

SUIVA: In all the mountains of the world there is no man like him.

KOTWI: It's a good thing, my girl, that the God chose you, but, for my sake, I wish you'd married Mablo. If you'd said "yes" to him, Amburi would have got me back my cattle. And now he will not. How am I to live?

SUIVA: I wonder why he chose me.

KOTWI: So do I. Old Waning Moon's a sly one. You don't know where you're at with that old grey-bird.

SUIVA: Mother!

KOTWI: You've been a good girl, though, I'll say that for you.

SUIVA: When I was no higher than your knee, you taught me fear of him. And every day I've said my prayers at sunrise and sunset. All my life I've feared him. I think that's why he chose me.

KOTWI: Partly for that, and partly, too, because we lost our cattle. He knows we're poor and that I am old. Maybe he'll whisper in your ear to feed your poor old mother twice a day.

SUIVA: If he does, I'll run and tell you!

KOTWI: Aie! And you'd best run fast. Or maybe I'll be dead of hunger before you get there. (*Whiningly*) You won't forget your poor old mother, Suiva?

SUIVA: Of course not, mother.

KOTWI: There's my own Suiva. I knew that's what you'd say. Where do they keep the meat?

SUIVA (*distastefully*): I don't know, mother.

KOTWI: No matter! No matter! We'll find out by and by! It is a fine thing to be the God's own daughter. A virgin priestess has great power for good. Pray him to slay our enemies and make their women barren.

SUIVA: Yes.

KOTWI: And when a deer is killed or a black bear comes or ducks or turtles come, remember that the God must have his share. If any man retain the whole of any bird or beast, the tribe will die of scurvy. Tell them that!

SUIVA: I'll tell them. And I'll pray that Yellow Snake may learn to fear the God so that he'll live to be your age and mine together . . . Mother!

KOTWI: Yes?

SUIVA: You'll see him as you go out by the gate.

KOTWI: Aie!

SUIVA: Go up to him and whisper in his ear.

KOTWI: I will not. I have no word to say to that young man.

SUIVA: Give him a message from me.

KOTWI: What is it?

SUIVA: Tell him that I love him; that I'll love him all my life. But he must go away and never try to see me any more.

KOTWI: I'll tell him the last part.

SUIVA: No, tell him all. If you do that for me, there is nothing I won't do for you.

KOTWI: Well, I see no harm. And you'll be good to me, I know you will. I'll tell him, Suiva.

(WANING MOON *enters from the left, carrying a jug of oil and a cup of wine.*)

SUIVA (*whispering*): Tell him now, mother, now, before the rites begin.

(SUIVA *goes to the altar and kneels on the stone steps, facing the image.* KOTWI *meets* WANING MOON *at the left entrance.*)

KOTWI: Old Moon!

WANING MOON: Yes?

(KOTWI *draws her aside to the left.*)

KOTWI: What made you choose her?

WANING MOON: Have you forgotten the five cows you promised?

KOTWI: So? It was my cows that did it. I said three, not five.

WANING MOON: It was five you said. If you go back on it I'll send her home. (*Indicating the God*) She's not his daughter yet.

KOTWI: All right! All right! I only hope I get the worth of them.

WANING MOON: That's your look out. Where are you going?

KOTWI: Only to the gate.

WANING MOON: Come when you hear the goat drums and tell the old women not to talk too much. The God dislikes their chatter. (KOTWI *goes out laughing.* WANING MOON *watches her with amused triumph; then approaches* SUIVA.) Young Moon, the time is near.

SUIVA (*rising*): Yes, Holy One.

WANING MOON: All the old men and women are gathered at the gate. Here, take the wine cup. (SUIVA *takes it.*) Lay it at his feet. (*She does so.*) That's right. And here's the oil to light you on your way. (*She hands* SUIVA *the jug of oil.*) Put it on this side of the fire, where I can reach it without crossing over. (SUIVA *places it to the right of the fire basket.*) So. And now what else is there?

SUIVA: The twining of white blossoms.

WANING MOON: I put it by the pine bark. [*She goes to the right of the altar and picks up a chaplet of white blossoms and green leaves.*] When you have spoken the last word I'll place this on your head. You wear it as you walk backwards to the cavern. [*She holds it up.*] It's not until this crown is on your head that you're the God's own daughter. But when this touches you, your life is his.

SUIVA: Yes, Holy One.

WANING MOON: You'll tend his fire until you're old as I am. And if any man come near you, he will be killed. If you seek out any man to love him you will be killed.

SUIVA: I'll seek no man and none shall come to me.

WANING MOON (*indicating the image*): Do you know his ways?

SUIVA: Only what mother taught me.

WANING MOON: How did he make the hills?

SUIVA: By breathing on the clouds he made them hard. And with his right hand he set them on the earth.

WANING MOON: Where does he live?

SUIVA: He has two houses—one in the deep pool, the other in a land beyond the sea.

WANING MOON: We know this house. Tell me about the other.

SUIVA: The other house is a great Yellow Tent, higher than any mountain and ten times wider than the eye can see. Inside the tent are springs of water, and sweet berry wine, and herds of antelope, and flocks of fat, white ducks. Yes, and all other birds and beasts we hunt against our hunger. But there we do not hunt. When we are hungry they come and fall upon our spears. And all the stones are hot with hidden fire so that to roast our meat we have but to lay it on the nearest stone. And when we are fed we dance in many circles, the Great Chiefs in the centre, and then, the priestess, and then, in wider circles, all who have feared the God and done his will.

WANING MOON: How do we get there?

SUIVA: When a man dies his spirit perches like a bird on a fir tree above his grave. At the last moon, the great God gathers all these spirits in his hands, and those who feared him not, he crushes and they live no more. But those who fear him he gathers to his breast and takes with him to his great Yellow Tent beyond the sea.

WANING MOON: You know already something of his ways but you have much to learn. How does he make his will known to the tribe?

SUIVA: He speaks his wishes in the priestess' ear and she proclaims them to the people.

WANING MOON: And if the people disobey his will?

SUIVA: Then his great eyes grow red like burning logs. And all the tribe fall down before him and no man dare move until the fire has vanished from his eyes. And then they bring him gifts and do his bidding as the priestess tells, else he will strike them down as leaves in autumn.

WANING MOON: Do you believe all that?

SUIVA: I know it's true.

WANING MOON: And are you glad he chose you?

SUIVA (*after a slight pause*): I fear him and I'm glad to do his will.

WANING MOON: His priestess must not fear him overmuch.

SUIVA: Holy One!

WANING MOON: Only as a daughter fears her father. Not as the common people fear the God. If you fear him too much you can't help him.

SUIVA: How can I help him?

WANING MOON: He's very old and sometimes he forgets the kind of meat or fish that he likes the best. Then you must tell the people what you think he likes. And often when he's drunk and cannot speak you must speak for him as seems best to you. If we need rain, the tribe must bring gifts; and they must bring more gifts till the rain comes. And when the rain does come, they must bring him still more gifts in that he heard their prayer and sent the rain. It's the same thing with floods or fire or cattle sickness. I'll tell you more of these things by and by. But now you must make ready for the rites. Your hair is too tightly bound.

SUIVA: I'll loosen it.

WANING MOON: Do you remember all the words to say?

SUIVA: I think so.

WANING MOON: At the last, when I ask you if you renounce all men to serve the God, what answer do you make?

SUIVA (*raising her right hand*): I renounce all men, all love, all hope of home and children. I shall serve him now, all days and nights, all summers and winters, till I'm old as the Old Moon. I swear it by his hand.

WANING MOON: That's right. Now, come into the cavern and I'll unbraid your hair and sprinkle you with sweet oil.

SUIVA: Then may I pray the God to make me speak with a clear voice?

WANING MOON: Aie! You can pray until the people come.

(*They go into the cavern.* YELLOW SNAKE *is seen climbing down the rock chimney to the left. The descent is slow and hazardous but finally he reaches the grass-tufted top of the flat rock. Here he stands for a moment peering downward, then descends the remaining ten feet to the level of the stage. He prowls about in search of* SUIVA, *lingering for a moment by the cavern mouth. The voice of the two women are suddenly heard. He retreats swiftly to the altar. The voices grow louder. He climbs the altar steps and takes refuge behind the image of the God.* SUIVA, *with hair unbound, comes slowly from the cavern, advances to the centre of the scene, pauses for a moment, looking at the top of the flat rock, then proceeds to the altar and kneels on the first step.)*

SUIVA: Great God whom I have feared, now make me strong; strong to endure thy will; strong to forget my love.

YELLOW SNAKE (*unseen*): The ferns grow tall and deep beyond the ranges. The grass is green and heavy with the rain. I'll make my love a tent of leaning silver with birches whiter than the white moon stream. I'll make my love a bow that's straight and slender, with arrows plumed and fitted to her hand. I'll make my love a bed of sleeping cedar and lay a yellow fawn-skin at her feet.

My love is like the lark that sings to waking, and like the thrush that sings the leaves to sleep. My love is all the sun-time and the star-time. My love is waking and my love is sleep.

(*He steps from behind the altar and comes to meet* SUIVA.)

SUIVA: Yellow Snake!

YELLOW SNAKE (*with hands extended*): I have come for you.

SUIVA: You mustn't!

YELLOW SNAKE: Suiva!

SUIVA: No. The God!

YELLOW SNAKE: But you're my mate.

SUIVA: I'm the God's daughter.

YELLOW SNAKE: That stone thing isn't God.

SUIVA (*in terror*): Yellow Snake!

YELLOW SNAKE: How can that stone be God?

SUIVA: He'll strike you.

YELLOW SNAKE: Strike me? That! I'll show you! Then, you'll come.

(*He picks up a stick and mounts the altar.*)

SUIVA: He'll make you mad!

YELLOW SNAKE (*menacing the image*): Show now if you are God, and hold my hand!

SUIVA: He'll kill you!

(YELLOW SNAKE *strikes the image and throws away the stick.*)

YELLOW SNAKE: I struck you, God. Now, strike me! Kill me, God!

SUIVA: Don't kill him, God, don't kill him! Make him mad!

YELLOW SNAKE (*coming down from the altar*): Suiva!

SUIVA: Spare him as you spared Lerii! Make him mad!

YELLOW SNAKE: Would you lay madness on me?

SUIVA: He won't kill you.

YELLOW SNAKE: Suiva!

SUIVA: He chose me. He will hear me.

YELLOW SNAKE: He didn't choose. He bought you.

(LERII *enters unnoticed on the left.*)

SUIVA: Yellow Snake!

YELLOW SNAKE: Your mother sold you to him for ten cows.

SUIVA (*drawing away*): Yellow Snake!

YELLOW SNAKE: Ten cows for Shiny Bird!

SUIVA: For Shiny Bird?

YELLOW SNAKE: To keep old Waning Moon.

SUIVA: He's made you mad.

LERII (*unexpectedly*): Shiny Bird is driving ten cows to his pasture.

SUIVA (*startled*): Lerii!

YELLOW SNAKE: There!

LERII: But they're not Kotwi's cattle.

YELLOW SNAKE: Who's?

LERII: Mablo's!

YELLOW SNAKE: Mablo's!

LERII: Aie! But that won't help you! (*He laughs, and runs to the left.*)

YELLOW SNAKE: Mablo's!

SUIVA: Yellow Snake, go now while the God lets you.

YELLOW SNAKE: Mablo bought you. This is the trap he made. Now, will you come?

SUIVA: I'll pray the God to take his madness from you.

YELLOW SNAKE: Madness?

*(Suddenly, the goat drums sound on the left.)*

SUIVA: Yellow Snake!

YELLOW SNAKE *(trying to draw her away)*: Come quickly.

SUIVA *(freeing herself)*: No! *(She turns to him again and takes him in her arms.)* Yellow Snake! *(She kisses him and springs away.)* Now, go! They'll kill you!

YELLOW SNAKE: Come!

SUIVA: They'll kill me if they find you here. *(The drums grow louder.)* Do you want them to kill me?

YELLOW SNAKE: Suiva!

SUIVA: Go!

*(The drums grow louder.)*

YELLOW SNAKE: I'll come tonight.

SUIVA: You mustn't.

YELLOW SNAKE: Yes.

SUIVA: I'll be his priestess!

YELLOW SNAKE: No. Don't take the vows. Pretend the God has struck you. Say no word. Fall down upon the altar. Then, tonight, we'll go.

SUIVA: Yellow Snake.

YELLOW SNAKE: I'll watch you from the rock. Don't take the vows!

*(He goes to the flat-topped rock, climbs it, and lies on the top.* WANING MOON *comes from the cavern.)*

WANING MOON: Suiva, stand upon the altar. Face the God! *(*SUIVA *does so.* WANING MOON *mounts the steps and stands to right, the brazier between them. She picks up the jug of oil and pours some on the fire, lighting the scene with a flaring brilliance. The procession enters from the left. First come* AMBURI *and* MABLO*; then the two old men beating drums; then the worshippers, all old men and women dressed* *in coloured blankets and the skins of mountain animals. They arrange themselves in a large semi-circle around the altar, the Chief and* MABLO *standing apart at the extreme right. The drums cease, and, after a short pause,* WANING MOON *makes one step forward and raises her hand.)* Great Chief and Great Chief's son, and you old men and women, bow your heads! (*The worshippers do so simultaneously.*) Fear you the God?

THE WORSHIPPERS: We fear him.

WANING MOON: Has any man killed any beast today?

AN OLD MAN (*raising his head*): My son killed a black bear beyond the canyon.

WANING MOON: The God will take one shoulder for his part.

THE OLD MAN: My son shall bring it at tomorrow's dawn.

WANING MOON: And let him fear the God. The God is great.

THE WORSHIPPERS: He giveth us full bellies.

WANING MOON: The God is good to them that love his priestess.

THE WORSHIPPERS: We love you well.

WANING MOON: The God will hear her when she prays for you, and he will fill your bellies.

THE WORSHIPPERS (*raising their heads*): The God is great; he is the God of Gods.

WANING MOON (*addressing the image*): Great God of Gods, I was your priestess when the world was young. And now the world is old, and I am old. I am the Waning Moon and I have spent my brightness in your service. Already you have crooked your finger at me and soon you will take me to your Yellow Tent. There, you have made a place for me beside you and I shall sit all seasons at your feet. And, though I leave my place here to another, and go to live with Shiny Bird, the tribe must know that I'm no common person, that I am still your daughter. They must know that if they work me ill your hand will strike them. That you will shut them from your Yellow Tent. (*She turns to the worshippers.*) Hear you his will?

THE WORSHIPPERS: We hear it.

WANING MOON: Then, bide by it, and he will prosper you.

AMBURI: Even as we fear him, we shall bide by it.

WANING MOON: He willed it that the Old Moon should have rest. He whispered in my ear that I should work no more, and then he broke the sky with a loud thunder, and rent the sky with a bright spear of fire. And the loud thunder said to me, "Choose Suiva for the Young Moon;" and the bright spear was pointed at her house. And I made known to her the great God's bidding and she is come to take his holy vows. (*She turns to* SUIVA.) Stand forth. Young Moon. (SUIVA *turns, moves forward, and faces the worshippers.* WANING MOON *turns again to the worshippers.*) Here is a maiden with the Moon upon her. Before I lay the white flowers on her head, will any say that she's not fit to serve him? (*She pauses. There is no response.*) Will any say that she has lied or stolen? (*She pauses. There is no response.*) Will any say that she is not a virgin? (*She pauses. There is no response.*) Then, will you love her as you love the Old Moon?

THE WORSHIPPERS: Aie! We'll love her.

WANING MOON: And you will fear her as you feared the Old Moon?

THE WORSHIPPERS: Aie! We'll fear her as we feared the Old Moon.

WANING MOON: The God has heard you. He will not forget you. (*She turns to* SUIVA.) Young Moon, as the God spoke, the tribe has spoken. Do you wish them well?

SUIVA: I wish them well.

WANING MOON: In peace and war?

SUIVA: Their bellies shall be filled. The daggers of their enemies shall be broken.

WANING MOON: And when they die?

SUIVA: Those who have loved and feared me, shall be taken to his Yellow Tent.

THE WORSHIPPERS: We love you and we fear you.

WANING MOON (*handing her the oil*): Will you guard his fire?

SUIVA (*pouring on oil*): As now I guard it. (*She hands back the jug of oil.* WANING MOON *offers her the plate of meat.*)

WANING MOON: And will you feed him?

(SUIVA *takes a scrap of meat and lays it on the fire.*)

SUIVA: As now I feed him.

(WANING MOON *lays down the meat and takes up the sacrificial knife which she hands to* SUIVA.)

WANING MOON: And will you shear the foeman's hair to fill his nose with incense?

SUIVA (*taking the knife*): With this knife will I shear it.

(*She hands back the knife.* WANING MOON *extends the cup of wine in which* SUIVA *dips her fingers.*)

WANING MOON: And will you give him the sweet wine to drink?

SUIVA: As now I give it.

(*She turns to the image and wets its lips with her fingers.* WANING MOON *puts down the goblet and takes up the wreath of white flowers.* YELLOW SNAKE, *unable to control his agony raises himself on his knees and peers downward at the altar. He is easily discerned by the audience, but is not, as yet, discovered by the worshippers. But* SUIVA *sees him, as she turns and comes forward to the front of the altar.*)

WANING MOON (*holding the wreath*): These are the sacred flowers; the flowers of the God. Before I lay them on your head, make prayer. (SUIVA *closes her eyes for a moment, then raises them to* YELLOW SNAKE, *who holds out his arms to her; then, looks at* WANING MOON.) Do you renounce all men to serve the God?

SUIVA (*raising her right hand*): I renounce all men, all love, all hope of home and children. I shall serve him now, all days and nights, all summers and all winters, till I'm old as the Old Moon. I swear it by his hand.

(*A sound escapes* YELLOW SNAKE. MABLO *hears it, discovers him, and points him out to* AMBURI. *He is about to give the alarm when* AMBURI *puts his hand over his mouth.* AMBURI *removes his hand and seizes his arm. The two men never take their eyes from* YELLOW SNAKE *until the ceremony is finished.* YELLOW SNAKE *is not seen by any of the worshippers.* WANING MOON *places the crown on* SUIVA's *head; then turns to the worshippers.*)

WANING MOON: The crown is on her. The Young Moon is here.

(*The drums sound. The worshippers with bent heads, and arms extended, go out backwards to the left.*)

THE WORSHIPPERS: The Moon, the Moon is here! Young Moon, we fear you.

(SUIVA *and* WANING MOON *come down from the altar, and, facing the retiring worshippers, walk backwards to the cavern into which they disappear at the same time as the drumbeaters, the last of the worshippers, go out left.* MABLO *and* AMBURI *remain as they were with eyes fixed on* YELLOW SNAKE, *who, thinking himself unobserved, begins to climb upward. They watch him until he is out of sight. Then,* AMBURI *releases* MABLO's *arm.*)

AMBURI: Go and kill him.

MABLO: I?

AMBURI (*disdainfully*): Tell the young men to kill him and bring his body here.

(MABLO *hurries out to the left.* AMBURI *folds his arms in an attitude of waiting.*)

CURTAIN.

## ACT III

SCENE—*The same as Act II. Fifteen minutes have elapsed. It has grown a little darker. Otherwise, the scene is unchanged. As the curtain rises,* SUIVA *enters from the cavern, goes stealthily to the base of the flat rock, and calls softly.*

SUIVA: Yellow Snake! . . . Yellow Snake! Go now, the way is clear.

(*She turns, goes to the altar, climbs the steps, and looks across the top of the rock. Realizing that* YELLOW SNAKE *has gone she utters a sigh of relief; then, extends her arms as though he were still there and lets them fall with a gesture of resignation.* WANING MOON *comes from the cavern and approaches her. She is carrying a pot containing sulphurous paste.*)

WANING MOON: The fire is low.

SUIVA: I'll tend it.

(*She picks up the jug of oil.*)

WANING MOON: Not oil! Not oil! That's only for the rites. Lay pine bark on it. (SUIVA *replenishes the fire with pine bark.*) So. Don't smother it. It's good dry bark and full of gum. The trouble is, it burns too quickly. When you want to sleep, you must use green wood. Only be careful that it doesn't die.

(WANING MOON *picks up the cup and drinks.*)

SUIVA: I know the law. If the fire dies the God will kill me. And the tribe will suffer for two seasons.

WANING MOON: There is nothing like old wine. What's that you said?

SUIVA: I said the God would kill me.

WANING MOON: If that were so, I'd be already dead.

SUIVA: You let it out!

WANING MOON (*drinking again*): How can I wake to tend it when I'm drunk? No harm has come. And none will come unless the tribe find out. For that I keep a firestick in the cavern.

SUIVA: Was there no famine?

WANING MOON: Famine? No! But the tribe might have killed me. You had better be careful. Amburi fears the God as a blind man fears thunder. No matter what you tell him, he'll believe it. He's the best friend we have. He keeps the tribe in order. For fear of him they dare not slight the God. But he's a just man. It's all one to him, the priestess and the people. It's the God he fears.

So, if you speak from God to make a law, you'd better mind it, for if you break it, and he catches you, he'll kill you quickly as he would a squirrel.

SUIVA: Then it's the Chief who punishes the priestess?

WANING MOON (*slightly tipsy*): The God, the Chief, the priestess, how do I know? We're so mixed up together, who can tell? The wine is good. Will you not drink? (*She proffers the cup.*)

SUIVA: I thought the wine was sacred.

WANING MOON: No more than we are. Drink.

SUIVA: I don't like it.

WANING MOON: You'll learn to like it. And you'll tell the tribe to bring the God his goat-skin every month. And it must be old wine of such a colour; old wine that warms the heart. The God hates new wine as he does old meat!

SUIVA: Does the God hate it, or do you?

WANING MOON: What he likes, I like; but what I hate, he hates. We do not differ, the old God and I. He speaks, I answer. I speak, he answers. It is the same word always.

SUIVA: When does he speak to you?

WANING MOON: Most often when I've had three cups. It's then I hear him roaring in the wind. At least, I think I hear him. Who can tell?

SUIVA: You told me that you heard him every day.

WANING MOON: Maybe I do.

SUIVA: But do you?

WANING MOON: I'd say so anyway, and so must you.

SUIVA: Why must I if it isn't true?

WANING MOON: The tribe expects the God to speak to you. If he does not, they'll think that you displease him. And if they think that you displease him, they'll find another priestess.

SUIVA (*eagerly*): Will they let me go?

WANING MOON (*sardonically*): Aie! They'll let you go into the pool to feed him! But if you listen you may hear his voice.

SUIVA: I've always feared him. He should speak to me.

WANING MOON: Maybe he will. But if he doesn't, I'll be here. I'll tell you what to say.

SUIVA: You're not the God.

WANING MOON: My ways have been his ways for fifty years. I know his will, and you'd do well to listen when I speak.

SUIVA: Then, tell me this: If there should come a man, a young man, here, and take a stick and strike the God with it, what would he do?

WANING MOON: The Chief would kill him for his blasphemy.

SUIVA: Yes, but the God? What would the God do? Would he lay madness on him?

WANING MOON (*judicially*): The priestess might pour poison in his cup.

SUIVA: But would the God himself lay madness on him?

WANING MOON: Not without your help.

SUIVA: But, if I prayed to him?

WANING MOON: Prayers are not enough.

SUIVA: Has he no power to act without my help.

WANING MOON: You and he are one. You have your strength together.

SUIVA: But he has strength alone. I have seen his red eyes gleam.

WANING MOON: I'll show you how they gleam. I came to show you that, but I forgot. (*She mounts the altar. Dabs her fingers in the pot of paste and bends down to* SUIVA.) You see this paste, now watch what I can do! (*She smears two thick circles about the eyes of the image.*) Lay it on thick, so they shine the brighter!

SUIVA: But they don't shine.

(WANING MOON *lays down the pot, picks up the cup of wine and dips her fingers in it.*)

WANING MOON: Now, look. (*She exhibits her fingers, which glow with a soft light.*)

SUVIA (*terrified*): His fire is on you!

WANING MOON (*laughing creakily*): Aie! His fire is on me. And there is another pot inside the cavern. If you want more I'll show you how to make it. (*She twiddles her fingers.*) Don't be afraid. It doesn't burn. I get it from the mountain.

SUIVA: What is it?

WANING MOON: I don't know. I saw it gleaming in the rain one night. And then I learnt to make it strong by baking it in an oven of hot stones. Some day I'll show you. (SUIVA, *overcome with her disillusion, sinks down on the altar steps.* WANING MOON *continues.*) If any slight the God, then wet his eyes and they'll fall down before him on their bellies. They'll fear his anger, and they'll mend their ways. They'll bring him gifts, as many as you tell them. (*She pauses, glances down at* SUIVA.) What's the matter? Are you sick?

SUIVA: I want to go away.

WANING MOON (*not unkindly*): You can't go now.

SUIVA: I want my mother.

WANING MOON: She'll come to you tomorrow. She'll come every day. You'll feed her with the God's meat.

SUIVA: Was it for that she sold me?

WANING MOON: Sold you?

SUIVA: Yes.

WANING MOON: Who said your mother sold you? (SUIVA *does not reply.*) Your mother did not sell you. But if she had there'd be no harm. There's not a girl in all the tribe who does not envy you. You'll never come in hungry from the hunt and have no meat. Those days are gone.

SUIVA: My lover's gone.

WANING MOON: Aie! It's not sweet to live without a man. And none come here except the old men. Only the old men, and Mablo.

SUIVA: Mablo!

WANING MOON: Aie! And it was he that wanted you to mate. Don't be too sad. He comes here when he likes. And he's a fine man.

(*She pats her consolingly on the shoulder, and crosses to the cavern, which she enters carrying with her the pot of paste. There is rather a long interval during which* SUIVA *sits motionless, occupied with her thoughts.* MABLO, *carrying a bow and arrows, comes in quickly from the left. After glancing about the place he discovers her and approaches. She rises to meet him.*)

MABLO: Have you seen my father?

SUIVA: No.

MABLO: I left him here. I thought he'd wait.

SUIVA: He may come back.

MABLO: Aie! He'll come back. I have some news for him. Some news he'll like to hear. (SUIVA *tries to walk past him into the cavern.*) Where are you going?

SUIVA: What is that to you?

MABLO: I'll be your friend, Young Moon.

SUIVA: Then, let me pass.

MABLO: Wait till my father comes.

SUIVA: I want to go into the cavern.

MABLO: It isn't late.

SUIVA: I am tired.

MABLO: Do you sleep lightly? Would you hear me if I called you?

SUIVA: This morning I whipped you. If you come tonight I'll use a knife.

MABLO: You're not so wild as that. And if you were I'd tame you. (*He thumps his chest.*) I'm a man.

(AMBURI *enters from the right.* SUIVA *sees him.*)

SUIVA: There is your father.

(*She goes quickly into the cavern.* MABLO *joins his father. They meet down left.*)

AMBURI: Well?

MABLO: I killed him, father!

AMBURI (*incredulously*): You!

MABLO: The others would not for the songs he makes.

AMBURI: You say you killed him! You killed Yellow Snake! (*He lays his arm affectionately on* MABLO*'s arm.*) My son! I'm so proud of you! How did you kill him?

MABLO: Alone I did it.

AMBURI: How?

(MABLO *contorts himself indicating the small of his back.*)

MABLO: I shot him here.

AMBURI: Behind!

MABLO: He never saw me. He never knew that I was there.

AMBURI: You shot him in the back?

MABLO: While he was climbing. He fell and is twice dead. Did I not well?

AMBURI: Aie! You did well! You did so well the squaws shall spit on you.

MABLO: Father!

AMBURI: You, my son!

MABLO: You said to kill him!

AMBURI: Yes, but kill him so! An arrow in the back! Is that the Chief's way? Can't you use the knife?

MABLO: But he'd have killed me with the knife!

AMBURI: What of it?

MABLO: What of it?

AMBURI: Yes.

MABLO: But . . . but, father, I'd be dead!

AMBURI: Aie! You'd be dead. But dead as a chief dies; not living like the groundhog coward you are. You shall have women's clothes!

MABLO (*in agony*): No! No!

AMBURI: You shall have women's clothes and wear them for the passing of one moon. And I shall tell the squaws to spit on you; and the children, they shall spit on you.

MABLO: I will not!

AMBURI: What!

MABLO: Yes! Yes! I'll wear them!

AMBURI: Your shame has poisoned me. The man you killed broke the God's law, but he was not a coward. And for a son, I'd rather have him dead than you alive.

MABLO: They've brought his body to the gate. What shall I tell them?

AMBURI: Tell them to make it ready for the rites. (MABLO *slinks out left.* AMBURI *pauses for a moment in meditation, then turns to the cavern and calls*) Old Moon!

(WANING MOON *comes scurrying out.*)

WANING MOON: Great Chief!

AMBURI: Is the God hungry, Old Moon?

WANING MOON: The God is hungry. He said at sunrise that he wanted fresh meat.

AMBURI: Is the time good for sacrifice?

WANING MOON: The time is good. The sun was red tonight.

AMBURI: The sky was red with streaks of yellow gold. What does that mean?

WANING MOON (*glibly*): Great good will follow on the sacrifice. He'll send the buffalo to the near water holes.

AMBURI: What would he do for the great sacrifice?

WANING MOON: The great sacrifice?

AMBURI: You heard me.

WANING MOON: Is it a man or woman?

AMBURI: It's a man.

WANING MOON: For a man-sacrifice, he'll send the caribou again across the ranges.

AMBURI: Good! Have the Young Moon make ready for the rites.

WANING MOON: Tonight?

AMBURI: His body's at the gate.

WANING MOON: Is it a young man?

AMBURI: A young man from the Blue Sea country, caught on our hunting-ground. You tell her that.

WANING MOON (*turning*): I'll tell her.

(*She goes part way to the cavern.*)

AMBURI: Come here! (*She returns.*) You'll tell her, but it's not the truth.

WANING MOON: Great Chief!

AMBURI: Was there a young man here today?

WANING MOON (*with genuine surprise*): A young man here!

AMBURI: Within the gate?

WANING MOON: How could there be?

AMBURI: There was a young man here!

WANING MOON: I didn't know it!

AMBURI: Your face is like your words. I hold you guiltless.

WANING MOON: He must be killed.

AMBURI: He has been killed.

WANING MOON: Who is he?

AMBURI: Yellow Snake.

WANING MOON: The singer? . . . That is good!

AMBURI: They say he loves the Young Moon.

WANING MOON: It may be.

AMBURI: Does she love him?

WANING MOON: I don't know.

AMBURI: Can you find out?

WANING MOON: She might not tell the truth.

AMBURI: It may be that she knew that he was here. She may have called him to her. If she is guilty and I let her live, the God will take his favour from the tribe. Is not that his word?

WANING MOON: That was the word he spoke.

AMBURI: We cannot change it. But it may be that she is innocent. She may not love him; she may not know that he was here.

WANING MOON: How can you tell?

AMBURI: The old men shall bring in the sacrifice. And I shall judge her as she pulls back the white cloth from his face.

WANING MOON (*admiringly*): Aie!

AMBURI: Now, make her ready while I lead them in. (AMBURI *goes left, pausing at the exit.*) If you should tell her to beware . . .

WANING MOON: May the God strike me!

AMBURI: With my hand!

WANING MOON: So be it! (*He goes out left.* WANING MOON, *who has bowed before him, straightens up, gasping. She has had a very real fright. There is a momentary pause during which she composes herself. Then she goes towards the cavern calling*) Young Moon! Come out here!

(SUIVA, *dressed as before, comes from the cavern.*)

SUIVA: What is it?

WANING MOON: The great sacrifice.

SUIVA: A man?

WANING MOON: A hunter from the Blue Sea country. Our young men killed him where the hills divide.

SUIVA: When did they kill him?

WANING MOON: When the sun was high. Their arms are sore from carrying his body.

SUIVA: I hadn't heard there was a hunter killed.

WANING MOON: They have just come in. The way was long and steep.

SUIVA: Is he a young man?

WANING MOON: I don't know.

SUIVA: Where have they laid his body?

WANING MOON: At the gate. The old men make it ready for the rites.

SUIVA: So soon?

WANING MOON: The beaters hold the death drums in their hands. Come quickly and I'll show you what to do.

SUIVA: Must I?

WANING MOON: Who else?

SUIVA: You do it for tonight.

WANING MOON: I am no more his priestess. (*They go to the altar.* WANING MOON *hands her the knife.*) Here's the knife. (SUIVA *takes it.*) Now, stand upon the altar! (SUIVA *mounts the altar.*) Further back! (SUIVA *moves back a step.* WANING MOON *indicates the forward part of the altar.*) They lay it here, and when the drums have ceased you pour a flame of oil upon the fire. Now, do you know the rites?

SUIVA: Yes, we used to play them when I was a child. We took turns being priestess. But, then, I never thought . . . (*The drums sound. The weird, monotonous muffled beating grows louder and louder as the worshippers approach.*) They're coming!

WANING MOON: Speak up boldly!

SUIVA: Yes, I'll try.

WANING MOON: When you have cut the burning of his hair, and offered it, what then?

SUIVA: I draw the white cloth from his face and say, "This is my enemy. He shall feed the God." And then the old men throw him in the pool.

WANING MOON: You know the rites. I have no more to tell you.

*(She goes to the right.)*

SUIVA: Stay with me!

WANING MOON: I cannot.

SUIVA: Why?

WANING MOON: Now you must stand alone.

*(She takes her place at some distance to the right. There enter from the left in procession.* AMBURI *and* MABLO*, the bearers of the death drums, eight old men carrying the body of* YELLOW SNAKE*, and a large following of old men and women. The bearers lay the shrouded body on the altar, and the procession arranges itself to left and right in the form of a V of which the altar is the apex. The drums cease.* SUIVA *pours oil on the fire, lighting the scene with a weird, flaring brilliance.)*

SUIVA: Fear you the God?

THE WORSHIPPERS *(with bent heads)*: We fear him.

SUIVA: The God will hear me when I pray for you and he will fill your bellies.

THE WORSHIPPERS *(raising their heads)*: The God is great; he is the God of Gods.

SUIVA: Where do the hunters go with swift brown feet?

AMBURI *(stepping forward)*: Over all lands to serve the God.

SUIVA: Are the God's hunters home from the far lands?

AMBURI: From the far lands the hunters are all home.

SUIVA: Do their swift arrows cling to the light deer?

AMBURI: They cling not to the deer or bear or cougar.

SUIVA: Did their spent arrows fall upon the mountain?

AMURI: Their arrows did not fall upon the mountain.

SUIVA: Where did their arrows fall?

AMBURI: They fell upon the white thing at your feet.

(SUIVA *pretends not to have seen it before.*)

SUIVA: What is this white thing? . . . Is it the body of a fish or bird?

AMBURI: It did not live in water or in air.

SUIVA: Is this a body that stood straight and strong?

AMBURI: A brown snake crawls but this one did not crawl.

SUIVA: Is this a cunning body with bound hair?

AMBURI: We caught no wild sheep in the twisted thorn.

SUIVA: Is this a body with a voice to speak?

AMBURI: The hill dog barks but this one did not bark.

SUIVA: It is not fish or bird or beast. What is it?

AMBURI: Honour to God and favour to the tribe.

SUIVA: Speak, that the God may know! What is this white thing?

AMBURI: The white thing is a man.

SUIVA (*greatly surprised*): A man!

AMBURI: He was our enemy that loved us not.

SUIVA: He is my enemy. The God has struck him.

AMBURI: He was our enemy that feared us not.

SUIVA: He was our enemy. The God shall eat him.

AMBURI: He was a fighter but he'll fight no more.

SUIVA: He was a hunter but he'll hunt no more.

AMBURI: He was a singer but he'll sing no more.

SUIVA: He was a lover but he'll love no more.

AMBURI: In all the moons his mate shall find him not.

SUIVA: Her feet are weary but she'll find him not.

AMBURI: Will the God breathe the burning of his hair?

SUIVA: The knife is sharp. The flame is hot and bright.

AMBURI: Then cut, and may the great God prosper us!

(SUIVA *takes the sacrificial knife, kneels by the body and without uncovering the face, seizes the hair with her left hand.*)

SUIVA (*addressing the body*): My hand is in your hair. Why don't you strike me? (*She threatens it with the knife.*) Am I your mate that you fear not my hand? . . . Are you asleep? (*She shakes him.*) Wake up! . . . Or are you dead? (*She pauses. Then, tauntingly*) Strong man, you're dead! You're dead! You'll wake no more! My enemy is dead. He cannot harm me. My hand is in his hair. He cannot strike me. My enemy is dead. He'll wake no more. (*Again addressing the body*) You were a fighter but you'll fight no more. You were a hunter but you'll hunt no more. You were a singer but you'll sing no more. You were a dancer but you'll dance no more. You were a lover but you'll love no more. You'll toss no more your dark hair to the sky! (*She severs a lock of hair and springs to her feet brandishing it.*) See now, my enemy, how weak you are! And I, the daughter of the God, am strong! And as I hold your cut hair in my hand, so does he hold your spirit. And as I crush your hair in my hand, so shall he crush your spirit. (*She holds the severed lock above the fire and addresses the image.*) Great God! Make wide your nostrils! Breathe it deep! (*She scatters it on the fire.*) And have more hunger for the sacrifice!

THE WORSHIPPERS: The sacrifice!

(*SUIVA prods the body with her foot.*)

SUIVA: Strong man, strong man, my foot is on your heart. The great God struck you and you've come to naught. And now, the God will look upon your face, and shut your spirit from his Yellow Tent.

(*She kneels by the body.*)

THE WORSHIPPERS (*at high tension*): The face! The face!

SUIVA (*withdrawing the cloth*): You are my enemy. You shall feed the God. (*She recognizes him. There is a long, tense, motionless pause. She lays her hand on his head and turns to the worshippers with childish bewilderment.*) This is no enemy. This is my beloved. (*They jeer at her. She looks at them uncomprehendingly, then at the image, then at YELLOW SNAKE.*) What have they done to you? (*More jeers.*) This is my mate.

KOTWI (*shrieking*): He's not your mate!

SUIVA: Mother! . . . He is my mate. (*She turns again to the body and strokes the hair.*) Yellow Snake! Speak to me! I'm your mate!

AMBURI (*harshly*): Since when has the God's priestess had a mate?

(*SUIVA ponders his words for a moment, glances at her white vestment, gets up and loosens it at the shoulders. It falls from her, leaving her clad in the fawn-skin.*)

SUIVA (*with childish relief*): Is that it? (*She kneels by the body.*) Now, will you speak to me? I am no more his daughter. I'm your mate. I am your Suiva as I used to be. Now, if you ask me I will go with you. Will you not ask me? Speak . . . Or are you angry with me? . . . (*Pleadingly*) Yellow Snake! Look at me. Be not angry. (*With arms outstretched*) See! I am your mate again. And all is well . . . Be no more angry. Speak! Tell me of Hidden Water! Take me there! Take me to Hidden Water! (*She turns to the worshippers.*) He doesn't hear me. (*They jeer more loudly. She bends over him again and feels the coldness of his face. She gets up and faces them with dawning realization.*) What have you done to him? (*More jeers, silenced by* AMBURI's voice.)

AMBURI: Why did he come here?

SUIVA: He came because he loves me and I love him. What have you done to him?

AMBURI: Your lips have spoken. (*He turns to the bearers who are crouching by the altar.*) Make the sacrifice!

THE WORSHIPPERS: The sacrifice!

(*The bearers spring forward and seize the body.* SUIVA *tries vainly to withhold them.*)

SUIVA: He's mine! You shall not! (*They topple the body from the altar into the pool. A great cry goes up. The bearers crouch back to their former places.* SUIVA *bends over the pool and when the body strikes the water, some sixty feet below, she flings up her hands and turns shrieking on the worshippers.*) You! You! My people! You have killed my mate!

AMBURI: Old men, make ready!

*The old men by the altar draw their knives.*

SUIVA: Will you kill me too?

AMBURI: Kill her!

(*The old men rush forward.* SUIVA *stoops, picks up the silver moon and confronts them with it.*)

SUIVA: Kill me! (*They waver and fall back.*) Cowards!

AMBURI: Kill her!

(*The old men hesitate.*)

SUIVA: Come!

THE OLD MAN (*to* AMBURI): We dare not.

SUIVA: Why? (*She indicates the image.*) The God won't hurt you. (*She picks up the wine cup.*) Look! (*She dashes the wine in the face of the image.*) His name is fear! (*She drops the cup.*) Now, kill me!

THE WORSHIPPERS (*recoiling*): Profane!

SUIVA: This is not God. The God is dead. You killed him. He walked among you but you did not know him. He was God.

THE WORSHIPPERS: Profane! Profane!

SUIVA: He was the singer of the joy of life. His name was love. You killed him. He was God.

AMBURI: Kill her!

(*The old men again rush forward.* SUIVA *seizes the fire basket and draws it to the edge of the pool. The old men again draw back.*)

THE WORSHIPPERS (*whimpering*): The fire!

SUIVA (*balancing it on the edge*): Now will you kill me?

THE WORSHIPPERS: No!

SUIVA: Amburi, will you spare me?

AMBURI: Yes.

SUIVA: Cowards! You are more dead than he is.

(*She topples the fire basket into the pool.*)

THE WORSHIPPERS: The fire! The fire is gone!

(SUIVA *bends over the pool. Her voice is low, sweet, caressing.*)

SUIVA: My mate! My mate! My singer! My beloved! You had no fear. (*She stands proudly erect.*) And now . . . I have no fear. (*She steps from the altar into the pool.*)

THE WORSHIPPERS (*ignoring her completely*): The fire! Famine and death!

(*The eyes of the image, smeared with sulphur and wet with wine, have begun to glow. An old squaw first notices them.*)

THE SQUAW (*shrieking*): The eyes!

THE WORSHIPPERS (*in mortal terror*): The eyes! The eyes!

AMBURI: Fall down before him! Fear him! He is angry!

*(As they prostrate themselves,* LERII *emerges from the throng. He stands looking down at them, and up at the image, and laughs his insane laugh. Then, all is quiet for a moment and the curtain falls.)*

# Explanatory Notes

The explanatory notes, which are marked by page and line number (page.line), offer elaboration on cultural references, geographical locations, and theatre terminology. Production differences, including set design and stage directions, are also annotated in the explanatory notes, as suggested by the theatre playbills, reviews, and photographs. The introduction and dossier offer a detailed account of the different productions' performance variants as indicated by photographs, programs, and reviews.

## ACT I

**7.3–8 The scene represents the edge of a grassy, pine-clad plateau [. . . ] At right-centre is a fallen log, and above it an old pine with heavy foliage**: The Birmingham and Hart House productions offer variants on this set design. Whereas Hart House represents the "*pine-clad plateau*" and "*range of mountains*" with a painted backdrop (see fig. 8), the 1919 and 1920 Birmingham productions include three-dimensional rocks and trees. Birmingham's 1919 set features a tree-lined backdrop with a notable absence of mountains (see fig. 11), while the 1920 production includes more three-dimensional rocks, mountain ranges in the backdrop, and large, darkened pine trees upstage right. Both Birmingham productions place a large tree on centre stage with a branch halfway up the trunk for Yellow Snake to climb (see fig. 7), but with one distinction: the 1919 production uses a branch on the stage-right side of the tree while the 1920 production image shows a branch on the stage-left side. The two Birmingham set designs seem to forgo the "small circular tepee" and the centre-stage pine tree's "heavy foliage." The Hart House production, by contrast, uses a markedly sparser stage design with one log (with Waning Moon sitting on it in fig. 9) and some dirt on the ground. Although there may be some parts of the Hart House stage outside of the photograph's frame, there appear to be no other three-dimensional props or set elements. Hart House further differs from the two Birmingham productions by highlighting a detailed mountainous backdrop. See the critical introduction's

"Performing Ethnography and Primitivism" section for a more in-depth discussion of these differences in set design.

**7.13–14 He withdraws in a panic and, as the sneeze is followed by some further commotion, climbs a nearby tree and hides in the foliage:** The two Birmingham set designs use a single branch for Yellow Snake to climb, but they offer no "foliage," so Yellow Snake can clearly be seen by the audience while Suiva and Kotwi keep their backs to him. See fig. 6 for a photograph of this moment during the 1919 Birmingham production.

**7.15 a fat squaw:** The earliest documented usage of the term "squaw" dates back to 1634, in *New England's Prospect* by William Wood, in which Wood uses the word to indicate "a North American Indian woman or wife" ("Squaw," def. 1a) and, more broadly, a "female" ("Squaw," def. 1). While "squaw" most often refers to an aboriginal woman, it has also been "applied by Indians to white women" ("Squaw," def. 1b). The term also has strong derogatory connotations and, as early as the nineteenth century, is used to indicate "an effeminate or weak person" ("Squaw," def. 3).

**7.18–19 She is a thin old hag of a squaw and wears a ceremonial white garment ornamented with a silver crescent-moon:** Birmingham's 1919 production photos (see fig. 6) show a haggard Waning Moon in dark robes and a statuesque Suiva in a white dress with a crescent moon around her neck (which may have been worn by Waning Moon in the first act). In the 1922 Hart House production, Waning Moon does not appear to be wearing a ceremonial white garment; her dress is dark, and a crescent moon hangs around her neck (see figs. 8 and 9).

**7.23 The God is great. He giveth us full bellies:** This is the line that begins what Aikins refers to as Kotwi and Waning Moon's notably spiritual dialogue, which uses the English translation of the Islamic Arabic religious expression "Allahu Akbar" ("God is great") and echoes passages from Ecclesiastes (2:26).

**8.1 Their tones, which have been ritualistic, return to normal:** Although the play contains allusions to the Judeo-Christian Bible's rhetoric and imagery, Aikins's theosophical warnings against an anthropomorphised God and his description of a general "ritualistic" dialogue avoid singling out a specific religious work.

**8.4–5 And soon they'll grind our meat between two stones:** Kotwi's discussion of her impending death refers to the tradition of using two stones (such as a mortar and pestle) to grind grains and food for consumption. Kotwi's description of death in terms of food preparation gestures towards cannibalistic rituals. Documenting the significance of "cannibal," the Oxford English Dictionary explains that the noun "cannibal" was "a name given to the Carib people of the West Indies, who were said to eat human flesh (*obs.*)(n. 1a). In (later) extended use: a person who eats human flesh" ("Cannibal," n. 1., def. 1a). As a result of this history of the term, stereotypes of aboriginal peoples include cannibalism. Kotwi's following remark—"Have you eaten yet?"—further underscores the interconnection of death and food.

**8.10 The God will guide you to his Yellow Tent**: The play imagines a "Yellow Tent" as the place of God and the afterlife for those who fear him.

**8.21 You might as well believe the world is round like a sheep's bladder!**: Together with the "squaw" description, cannibalistic imagery, and faux-native dialogue, Kotwi's refusal to believe that the world is round establishes her ignorance.

**9.6–7 like the doe in springtime**: This phrase suggests that Suiva, "like a doe in springtime," is ready to mate.

**9.7 And yet I give her**: There is a marked repetition of the word "give" in this scene to mask Kotwi's true motive of self-profit. See the introduction for a discussion of the scene's rhetoric of gift giving in the context of the play's anti-materialism.

**9.10–12 When the fat deer are brought, and the bears' hearts, and the wild ducks and turtles, and burnt upon the altar, what does the God get of them?**: Waning Moon here refers to the religious sacrifice of animals, which has a long-standing tradition and can be found in a range of religions dating back to ancient Greece. For a discussion of sacrifice in North America, see George Franklin Feldman's *Cannibalism, Headhunting and Human Sacrifice in North America: A History Forgotten* (2008); for sacrifice and idolatry in Christianity, see Jonathan Sheehan's "The Altars of the Idols: Religion, Sacrifice, and the Early Modern Polity" (2006); for an examination of animal sacrifice in Sinhala Buddhism, see J. P. (Hans) Feddema's "The 'Lesser' Violence of Animal Sacrifice" (1995); for an overview of the history and function of Greek sacrifice, see J. N. Bremmer's "Greek Normative Animal Sacrifice" (2007).

**9.22 Old Coyote**: Coyote is one of the many names—as well as Crow, Raven, Rabbit, Spider, Monkey, Weesageechak, and Nanabush, among others—for the trickster figure in aboriginal cultures. As Monique Mojica and Ric Knowles explain, Coyote is "one embodiment of the Sacred Clowns, Tricksters, and Contraries of so many different First Nations cultures who enter sacred ceremony to scandalize, scare, ridicule, and make people laugh" (iii). In short, the trickster figure is "the outlaw, the critic, the teacher, the disturber, the cultural hero and the buffoon" (Mojica and Knowles iii). Through the name "Old Coyote," Aikins gestures towards the significance of Coyote as a popular figure in aboriginal drama.

**10.3 groundhog**: Throughout the play, Aikins associates the groundhog with negative characteristics of being "very fat," "sly," and a "coward." In later scenes, Yellow Snake and Amburi describe Mablo as a "sly groundhog" and "groundhog coward," respectively.

**10.10 warm stones in my bed**: Hot stones are a natural bed-warmer.

**10.20 died of the mouth sickness**: Aikins is likely referring to foot-and-mouth disease, which is a sometimes-fatal viral disease that affects cloven-hoofed animals such as cattle, sheep, pigs, and deer.

**10.27 never a man has touched her ankle-ring**: An idiom that suggests that Suiva is a virgin. Aikins uses ankle rings as a sign of wealth (Mablo later promises to adorn his future wife with ankle rings that will go up to her knee) and affiliates this piece of jewellery with marriage.

**10.29 grouse**: A type of bird with feathered feet (the family Tetraonidæ to many naturalists, of which the largest genera are *Tetrao* and *Lagopus*) ("Grouse," def. 1a); also commonly known as moor fowl or moor game. The Canada grouse (Canace or *Dendragapus canadensis*), also known as the spotted grouse, is a variety specific to Canada ("Grouse," def. 1b).

**11.2 The fingers of four hands**: Idiom of counting by hands and fingers; in this case, twenty.

**11.23–25 And when Amburi dies, he'll be the Chief. Chief of the Seven Feathers! He'll smoke the silver pipe, and wear the yellow on his cheeks!**: While "yellow" can be used as a adjective that signals cowardice, Aikins uses the colour yellow to demarcate the high status of a chief. Yellow Snake's name, as a result, suggests that he is of high moral character despite the fact that other characters (Mablo, Waning Moon) see him as a threat and an interloper.

**12.24 A grouse with yellow on his cheeks**: A grouse is commonly known as a "red" bird and even referred to as a "red grouse" ("Grouse," def. 1b). Because grouse are "restricted almost entirely" to the "British Islands," audiences at the Birmingham and London productions would have anticipated Suiva's objection that there are no yellow grouse.

**12.26 meadowlark:** A meadowlark is a bird known for its melodious songs and distinctive bright yellow breast. Kotwi uses a meadowlark as a symbol for Yellow Snake because of the bird's singing voice and yellow markings.

13.12 The stage direction "***emerging on hands and knees***," together with Aikins's use of "SUIVA'S VOICE" (MS) suggest that Suiva does not exit the tepee and make a full appearance until this moment.

**13.15–14.3 You needn't tell me that!:** Suiva's monologue reflects the sensual Song of Solomon as she describes her "mate," a "twisted vine," "sweetness," "balsam," "oil," "breast," and "incense" in a prayer to her God. Despite the overt sexual imagery, the final lines of Suiva's prayer define her as God's "slave." Together, the ritual of prayer and the sensual nature imagery challenge the expectation that God will punish Suiva for engaging in sexual acts.

**14.18 (He kisses her ardently. She struggles to free herself.):** In identifying himself as "Your lover" and kissing her "ardently," Yellow Snake challenges the God of Gods' strict sexual mores and the expectation that virginity signals spiritual purity. Whereas Yellow Snake challenges the God of Gods' doctrine and vocalizes a more progressive view of sex, Suiva at once fears the God and her own physical displays of sexuality. Although Yellow Snake acts as the arbiter of a new religion founded on nature, equality, and sexual freedom, his poetic descriptions of Suiva (with "breath [ . . . ] like crushed lilies") often echo natural imagery from the Song of Solomon; for instance, the Song of Solomon describes "my love" as "the lily among thorns" (2:2) and with "lips like lilies" (5:13). Yellow Snake's descriptions of the nature-laden Hidden Waters as a utopia for lovers where some birds "are only voices" (13) also resemble the Song of Solomon's garden, wherein lovers meet and "the companions harken to thy voice" (8:13). Aikins suggests that the tribe's religion imposes artificial restraints on something that is natural—female sexuality.

**14.28 Your hair is like the thunder-clouds! Your breath is like crushed lilies!:** Along with Suiva's talk of a "twisted vine," Yellow Snake's descriptions of "thunder-clouds" (12), "crushed lilies" (12), and Hidden Waters further echo the Song of Solomon.

**15.28 Grey Mountain:** There is a Grey Mountain in Whitehorse, Yukon Territory of Canada, which is approximately "a two days' journey" by foot from Naramata, B.C. Aikins's stage directions describe a mountainous backdrop to the aboriginal reserve, which is suggestive of the Naramata landscape where Aikins wrote the play and spent much of his life.

**16.27–31 And when you look on it your eyes are stars, your hair is waving grass, your arms have bark like fir trees, and your legs are like polished stones in the creek bottom [ . . . ] even the stones and the fishes**: Yellow Snake's descriptions of Hidden Waters warrant comparison with the Song of Solomon. See especially the passage when the bridegroom praises the bride and compares her eyes to doves, her hair to goats, and her teeth to sheep (Song of Solomon 4:1).

**18.3–4 the ptarmigan turn white**: A grouse that lives in the rocky landscape of the northern hemisphere, with mottled grey-brown feathers that turn white in the winter season, and a black tail ("Ptarmigan," def. 1).

**18.20 a three-years' skunk**: Generally, the oldest age of a skunk in the wild.

**19.9 oily tongue**: Idiom meaning smooth talker or flatterer.

**20.1 bear's grease!**: Bear fat or lard, which can be used as a lubricant and in medical or cosmetic preparation.

**24.15 fore-right**: Downstage right.

**24.15 rear right**: Upstage right.

## ACT II

**30.2 The scene represents a rocky canyon . . . stunted pine trees**: See fig. 2 for an image of the second act's set in Birmingham's 1919 production. Aikins notes that "*To the left, well forward, is a high, flat-topped rock*" and "*To the right is a sheer cliff, pierced by a cavern with a door-like opening*," but the 1919 Birmingham production interprets Aikins's "left" as "stage right" and Aikins's "right" as "stage left."

**31.19 Pantherhead**: Panthers are common in aboriginal mythology.

**33.5–6 She lays it deftly among the flames of the brazier**: A brazier is a portable grill; in this case, it is set in a fire pit (see fig. 7 for a Birmingham production photo of what appears to be a downstage fire pit surrounded with stones).

**34.9 (pointing in the pool)**: Fig. 2 depicts this scene from Birmingham's 1919 production.

**39.19–21 When a man dies his spirit perches like a bird on a fir tree above his grave. At the last moon, the great God gathers all these spirits in his hands, and those who feared him not, he crushes and they live no more**: Birds here represent the soul, and while the Yellow Tent offers an afterlife for obedient servants of God, there is only an absence of any afterlife for those who do not fear him.

**40.30–32 YELLOW SNAKE is seen climbing down the rock chimney to the left. The descent is slow and hazardous but finally he reaches the grass-tufted top of the flat rock**: Yellow Snake's position on "*top of the flat rock*" can be seen in the left-hand side of the photograph from Birmingham's 1919 production (see fig. 6).

**41.8–15 The ferns grow tall and deep beyond the ranges . . . my love is sleep**: Yellow Snake's language of love invites further comparison with the Song of Solomon. For instance, his promise "I'll make my love a tent of leaning silver with birches whiter than the white moon stream" echoes the Song of Solomon's description of a house made from cedar and pine.

**45.31–32 And will you shear the foeman's hair to fill his nose with incense?**: Waning Moon references a traditional smudging ritual of burning incense and using the cleansing smoke for purification; it is a holy act performed during sacred rituals.

**46.18–19 A sound escapes YELLOW SNAKE. MABLO hears it, discovers him, and points him out to AMBURI**: This seems to be the moment depicted in fig. 6 (with Mablo pointing behind Suiva); in the photograph, however, Suiva wears a crown of flowers, but, according to the play's stage directions, Waning Moon has not yet placed them on her head.

## ACT III

**53.14 You shall have women's clothes!**: Forcing men to wear women's clothes as punishment dates back to ancient Greece and the Middle Ages (see Vern L. Bullough's "Transvestites in the Middle Ages").

**54.19 Blue Sea country**: Conversations between Suiva and Yellow Snake (see Act I) explain that the "blue sea" is only "A two days' journey." The Blue Sea country, which is capitalized here and could be distinct from the earlier descriptions of the "blue sea" area, either references the Pacific Ocean or, most likely, Naramata's Lake Okanagan.

**61.5 The God is dead**: a famous line by Frederick Nietzsche in *The Gay Science*. See the critical introduction for an examination of the play's Nietzschean contexts.

**61.8 He was the singer of the joy of life. His name was love**: Suiva echoes the love rhetoric from the Song of Solomon and her earlier scenes with Yellow Snake.

# Textual Notes

The version of *The God of Gods* published in *Canadian Plays from Hart House Theatre* (Volume 2, 1927), edited by Vincent Massey, serves as the copy text for this edition. The textual notes account for differences between the Hart House version and the original manuscript. Each textual note offers the present text before the square bracket (]), which is followed by the alternate reading from the original manuscript. If the present text varies from its copy text, then the notation "ed;" appears after the square bracket to highlight the editor's emendation to the copy text, and the Hart House (HH) version follows the square bracket marked by the abbreviation HH; if the emendation also differs from the manuscript, then the manuscript (MS) version also follows the square bracket. For instance, the following note signals a spelling change to both the copy text and the manuscript: groundhog] ed; ground-hog (MS, HH).

Spelling (e.g., "fawn-skin" versus "fawnskin") and punctuation inconsistencies (e.g., comma versus period) as well as overt typographical errors have been corrected and noted in only the first instance. All spelling errors and inconsistencies have been corrected according to the Canadian spellings (e.g., "color" has been changed to "colour" and "gray" to "grey") in the *Oxford English Dictionary* (online edition). Unless misspelled, variants in spelling have been modernized (e.g., "to-night" has been changed to "tonight") and unified to accord with the Hart House version. For example, "groundhog" has variant spellings (groundhog, ground-hog) in both the Hart House script and the original manuscript, but it has been standardized to "groundhog" because it appears more often in the Hart House version; subsequent occurrences have been silently corrected. Minor variants in punctuation or contractions in the copy text and differences between the copy text and manuscript are noted because they may have impacted the delivery and performance of the lines.

The Hart House script and original manuscript have been formatted according to University of Ottawa Press house style. For instance, the ellipses in this edition have been standardized to three periods, whereas Aikins's manuscript includes varying lengths of ellipses (ranging from three to five periods) and the Hart House version usually includes four periods. Also, the original manuscript does not italicize stage directions, but the present version italicizes all stage directions.

Finally, word choices, punctuation, grammar, and sentence structures have not been altered in order to account for Aikins's use of faux-aboriginal dialect.

**3.1** *The God of Gods: A Canadian Play* ] This subtitle is taken from the Hart House Theatre's playbill and advertisements (1922) and indicates how the play was presented to Canadian audiences. The subsequent collection, *Canadian Plays from Hart House Theatre*, does not include a subtitle for *The God of Gods*. Aikins's original manuscript, by comparison, entitles his play *The God of Gods: A Play in Three Acts*, whereas Birmingham Theatre uses the subtitle "An American-Indian Play" (1919) and Everyman Theatre's playbill cites the play as both *The God of Gods: A Drama in Three Acts* and *The God of Gods: A Drama* (1931).

**3.2** CHARACTERS ] Persons of the Play

**3.10** OLD MEN, worshippers ] OLD MEN

**3.11** OLD WOMEN, worshippers. ] OLD WOMEN

**4.12** Set Design - - - - - - - - - - - - - - - - - - - - -BARRY JACKSON ] The playbill does not list the name of the set designer for Birmingham's productions, but one 1919 reviewer credits Barry Jackson. A note on the back of a photo from the 1920 production credits Paul Shelving.

**4.23** Worshippers ] The original manuscript does not list "worshippers" in the cast, and only includes "Old Men. Old Women" to indicate the supporting cast (1).

**5.16** Old Men and Women ] The Everyman Theatre does not attribute any specific actor(s) to the roles of the Old Men and Women, which suggests that the actors may have performed their individual roles (as Amburi, Kotwi, Waning Moon, etc.) while also playing a role in the ensemble of Old Men and Women.

**7.2** ACT I ] After the list of characters, the original manuscript provides a summary of the setting, before the more detailed stage directions that begin Act I, as follows:

Act One—A pine-clad plateau.
Act Two and Three—An altar to the God of Gods.
Time—In the summer of the God.
Place—A mountain valley. (1)

**7.4** *birch bark* ] birchbark

**7.10** ] "*The curtain rises*"

**7.13** *panic and,* ] *panic and*

**7.14** *commotion,* ] *commotion*

**7.17** *about grunting* ] *grunting about*

**8.13** No! ] No! No!

**8.24** eyes, then. ] eyes then.

**8.24** sly one—ough! ] sly one . . . ough!
**8.27** Eh? Is it Suiva? ] Eh, is it Suiva?
**9.1** God, and ] God and
**9.7** give her. ] give her!
**9.18** eat! ] eat?
**9.19** sick, ] sick
**9.23** liar, ] liar
**10.3** groundhog ] ed; ground-hog (MS, HH)
**10.14** here, ] here
**10.29** grouse, ] grouse
**10.30** *with interested* ] *with an interested*
**11.10** so, ] so
**11.16** Chief's ] chief's
**11.24** pipe, ] pipe
**11.25** little ] littl [sic]
**11.27** him. ] him!
**12.5** *behind her.)* ] *behind it.)*
**12.11** Gods! ] Gods.
**12.13** *and calls)* Suiva! Oh, ] *and calls.)* Suiva! Oh!
**12.14** SUIVA (*off, sleepily*) ] SUIVA'S VOICE (*sleepily*)
**12.16** SUIVA ] SUIVA'S VOICE
**12.18** SUIVA: I am putting on my tunic . . . Your voice is happy. Have you snared a grouse? ]
SUIVA: I am putting on my tunic. Or shall I come out naked?
KOTWI: Hush! For shame! Don't be a child!
SUIVA'S VOICE: Your voice is happy. Have you snared a grouse?
**12.21** SUIVA ] SUIVA'S VOICE
**12.23** SUIVA ] SUIVA'S VOICE
**12.25** SUIVA ] SUIVA'S VOICE
**12.27** KOTWI: That smokes a silver pipe.
SUIVA: Just now I dreamt that I heard voices. ]
KOTWI: That smokes a silver pipe.
SUIVA'S VOICE: You told me not to be a child.
KOTWI: Well! Well! We'll see!
SUIVA: Just now I dreamt that I heard voices.
**12.30** SUIVA ] SUIVA'S VOICE
**13.4** SUIVA: What did she want? KOTWI: To talk of cows ] These lines are in reverse order in HH (giving KOTWI two lines in a row).
**13.6** SUIVA ] SUIVA'S VOICE

13.8 SUIVA ] SUIVA'S VOICE
13.13 KOTWI *(going left)*: ] KOTWI *(going out to the left)*:
13.13 spring ] spring,
13.16 *fawn-skin* ] *fawnskin*
13.18 *turns,* ] *turns*
13.18 *outstretched,* ] *outstretched*
13.18 *half risen* ] *half-risen*
13.19 torchbearer ] torch bearer
13.21 *(She turns, comes forward, and kneels.)* ] *(She turns, comes forward and kneels.)*
13.22 tongue of fire ] tongue fire
13.29 season, ] season
13.33 fire, ] fire
14.1 I am thy slave. I fear thee! ] "I am thy slave. I fear thee."
14.2 *up,* ] *up*
14.15 *him,* ] *him*
14.18 *She struggles to free herself.* ] *(struggling)*
14.20 *(laughing and continuing his embrace)* ] (laughing and continuing)
15.9 water, but ] water. But
15.13 blood, and I'll bathe mine too, and then ] blood. And I'll bathe mine too. And then
15.30 days' ] days
16.4 *resting her cheek on her hand* ] *resting cheek on hand*
16.8 nest in them ] nest with them
16.10 smoothed with sand, and some are pictures made with blood on birch-bark, and some are only voices. But when they sing it is like quick water under the white moon. ] smoothed with sand. And some are pictures made with blood on birch-bark. And some are only voices, but when they sing it's like quick water under the white moon.
16.16 kill the trees; and if you kill the trees, you have no shelter from the sun and storm; and though you live, life will be dull as sleep is without dreams; and you'll be glad to die. ] kill the trees. And if you kill the trees you have no shelter from the sun and storm. And though you live, life will be dull as sleep is without dreams. And you'll be glad to die!
16.20 There is grass—like this grass, and flowers, and berry-bushes . . . And when they are hurt they cry as your children do. And when the wind runs through them and they're glad, you hear ] There is grass, like this grass, and flowers and berry-bushes . . . And when they're hurt they cry as children do. And when the wind runs through them and they're glad you hear
16.24 sky, with ] sky; with

**16.29** creek bottom—you ] creek bottom . . . . you
**17.6** come. ] come?
**17.7** days' journey? ] days journey?
**17.20** nest and ] nest, and
**17.21** He must have no fear of any beast, or man, or God. ] And he must have no fear of any beast or man or God.
**17.23** God, then ] God then
**17.28** traps and curves ] traps. He curves
**17.30** you. But if you fear him not, ] you, but if you fear him not
**17.31** you, or ] you or
**18.3** fed, ] fed
**18.7** Only the God. ] Only the God!
**18.29** gates—they ] gate. They
**19.13** singer, but ] singer but
**19.15** house, too, ] house too
**19.18** Eh? ] Eh!
**19.23** coming, we must have a house; and ] coming; we must have a house. And
**19.25** you will ] you'll
**20.9** Yes! Yes, and ] Yes! Yes! And
**20.12** The ground's ] And the ground's
**20.14** mate, ] mate
**20.21** *her, and* ] *her and*
**20.22** again, and ] again and
**20.23** *pieces, and* ] *pieces and*
**21.7** *form of* ] *for mof* [sic]
**21.14** *framework* ] *frame work*
**21.18** saplings do. ] saplings.
**21.20** *joists. Across the joists they lay rafters,* ] *joists, and across the joists they lay rafters*
**21.26** *his hand on hers* ] *He takes her hand*
**21.27** *(rather shyly, taking* ] *(Rather shyly, but taking*
**21.28** *up.* SUIVA *laughs.)* ] *up.)*
SUIVA *(laughing):*
**21.29** man, nor beast, nor ] man or beast or
**22.3** *run off to the right.* KOTWI *comes in from the left, grunting. She glances* ] *run together to the right.* KOTWI *comes grunting in from the left, glances*
**22.5** *There is no reply* ] *No reply*
**22.7** *right. She turns to scold her daughter but discovers* AMBURI, *the old Chief, and his son,* MABLO. *They enter.* ] *right and she turns to scold her daughter but there enter instead Amburi, the old Chief, and his son Mablo.*

**22.8** AMBURI ] *Amburi*
**22.8** *courtly, old man,* ] *courtly old man*
**22.11** KOTWI, *her expression changed to one of gratified surprise, goes forward to meet them.)* The Great Chief and his son, Mablo, do me much honour. ] KOTWI: The Great Chief and his son do me much honour.
**22.20** there . . . ] there. *(a slight pause)*
**22.23** are gentle ] ar [sic] gentle
**23.2** I'd ] I had
**23.4** girl, though, ] girl though
**23.8** baskets, too, ] baskets too
**23.9** stream-polished stones. ] stream polished stonne [sic].
**23.10** sheds ] shed
**23.14** Or a ] Or the
**23.20** wine, ] wine
**23.20** it, and ] it and
**24.11** killed, ] killed
**24.14** *out left.* ] *out by the left.*
**24.17** *She pauses for an answer, then turns and discovers* MABLO. ] *(Silence. She turns and discovers Mablo.)*
**25.5** one-tenth ] one tenth
**25.9** brown-grey ] brown-gray (HH)
**25.13** go, all gold and silver, to your knee, ] go all gold and silver to your knee
**25.29** so soon ] how soon
**26.2** *leafy branch* ] *leafy birch branch*
**26.7** *abruptly, and* ] *abruptly and*
**26.9** *her. She* ] *her; she*
**26.12** then, ] then
**26.14** that. ] that!
**26.15** fall. ] fall!
**26.16** *pursuit in earnest, but* ] *He sets about the pursuit in earnest but*
**26.19** me, ] me
**26.21** *around a tree.)* Oh, no, you don't! . . . The leaves are falling fast. . . . he'd catch me ere ] *round a tree.)* Oh, no! You don't! . . . The leaves are falling fast! . . . he'd catch me e'er
**26.26** squirrel. ] squirrel!
**26.30** *course,* ] *course*
**27.7** *her, then, hesitates, turns,* ] *her; then, hesitates, turns*
**27.8** *runs at it,* ] *runs at it*
**27.9** *bruised foot* ] *damaged foot*

**27.10** WANING MOON *enters from the right.* ] Waning Moon *enters from the right;*
**27.11** my legs ] me on the legs
**27.16** proper and ] proper. And
**27.24** kill *him.* ] kill him.
**28.10** Eight! ] Eight.
**28.11** you will . . . If you want her then, no ] you'll . . . If you want her then. no [sic]
**28.16** them, but . . . We'll watch them. ] them! But . . . We'll watch them!
**28.22** rabbit. ] rabbit!
**29.2** his nest ] your nest:
**29.3** go? ] go.
**29.11** you, as ] you. As
**29.12** teeth. ] teeth
**29.14** it, so that we hate no man, and ] it. So that we hate no man and
**29.15** today ] ed; to-day (HH)
**29.22** What brings you here? ] What brings you here!
**29.28** YELLOW SNAKE, *who* ] YELLOW SNAKE *who*
**29.29** *arms.* ] *arms;*
**30.4** *basket is* ] *basket, is*
**30.5** *meat scraps, a cup of wine* ] *meat-scraps, a cup of wine,*
**30.6** *thrashes* ] *crashes*
**30.9** *door-like* ] *doorlike*
**30.13** *It is sunset* ] *The time is sunset*
**30.13** *rises,* ] *rises*
**30.15** *finished;* ] *done;*
**30.16** *altar,* ] *altar*
**30.21** by, I will. ] by I will.
**30.26** farther ] far
**31.7** you his ] you now his
**31.8** God. Set more deer in his path! ] God; Set more deer in his path.
**31.17** I am tired of watching the pool, and ] I'm tired of watching. And
**32.11** WANING MOON *is shocked* ] WANING MOON, *shocked*
**32.14** LERII, *completely shattered* ] LERII, *his assurance completely shattered*
**32.18** *it,* ] *it*
**32.23** likely. At the rites, she wets ] likely; at the rites. She wets
**32.24** tonight ] ed; to-night? (HH)
**32.26** in, ] in
**33.1** I have . . . hungry and ] I've . . . hungry. And
**33.12** You had better wait. You'll see her at the rites and afterwards ] You'd better wait. You'll see her at the rites [sic] And afterwards,

**33.20** *vestment, and,* ] *vestment and,*
**34.2** whirlpool ] suckhole
**34.4** Poor Lerii. ] Poor Lerii!
**34.13** Now ] Now,
**34.21** mind, you'll ] mind. You'll
**34.21** if ] iff [sic]
**35.6** nothing, even ] nothing. Even
**35.9** God, and ] God. And
**35.15** *turns slowly.* ] *gyrates slowly.*
**35.24** to catch ] t ocatch [sic]
**35.30** couldn't, mother, I ] couldn't mother. I
**36.15** you, but, for my sake, ] you. But, for my sake
**36.16** him, Amburi ] him Amburi
**36.17** KOTWI: And now he will not. How am I to live?
SUIVA: I wonder why he chose me. ]
KOTWI: And now he will not. How am I to live?
SUIVA: The God will pity you. You'll find a fat deer with a broken leg.
KOTWI (dryly): Aie! Maybe.
SUIVA: I wonder why he chose me.
**36.20** grey-bird ] greybird
**36.22** girl, though, ] girl, though.
**36.25** that's ] that't [sic]
**36.26** partly, too, ] partly too
**37.2** own Suiva. ] own Suiva!
**37.9** bear comes or ducks or turtles come, remember ] bear, or ducks or turtles, remember
**37.13** together . . . ] together.
**37.23** I'll tell him the last part. ] 'll [sic] tell him the last part!
**37.24** No, tell him all. ] No, tell him all!
**37.25** Well, I see no harm. And you'll be good to me, I ] Well. I see no harm in it. And you'll be good to me. I
**37.28** mother, now, ] mother. Now,
**37.29** *altar* ] *altar,*
**37.29** *steps* ] *step*
**38.7** *Indicating* ] *Indicates*
**38.9** That's ] That't [sic]
**38.11** goat drums and . . . talk too ] goat drums. And . . . talk
**38.12** *out laughing* ] *out to the left*
**38.24** word I'll place ] words I lay

38.29 him you will ] him, you'll

39.6 houses—one in the deep pool, the ] houses. One in the deep pool; the

39.10 springs of water, and sweet berry wine, and herds of antelope, and flocks of fat, white ducks. . . . we do not hunt. . . . we are fed . . . in the centre, and then, the priestess, ] springs of water and sweet berry wine and herds of antelope and flocks of fat white ducks. . . . we do not hunt them. . . . we're fed . . . in the centre and then, the priestess

39.19 dies . . . a fir ] When a man dies, . . . the fir

39.20 moon, ] moon

39.20 hands, ] hands

39.21 not, ] not

39.24 something ] some thing

39.29 red like ] red lie

39.29 fall ] falls

40.7 can't ] cannot

40.12 bring gifts ] bring him gifts

40.13 come, they . . . gifts in ] come they . . . gifts for

40.16 hair is ] hair's

40.24 winters, ] winters

40.30 *seen* ] *seet* [sic]

41.1 *heard. He retreats swiftly to the altar* ] *heard in conversation; he retreats swiftly to the proximity of the altar*

41.4 *pauses for a moment, looking* ] *pauses and gazes for a moment*

41.7 love ] lover

41.10 moon stream ] moon-stream

41.14 sun-time and the star-time ] sun time and the star time

41.16 *He steps from behind the altar and comes to meet* SUIVA. ] *He discovers himself and comes down from the altar.*

41.18 I have ] I've

41.28 you! ] you.

42.4 God, don't ] God! Don't

42.24 Who's? ] Whose?

42.27 *laughs,* ] *laughs*

43.6 *sound on* ] *soun dfrom* [sic]

43.8 quickly. ] quickly!

43.23 Snake. ] Snake!

43.25 it, ] it

43.29 *scene* ] *wild place*

43.30 First ] First,

**44.1** *coloured* ] *colored*
**44.2** *large* ] *deep*
**44.3** *cease, and, after a short pause,* ] *cease and after a short pause*
**44.5** *simultaneously* ] *with a single motion*
**44.11** tomorrow's ] (MS); to-morrow's (HH)
**44.16** you, and ] you. And
**44.24** And, though ] And though
**44.33** more, and ] more. And
**45.3** bidding ] bidding,
**45.5** *forward,* ] *forward*
**45.14** forget you. ] forget.
**45.19** shall ] they shall
**45.23** Will ] And will
**46.7** SNAKE, *unable* ] SNAKE *unable*
**46.11** *holding* ] *with*
**46.11** of the God ] of God
**46.12** head, ] head
**46.13** SNAKE, *who* ] SNAKE *who*
**46.17** winters, ] winters
**46.18** *him, and* ] *him and*
**46.20** *arm. The two* ] *arm. He lowers his hand after a moment and seizes his arm. The two*
**46.21** *is finished* ] *concludes*
**46.21** YELLOW SNAKE *is not seen by any of the worshippers.* WANING MOON *places . . . then turns* ] *None other has discovered him.* WANING MOON *lays . . . then, turns*
**46.25** *heads,* ] *heads*
**46.25** *extended,* ] *extended*
**46.27** Moon, ] Moon
**46.28** *altar,* ] *altar*
**46.29** *into which they disappear at the same time,* ] *which they enter*
**46.30** *out left.* ] *out to the left.*
**46.32** *Then,* ] *Then*
**47.3** *waiting.)* CURTAIN. ] waiting and the curtain falls.) End of Act Two.
**48.2** *The same as Act II. Fifteen minutes have elapsed. It has grown a little darker. Otherwise, the scene is unchanged. As the curtain rises,* SUIVA *enters* ] *Since the preceding act fifteen minutes have elapsed. The scene is vacant, slightly but otherwise unchanged. As the curtain rises,* SUIVA *comes*
**48.5** Yellow Snake! . . . ] Yellow Snake! (a pause)
**48.6** *She turns, . . . steps, and looks across the top of the rock. Realizing that* YELLOW SNAKE *has gone she utters a sigh* ] *A further pause. She turns, . . . steps, and from*

*that place looks across to the top of the rock and discovers that he is gone. She utters a perceptible sigh*

48.8 *there and* ] *there; then*

48.9 *containing sulphurous* ] *which contains a sulphurous*

48.18 dies the . . . suffer for ] dies, the . . . suffer famine for

48.28 You had ] You'd

49.1 it, for if you break it, and he catches you, ] it. For if you break it and he catches you

49.5 together, ] together

49.8 Drink. ] Drink!

49.11 wine that warms the heart ] yellow wine that warms the heart and belly

49.13 it, ] it

49.14 but what I hate, he hates. . . . I answer. I speak, he answers. It is ] what I hate, he hates. . . . I answer; I speak, he answers. It's

49.29 go into ] go! Into

50.19 *altar.* ] *altar,*

50.20 can ] shall

50.26 there is ] there's

50.31 make it strong ] make strong

50.31 baking it in ] baking in

51.1 *disillusion* ] *disillusions,*

51.2 eyes and ] eyes. And

51.3 anger, and . . . gifts, as . . . (*She pauses, glances down at* SUIVA.) ] anger and . . . gifts as . . . (*She pauses and glances down at her.*)

51.14 *does not reply* ] *makes no answer*

51.15 harm ] harm in it

51.16 does not ] doesn't

51.24 *shoulder,* ] *shoulder*

52.1 for him. ] for him!

52.2 hear. . . . *past him into* ] hear! . . . *by him to*

52.9 I am ] I'm

52.15 There is ] There's

52.16 *down left.* ] *at the left-front corner of the scene.*

52.26 *indicating* ] *to indicate*

53.6 Yes, but ] Yes! But

53.17 you; and ] you, and

53.22 law, ] law

53.23 a son ] my son

53.26 *out left* ] *out to the left*

**54.1** wanted ] wants
**54.19** hunting-ground ] hunting grounds
**55.6** singer? . . . ] singer! *(A slight pause)*
**55.14** live, ] live
**55.23** *goes left, pausing at the exit* ] *starts for the left exit, then pauses*
**55.29** *herself. Then she goes towards the cavern calling* ] *herself, then she goes toward the cavern, halts and calls*
**56.3** man? ] man!
**56.10** They have ] They've
**56.16** death drums ] death-drums
**56.24** here, ] here
**56.27** Yes, ] Yes
**57.14** *in the form of a* ] *on the outskirts of an imaginary*
**57.15** *cease.* SUIVA *pours oil* ] *cease and* SUIVA *pours oil upon*
**57.19** you and ] you. And
**57.20** great; he ] great. He
**57.22** *(stepping forward)*: Over all lands ] *(standing forth)*: Over all lands they go
**58.2** thing? . . . ] thing? *(A pause. No response.)*
**58.7** thorn. ] thorns.
**58.8** *body* ] *body,*
**59.3** . . . Are you asleep? *(She shakes him.)* Wake up! . . . Or are you dead? *(She pauses. Then, tauntingly)* ] *(a pause)* Are you asleep? *(She shakes him.)* Wake up! *(a pause)* Or are you dead? *(A pause, then tauntingly:)*
**59.8** You were a dancer but you'll dance no more. You were a lover but you'll love no more. ] You were a lover but you'll love no more. You were a dancer but you'll dance no more!
**59.13** your hair in my ] your cut hair in my
**59.14** *addresses* ] *addressed*
**59.18** SUIVA *prods the body* ] SUIVA returns to the body and *prods it*
**59.20** naught ] nought
**59.25** *tense, motionless* ] *motionless*
**59.27** *uncomprehendingly, then at the image,* ] *uncomprehendingly; then at the image;*
**59.31** Mother! . . . ] Mother! (A short pause.)
**59.35** *fawn-skin* ] *fawn-skin from Act One*
**60.3** Speak . . . Or are you angry with me? . . . *(Pleadingly)* ] Speak *(A pause)* Or are you angry with me? *(Pleadingly)*
**60.5** well . . . ] well *(A pause)*
**60.7** (She ] (A pause. She
**61.2** *the face of the image.)* ] *his face.)*

**61.3** *the cup* ] *the wine cup*

**61.11–12** *the pool* ] *the void*

**61.29** him! Fear him! He is angry! ] him. Fear him. He is angry.

**62.1** LERII *emerges from the throng. He stands looking down at them, and up at the image,* ] *Mad* LERII *emerges standing from the throng. He looks down at them, up at the image*

**62.2** *all is quiet for a moment and the curtain falls.)* ] *silence, a short pause and the curtain falls.)* THE END.

# *Dossier*

## REVIEWS, PLAYBILLS, AND MEDIA

All reviews, playbills, and media are arranged in chronological order by date of publication.

### THEATRE REVIEWS

**Anonymous. "A New Production at the Repertory Theatre: Magic at the Empire."** ***Birmingham Gazette*** **7 November 1919.**

A play of unusual interest will be produced at the Birmingham Repertory Theatre to-morow (Saturday) night, in "The God of Gods," by Carroll Aitkins [sic] of British Columbia. It will be the first time this has been seen on any stage. It is a powerful tragedy of love and malice, and quite different to anything that has been seen on the Repertory stage. All the characters are American Indians. The play is in the hands of a strong company, including Susan Richmond, Margaret Chatwin, Isabel Thornton, Stuart Vinden, Frank Moore, Melville Cooper, and Eric H. Messiter. The play is produced by A.E. Filmer, and the scenery designed by Mr. Barry Jackson.

**E. C. "Feathers and Faith: Red Indian Play at the Repertory."** ***Birmingham Gazette*** **10 November 1919.**

Tribal religion, a devout Indian maiden, her two lovers—"a worthless singer of mad songs," and a rich chief's son with appetites of a ground hog—and a cunning old priestess who works as oracle, are the materials from which Mr. Carroll Aikins has made his interesting play, "The God of Gods," which Birmingham Repertory Theatre Company produced on Saturday night for the first time on any stage.

The devout maiden Suiva loves the singer Yellow Snake. Mablo, the chief's son, wants her, but in spite of the prospect of many cows for herself and her aged mother, she flouts him. Waning Moon, the priestess whose ways and wants have been the god's for 50 years, elects Suiva as her successor, so that Mablo, who has entry to the sacred precincts, may make her his, and kill Yellow Snake when he trespasses.

In the last act Suiva receives the body of Yellow Snake for sacrifice to the god, then defies both tribe and god, and flings herself after her lover into the hidden pool.

A SAWDUST GOD

The love scenes and the conflict in Suiva are finely treated. There are echoes of Dunsany in the character of the crafty, wine-bibbing priestess; but on the whole it is good, original work. The first act has rather a heavy burden of poetry, and though the pantheistic singer is well conceived, some of his speeches would stand cutting.

The acting throughout was admirable. Miss Susan Richmond interpreted the duty of the central figure with insight, and Miss Margaret Chatwin's priestess was a very clever study. These two have seldom done better work, and to them the play's success was principally due. Mr. Vinden's romantic handling of Yellow Snake deserves praise, and Mr. Melville Cooper got the right mixture of grossness and sheepishness into Mablo. Mr. Frank Moore played the chief with massive dignity. A little more subtlety on the part of Miss. Thornton would have made Suiva's mother more convincing. The setting was worthy of Mr. Filmer's record as producer, but the god was rather too palpably sawdust stuffed.

**Anonymous. "The God of Gods." *Birmingham Evening Despatch* 10 November 1919.**

Mr. Carroll Aikins, in "The God of Gods," produced for the first time at the Repertory Theatre on Saturday night, has written a play which deserves a wider popularity than, we fear, it will achieve. It is one of those rare artistic delicacies reserved for the favour of the comparatively small band of enthusiastic people who delight in "art for art's sake." And these should find in Mr. Aikin's play not only aesthetic nourishment, but matter enough to satisfy that eternal craving which animates all humans for "something new," which here is given us, not in the story, which is as old as anything else under the sun, but in the people concerned—a Red Indian tribe—and in their manner of dealing with some of the problems of life.

THE STORY

Suiva, a girl of the tribe, is loved by Yellow Snake, an outcast singer, who no more reverences the stone god than does the priestess Waning Moon, whose wishes have been the god's for many moons past. In fact, the gigantic fraud perpetuated on the believing tribe by the priestess, under the cover of the god, provides the only humour to relieve the pervading gloom of the tragedy.

The Chief's son also desires Suiva, but he is repulsed (and even whipped) by the girl. But the crafty Waning Moon has the power to select her own successor as priestess. By choosing Suiva she confines her to the immediate precincts of the god, to which only old men and women (and the Chief's son) are admitted. Interlopers are killed, so are priestesses who break their vows, one of which is to renounce all men and all love for ever.

At the hour before Suiva takes the vows before the god, Yellow Snake appears and, in a tense scene of passion, implores her to feign illness at the critical moment, and that night he will come and take her away. But Suiva, who has been brought up in the "faith," and, in spite of her love, is horrified at his blasphemous treatment of the God performs all the rites and becomes the successor to the scheming Waning Moon.

Yellow Snake is observed in his hiding place by the Chief's son, and unknown to Suiva, is ordered to be killed. When her lover's body is brought in to the sacrifice, she, as the new priestess, is called upon to perform the rites—to denounce unknowingly her dead lover as "mine enemy" and "the enemy of the God."

The climax of the tragedy is reached when she uncovers the face of the dead man. She scorns the god, and throws the eternal fire into the lake. Love, after all, is revealed as the god of gods. She follows her lover's body into the deep waters.

FINE ACTING

Of Miss Susan Richmond's acting as Suiva we have nothing but unqualified praise. It is without doubt the finest work she has done since joining the company. In the final scene she showed exceptional emotional power, her mourning for the dead lover mingled with her rage against the tribe and the fake god being wonderfully interpreted.

Miss Margaret Chatwin is *always* good, but seldom has she given us anything so consistently good and impressive as in this old hag who hoodwinks the tribe by her subterfuges. Her revelations when drunk of "how it is done" to Suiva was notable for its magnificent restraint. Mr. Stuart Vinden played Yellow Snake with a fine ardour and depth of expression.

**Anonymous. "The God of Gods: American-Indian play by Carroll Aitkins [sic]. Produced for the first time on any stage at the Birmingham Repertory Theatre on Sunday, Nov. 9." *Era* 12 November 1919.**

Yellow Snake................................E. Stuart Vinden
Amburi .......................................Frank Moore
Mablo .........................................Melville Cooper

Leril .......... Eric H. Messiter
Suiva .......... Susan Richmond
Kotwi .......... Isabel Thornton
Waning Moon .......... Margaret Chatwin

Mr. Carroll Aitkins [sic] is, we believe, a British Columbian, and has succeeded in breaking fresh ground with plenty of local colour. Waning Moon, the aged princess of the God of Gods, is about to resign her office, and suggests that for the consideration of ten cows she might nominate the beautiful Suiva as her successor. Suiva is the daughter of a covetous old woman, Kotwi, who recognizes the personal benefits likely to accrue from the suggested appointment. She offers five cows, and even seven, but cannot rise to ten. She soon sees another possibility of making capital of her daughter's beauty, for she is wooed by Mablo, the worthless and greedy son of the chief of the tribe. But Suiva is in love with Yellow Snake, the singer, an irresponsible poet, who is incapable through laziness of providing a home for her. When she rejects Mablo's overtures he sees that if she will not consent to become his wife his position as the chief's son will enable him to attain his desires if she becomes the priestess, and accordingly he gives Waning Moon the ten cows, and Suiva is consecrated to the God of Gods. The climax of the play is reached when Suiva as priestess offers the great sacrifice of a human body to the God. The body is Yellow Snake's, but Suiva does not know this until the end of the ceremony, when she uncovers the face and beholds that over her lover. Then her pent-up love breaks out, and she passionately throws herself on the corpse of Yellow Snake, denouncing the idol and crying out that the God of Gods is Love. The chief calls on the horrified worshipers to put her to death, but she saves herself from their hands by seeking her death in the lake.

The acting and staging were alike admirable. Miss Margaret Chatwin as Waning Moon, Mr. Stuart Vinden as Yellow Snake, and Miss Susan Richmond as Suiva equally bear the burden of the play, and all acted with intelligence and distinction.

**Anonymous. "The God of Gods." *Stage* 13 November 1919.**

At the Birmingham Repertory Theatre "The God of Gods" by Carroll Aikins was presented on November 8, 1919. The following was the cast:

Yellow Snake .......... Mr. E. Stuart Vinden
Amburi .......... Mr. Frank Moore
Mablo .......... Mr. Melville Cooper
Leril .......... Mr. Eric H. Messiter
Suiva .......... Miss Susan Richmond
Kotwi .......... Miss Isabel Thornton
Waning Moon .......... Miss Margaret Chatwin

"The God of Gods" is an American Indian play, and all having a place in it are coloured. The story is of an unusual kind. It is, in a sense, an allegory full of deep meaning, and it has the merit of reasonableness in conception. There is nothing impossible about this play, which belongs distinctly to the repertory class. The incidents might, in fact, have actually happened, although in these days, of course, many may regard them as improbable. There is undoubted originality and imagination about Mr. Aikins' work, which is mainly in prose, though the first act has a leavening of poetry. It lends itself to picturesque stage treatment, which Mr. Filmer has made extremely effective (the lighting effects are noteworthy), and there is a good deal of quaint and weird tribal music.

The God of Gods is an idol, in appearance crude and hideous, standing at the side of a sacred pool, in which he is supposed to live, and in front of him, on the altar, are the fires, which are served by Waning Moon, priestess to the God. She is a wine-bibbing, dissolute, and crafty creature. The time has arrived when she must be succeeded by a young woman, and ultimately her choice falls upon Suiva. She has great beauty, piety, nobility of character. The atmosphere of tribal religion, with its blind, unreasoning fear, runs all though the play. Suiva loves Yellow Snake, a singer, and Mablo, the chief's son, wants her for his mate. In spite of the prospect of many cows for herself and Kotwi, her aged mother, she flouts and beats him. Before Suiva had taken the final vows as priestess, came Yellow Snake to the template and entreated Suiva to fly with him. In his anger Yellow Snake strikes the God and defies him. He then hides on a rock in order to witness Suiva being admitted as Priestess. Amburi sees him, and directs Mablo, his son, idle and gross, to kill him; this is the penalty for trespass—the desecration of the temple. Mablo leaves, shoots Yellow Snake in the back, dead—for which cowardice he receives the castigation of his father. The latter then sets a trap for Suiva to try to ascertain if she had been a party to desecration of the temple. He calls on her to sacrifice to the God, and bids them bring in the lifeless body of Yellow Snake (whose face is covered), meaning to kill her even if she betrayed herself, for not even the priestess could break the law and live. She performs the strange rites, believing that the body is that of a young man of another nation; she cuts off the hair, and then removes the face covering, to realize that it is her lover. But Suiva had learnt many things from the drunken Waning Moon, and, apparently, no longer fears the God. So she turns on them all, reviling god, chief and tribe alike; and, in her frenzy, flings into the sacred pool the fire which, they all believed, contained the secret of life, and then plunges in herself to join her mate at last in death. Thus the play ends on a note of real moving tragedy, in which Suiva plays with great vigour and passion.

On the whole, the acting reaches a very high standard: it is thoroughly in acord [sic] with the best repertory tradition. Susan Richmond gives a convincing study; she brings out the beauty in the central figure, which is in itself an inspiration. Margaret Chatwin is at her best; the interpretation of the Priestess is one of the best things she has done; and Mr. Vinden's ardent and romantic treatment of Yellow Snake deserves [praise . . . ] Frank Moore plays the [ . . . ].

**Anonymous. "Repertory Theatre." *Midland Counties Herald* 13 November 1919.**
"The God of Gods" is a play of quiet, entrancing beauty and dignity, and is somewhat reminiscent of Mr. John Drinkwater's "The God of Quiet." The various parts were finely acted by the Repertory Company. Miss Margaret Chatwin added another dramatic triumph to her long list, and Mr. Vinden's performance was entirely excellent. The other artistes, viz., Miss Thornton, Mr. Frank Moore, Mr. Melville Cooper, and Mr. Messiter all did exceedingly well. "The God of Gods" is a play that should be seen by all those interested in the modern drama.

**Anonymous. "A Reader's Notes: Books are a finer world within the world." *Winnipeg Free Press* Saturday December [1919].**
Mr. Carroll Aikins, whose first volume of verse appeared two years ago, has written an Indian play, "The God of Gods," which has been produced by John Drinkwater's company in Repertory theatre, Birmingham. And by audience and critics it was well received. Barring distinguished dramatic novels, it is the first drama written by a Canadian to be presented in England. The god is a hideous stone idol, and the dramatic personal [sic] are: Yellow Snake, a singer (that is, a poet); Ambruri [sic], Chief of the Seven Feathers; his son Mablo, a fat and idle coward; Lerii, a mad old Indian; Suiva, a beautiful girl of the tribe whom Yellow Snake loves; Kotwi, her fat mother; and Waning Moon, drunken old priestess to the god.

Suiva, chosen priestess, must renounce her lover, Yellow Snake, who in fury strikes the god and hides himself in the pock to watch secretly the sacred ritual, a mortal crime for a young man. Detected, the chief orders his death, and he is shot in the back by Mablo, his body being brought [as] a sacrifice to the idol's altar. The chief degrades his son for shooting in the back. Suiva, now the Young Moon, must perform the ritual of the sacrifice, but she does not know until the cloth is removed that the offering is the dead body of her lover.

The Birmingham Post says that the ending of the play "touches the heights of tragedy." The season of the play, June, is in the "summer of the god," the action covers one day only, and the time is before the advent of the paleface on this continent. The text is contemporary English which in the ritual rise to poetry. The setting in the different acts, especially the dawn and sunset and racing clouds, was "by far the best we have seen in Birmingham," says the Post. "For those who want a play to mean something, "The God of Gods" is an allegory for the wits."

Mr. Aikins is a son of the late Mr. Somerset Aikins. He was born and grew up in this city. He has written dramatic short stories of the far west and about dramatic poems. In dramatic work, no matter what the form, he has a bright future.

**Charlesworth, Hector. "Rev. of 'The God of Gods.'" *Saturday Night* 29 March 1922.**

The most picturesque production given at Hart House Theatre this season was Carroll Aikins' tragic fantasy "The God of Gods," last week. While one swallow does not make it summer, it is a fairly good start for the Canadian drama. Mr. Aikins is a resident of the Okanagan Valley, British Columbia, and a member of a well-known Canadian family which has produced several professional and public men of wide repute; and obviously a man of distinctive individual talent with a real sense of the theatre. Though his story is laid in the Rocky Mountains of a pre-historic period, it would perhaps be stretching a point to claim that his play is essentially Canadian in atmosphere. It could be as effectively laid in any part of the great spine of the Western Hemisphere which includes both the Rockies and the Andes. In fact the story seems to owe its inspiration to legends of Andean tribes, in which the virgin priesthood and human sacrifice, appear as part of their religious ritual in the worship of the sun and moon. But folk-lorists will tell you that these rites have at one time or another been practiced by religious cults in every part of the earth. The presence of such traditions in the two Americas, is perhaps the clearest proof that the red aborigines derive from races of the older world.

However, the subject is too widely ramified to be taken up here: what one is concerned with is the use Mr. Aikins has made of the world-old traditions of a virgin priesthood and human sacrifice. They form the basis of his plot; but, as I read "The God of Gods," it is a Voltairean fable designed to expose the methods by which (in the view of the author) established religion has maintained its hold over the ignorant masses everywhere and in all ages. He has made his story of the tribal god of a small mountain people, a symbolical picture of this "system." The god is alleged to speak through his priestess; and she in turn uses her privileged position as his supposed mouthpiece to gratify her lust for power and gain. The tribe believes that her utterances are divine revelations and mandates. She knows it is a hoax; but personal interest and fear compel her to maintain that hoax. Otherwise fanatical believers would kill her. Moreover the tribe or human herd support the established or current religion not merely because it is the [ . . . ][i] through inherent fear; and also for the promise of reward; –starvation if the god is angry, plenty if he is well pleased. Thus the threefold elements of superstition, cowardice and greed are the foundation stones of the influence which Mr. Aikins' "God of Gods" exercises, through his priestess over the tribe. There can be little doubt that he intended his fable to serve as a criticism of anthromorphic conceptions of the deity generally; and that his ideas have a philosophic application entirely unrelated to the romance of the North American Indians. His hero, who is slaughtered and presented as a sacrifice, Yellow Snake, the singer, is frankly presented as a pantheistic free-thinker; his heroine, Suiva, whose accession to the honor of priestess has, unknown to her, been attained by purchase, becomes a tragic figure not merely because her lover is first denied to her and then slain; but because of the bitter disillusion she suffers in connection with her religious ideals.

The writing of "The God of Gods" is curiously uneven. At times it rises to real poetry and melodious clarity of exposition; at other times falls to crass banality,—as when the wicked old priestess says, "You know where you're at with him,"—but the climactic scenes are impressive. The production owed much to the beauty of its investiture as designed and painted by Kenneth Noxon, a young university student, and to the impressive groupings and stage business devised by Bertram Forsyth with the assistance of archaeological experts like Prof. Currelly. Unquestionably the main episodes had atmosphere and illusion.

In a play at once symbolical and romantic, it is necessary that the chief characters should be physically impressive and express in some sense sculptural beauty. From this point of Yellow Snake, the singer, as impersonated by R. de R. Acklom, and Suiva, the young priestess, as embodied by Lorna McLean were ideal. They appealed both to the eye and the imagination. Miss McLean was also called upon to do much vital acting; and her fervor and eloquence were of a high and moving character. E. A. Dale gave considerable dignity of a fanatical Indian chief. Dora McMillan suggested the degraded senility of the old priestess admirably and the other characters were picturesquely presented by G.F. McFarland, Winfred Mavor and Grace Webster.

**Anonymous. "Coming Attractions: What Playhouses and Concert Producers Say of Their Performances." *Globe* 13 April 1922: 14.**

THE GOD OF GODS

This Canadian play by Carroll Aikins will be at Hart House Theatre April 18th–22nd, matinee April 22nd. The author, although his work is too little known in Eastern

Canada, is Canada's most distinguished playwright. His home is in the Okanagan Valley, British Columbia, and he himself directs the perfectly equipped little theatre which he has constructed on his ranch. Here he conducts experiments in all departments of stage-craft, leads a company of strolling players who give productions through the Valley, and works at his own dramatic compositions, of which the "God of Gods" is the finest example.

The "God of Gods" is a romantic drama of Indian life in Canada. The play has not been published, but has been produced several times, notably in the Birmingham Repertory Theatre, where Mr. John Drinkwater's production won enthusiastic comment, and led to a subsequent revival.

The "God of Gods" is a piece of fine literature as well as an excellent play. The characters are boldly drawn, and their lines are full of poetic beauty. It has dramatic movement and color in a marked degree, and possesses an absorbing interest, which steadily increases until the final curtain.

**Anonymous. "Hart House Theatre: 'God of Gods,' Strange Mixture of Barbaric Mysticism." *Globe* 19 April 1922.**

Another play by a Canadian author was given last night by Hart House Theatre players. It was Carroll Aikens' [sic] "The God of Gods," a tragedy in three acts. The play has already been done by John Drinkwater's players in England, and it would be interesting to know what impression of the manners and customs of the Canadian redskin it left upon the minds of its English audiences. Mr. Aikens [sic] has drawn so lavishly upon his imagination that, with but a rudimentary knowledge of Indian mythology, romance and mysticism, one is safe in saying that the atmosphere of the play might be anything barbaric, but not Indian. The plot is surrounded by a strange mixture of idolatry, and voodooism savouring of African jungles, trimmed with ceremonies suggesting a curious blend of Aztec and Druidical rituals. To see the noble redman worshipping at the shrine of a foully grotesque image and indulging in orgies of human sacrifice, gives one a decidedly uncomfortable sensation. The story concerns Suiva, a young Indian maiden, who loves and is loved by Yellow Snake, a singer of tribal songs. Because of Suiva's young Indian maiden who loves and is loved by Yellow Snake, a singer of tribal songs [sic]. Because of Suiva's love for the young singer, Mablo, the Chief's craven son, bribes the aged priestess of the "God of Gods" to chose the maiden as her successor. By this ruse he hopes to immure her in the temple to which none has access but his father and himself. The plot succeeds, and the devout Suiva enters the temple to take the vows that will cut her off from marriage and dedicate her to lifelong attendance upon the idol. Ere her vows are taken, Yellow Snake invades the sanctuary and pleads with her to fly with him. She refuses. At the bidding of his father, Mablo kills Yellow Snake and his body is brought to the temple as a human sacrifice. Suiva, as the new priestess, officiates, but when she recognizes the body of her lover, she desecrates the idol and renounces her vows. Yellow Snake's body is cast into the sacred pool, and Suiva, defying her tribesman, plunges in after him and is drowned. The first act holds forth great promise. The wooing of Suiva by Yellow Snake is charmingly written, as also is the scene in which she teasingly flouts the chief's lazy son. But the two acts in the temple that follow are distinctly disappointing.

The movement is slow and the plot is dragged out interminably by the introduction of much unnecessary mummery before the idol. The last act also halts and stumbles until one writes with impatience. It should end swiftly with the death of Suiva, but is anti-climaxed by more mummery before the idol, which, despite the author's efforts to convince the audience that it is but a lifeless thing, suddenly develops glowing eyes, that burn horrifically as the curtain falls. The play, however, contains many beautiful lines and is full of truly poetic fancies. The characters are strongly drawn and in places, were they not supposed to be Indians, would be quite convincing. The Hart House Theatre production last night did all and more than could reasonably be expected. The settings and costumes were really beautiful, and the audience was treated to some lighting effects that deserve the highest praise. The two scenes, designed and painted by Kenneth Noxon, made colourful backgrounds for the barbaric action. Lorna McLean was the Suiva, and handled the part with much distinction and charm. It is no little praise to say that her work has progressed steadily during her association with Hart House Theatre, and that in this part she has reached a place in the very front rank of non-professional players. R. De R. Acklom gave an excellent performance as Yellow Snake, well poised, spontaneous and colourful. A piece of character work of outstanding excellence was contributed by Wilfred Mavor as Lerii, a mad old man. It is seldom one sees so much artistic abandon in a non-professional player. He shared the honours for characterization with Dora McMillan, who gave a most repulsively convincing interpretation of the old priestess. Grace Webster was Suiva's ambition old mother. Mablo was played by G. F. McFarland and E. A. Dale mad a dignified figure as the Chief.

**Anonymous. "Everyman Theatre: Reopening Under New Management." *The Times* (London) 12 August 1931.**

The Everyman Theatre at Hampstead has come under new management, and has been equipped with attractive new decorations, seats, and lighting for its reopening next Tuesday with a drama of Red Indian life entitled The God of Gods, by Mr. Carroll Aikins, a Canadian author. The scenery for the production has been designed by Mr. Michael Weight, and the costumes by Mr. Paul Shelving. The cast will include Miss Marie Ault, Miss Renée de Vaux, Miss Dorothy Barnes, Mr. Lewin Mannering, Mr. Arnold Riches, and Mr. Martin Walker.

Mr. A.E. Filmer will be the principle producer and Mr. Lionel Westlake the director for the new management, which hopes to present new plays of British authorship, as well as works by such established Continental playwrights as the Quintero brothers and Martinez Sierra. It is not proposed to run the Everyman as a repertory theatre; in general, no play will be taken off until it has run its course.

A new feature, initiated by Mr. Filmer at the Birmingham Repertory Theatre, will be the holding at the Everymen Theatre of art exhibitions, to which admittance will be free, in the daytime. As a beginning an exhibition of landscapes and other works by Mr. Charles Ginner and Mr. Ethelbert White will be on view from to-day onwards between 11 a.m. and 4 p.m. each week-day, except on Saturdays when it will close at 1 p.m.

**L., E. "'The God of Gods.' A Drama by Carroll Aikins." 18 August 1931.**

The new management of the Everyman, who "contemplate the production of new works by the most modern of British dramatists," have chosen a curiously remote play for their opening piece. Yet this story of primitive Red Indian superstition is written with a pleasant irony, and has so many good moments, that we wish that the author had chosen a subject nearer home. As it is, there is an air of charade about this business of the stone god, Waning Moon, his priestess, who never goes sober to bed, Suiva, the young vestal virgin, and her two painted and befeathered lovers.

There was some excellent acting, particularly on the part of Miss Renée de Vaux as Waning Moon, Miss Dorothy Barnes as Suiva, and Miss Marie Ault as her rapacious mother. As for the rest, anyone who has been properly brought up on Fenimore Cooper[ii] will warm to the sight of Indian chieftains in full war-paint with a paraphernalia of wigwams, moccasins, squaws, and scalps.

**W., H. M. "A Red Indian Theocracy: 'The God of Gods' at Everyman." *The Daily Telegraph* 19 August 1931.**

Redecorated, reupholstered, and under a new management, the Everyman Theatre reopened its doors last night with a new and rather remote but, in its way, quite interesting play by Mr. Carroll Aikins, called "The God of Gods," introducing us to a simple theocracy in which the natives dress like Red Indians and worship a stone god who is said (when sober) to have tremendous powers.

The lesser 'interest' in the drama is which lover shall finally win the beauteous virgin Suiva—the poet Yellow Snake, or the lazy but wealthier Mablo. The deeper one is the attitude of the sacred priestess towards the sculptured deity. In each the author carries the audience's interest along with him, but the outstanding quality of the play is the humour with which the latitudinarianism of the holy women comes out.

The note struck is "modern." It is also some thousands of years old. And it sounds to-day as amusingly from the other side of the Atlantic as it once sounded in the theatres of Athens.

In the part of the maid Suiva Miss Dorothy Barnes gives a particularly attractive performance, speaking her lines with beautiful clarity and suggesting the girl's innocence with delicacy and truth. Mr. Norman Shelley enacts a demented hanger-on of the God with much intensity; Mr. Arnold Riches cuts a pleasant figure in every way as the likable Mablo; and Mr. Lewin Mannering, Miss Marie Ault, and Miss Renée de Vaux give varied studies of old age in its less agreeable Red Indian aspects.

The admirably staged production was well received by a crowded house, and the new management may be said to have made a spirited start.

**P. P. "The God of Gods." 19 August 1931.**

The Everyman Theatre has now passed into new management, and one can obtain there chops and steaks and joints, wafting an attractive odour to one who has arrived at the theatre dinnerless.

Last night's new production, "The God of Gods," by Mr. Carroll Aikins, a Canadian dramatist, is sufficiently interesting to prevent even the hungriest flying to the restaurant department. A story of Red Indians, their loves and their superstitions, it starts rather slowly, with everyone talking far too much. Things move more quickly when Suiva, who loves and is loved by the poetic Yellow Snake, is made a priestess because she would not marry Mablo, son of the wealthy chief.

In spite of a tragic ending, the comedy element is much more to the fore than might be imagined, the bulk of it being contributed by Mr. Martin Walker as Mablo.

**Brown, Ivor. "'The God of Gods.' By Carroll Aikins." 23 August 1931.**[iii]

This drama of the virgin-martyr, victim of sacerdotal intrigue among the Redskins, was a curious choice as the opening salvo of the new campaign at the Everyman. Ritual in fine feathers has always spectacular possibilities, and Mr. Filmer, with the aid of Mr. Paul Shelving and Mr. Michael Weight, succeeded in revealing at the close the statuesque and colourful elements of idolatrous prostrations. But the piece had little life of its own, and began in wooden dullness. To establish the atmosphere of a civilization so remote on a tiny stage and at close quarters was beyond the power of the company; all the stamping, grunting, and spitting as accompaniment to prairie metaphor about the fat deer and leaping trout, produced only the effect of a charade in which palefaces were masquerading as copper skins. Miss Dorothy Barnes, as the heroine, spoke her lines with real beauty, and strove hard to banish one's disbelief in the whole affair, and Miss Marie Ault spared no effort to be a squaw of squaws. But it was all too difficult, and Mr. Martin Walker, on the night of my visit, appeared to be treating his part with scant regard, as thought he had no interest whatever in the prairie or in its problems. Actors cannot always enjoy their parts; but once they have taken them up, they should at least disguise their feelings.

**Anonymous. "Fresh Start at the Everyman." *The Western Morning News and Mercury* 27 August 1931.**

Once again the little Everyman Theatre at Hampstead has opened under new management, this time under the direction of Mr. A. E. Filmer, well known for his work at the Birmingham Repertory Theatre, the Abbey Theatre, Dublin, and the Champs Elysées, as well as in London, so we may look forward to some interesting productions. Apart from his own function of producer, Mr. Filmer has already imbued the theatre with some original features, such as a restaurant and an exhibition of pictures, and has introduced the increasingly-popular system by which those who subscribe a nominal sum per annum can obtain their seats at considerably reduced prices.

"THE GOD OF GODS"

"The God of Gods," the play with which the new regime opened, was not perhaps a very happy choice. It is a drama of Red Indians, not by any means always unimpressive, but written by Carroll Aikins without a great deal of invention or ingenuity and in prose that wavers between the colloquial and the mezzo-fallutin. However, with Mr. Paul Shelving's admirable costumes and Mr. Michael Wright's settings, it serves its purpose as a medium for Mr. Filmer's skill and imagination as a producer. The cast includes Miss Marie Ault, Miss Dorothy Barnes, and Mr. D. Lewin Mannering.

**Johnston, Lukin. "Canadian Playwright Meets With London Stage Success: Drama of North American Indian Life by Carroll Aikins, Presented at Everyman Theatre, Hampstead—Production Holds Interest of Appreciative Audience—Play Kindly Treated By Critics." *Province* 6 September 1931.**

London, Aug. 22—(By Mail)—About the hardest thing in stage-craft is to capture the atmosphere of barbaric romance, poetic imagery and simple, childlike innocence of the North American Indian, and present it convincingly to a sophisticated modern audience whose only conception of what an Indian looks like has been gained from story books. Why it should be easier to dramatize realistically the Hawaiian, Chinaman or Negro is difficult to determine. I only know that experience teaches it is so.

Carroll Aikins, well-known all over Canada as a theatrical producer and playwright, and an artist with a sensitive and penetrating touch, has essayed this most difficult task. He has met with such a degree of success that, at any rate, has brought his play, "The God of Gods," by way of the Birmingham Repertory Theatre, to the Everyman Theatre at Hampstead. To achieve so much is proof at least of unusual quality—for it is hard to recall any previous play by a Canadian author arriving at a London theatre. To gain a place in the Everyman list of productions is undoubtedly a proof of talent—for this little theatre has a reputation and a tradition to maintain.

### TRAGIC STORY

The opening night of "The God of Gods" drew a crowded and appreciative house. How far the appreciation should be apportioned between the novelty of the theme, the unusualness of the stage setting and the play itself, one need not attempt to estimate. Suffice it to say that the combination of all three factors held the attention to the final curtain.

The play is the love-story of Suiva, an Indian maid, whose mother has sold her (for her own ends) to be the new priestess of the stone deity of the tribe. Completely under the spell of the immemorial native faith in the power of the god, Suiva renounces her lover, Yellow Snake, for whose sake she has repelled the advances of the good-for-nothing son of the chief of the tribe. Her lover is shot in cowardly fashion by Mablo, the chief's son. Her first duty as the new priestess is to receive as human sacrifice the body of Yellow Snake. Of the identity of the swathed corpse she is unaware until the climax comes—when she throws herself into the sacred pool to be with her lover in the Happy Hunting Grounds.

There is the making of a real play here; a tragic story, with a dramatic, unexpected ending, which, but for the near-impossibility of recreating on the modern stage and the mentality of the Indian, might be expected to grip.

The play "interested" this sophisticated London audience—but just failed to "grip." The beauty of many of the lines, adorned with all the poetic imagery of native folklore—did not suffice to conjure up a convincing picture of the child-like mentality of the primitive savage, or to make realistic his faith in the power of the hideous stone image which spoke only through the mouth of a drunken, rapacious old priestess.

CRITICS SYMPATHETIC

Dorothy Barnes, who plays Suiva, gave an attractive performance, contriving to make real the sublime faith of the savage, and to suggest the innocence of the Indian maid with delicacy and restraint. As Yellow Snake, Arnold Riches made a gallant lover—though stage direction surely "slipped a cog" when it made this Red Indian brave wear round his shoulders the skin of a spotted cheetah which he was [ . . . ][iv] to believe, moreover, that Martin Walker, as Mablo, the chief's son, was carrying out the author's ideas in playing his part almost as burlesque, which brought a titter from the audience at almost every speech, and caused on London critic to say "the comedy element was much to the fore." Comedy in the part seemed hopelessly out of place.

Despite small defects, however, the play for the most part [was] kindly treated by London critics. Here are excerpts from some of them:

Daily Telegraph: It is perhaps rather remote, but, in its way interesting . . . The author carries the audience's interest along with him, but the outstanding quality of the play is the humor with which the latitudinarianism of the holy women comes out.

Morning Post: The unusualness of the play and the element of spectacle in it—though the latter was a little drawn out—partly no doubt count for the favourable reception it received, though it must be added, it is a well-told and well-written story.

Evening Standard: A story of Red Indians, their loves and superstitions, it starts slowly with everybody talking far too much . . . In spite of a tragic ending, the comedy element is much more to the fore than might be thought, the bulk of it being contributed by Martin Walker as Mablo.

The Star: Perhaps "The God of Gods" has dramatic qualities which escape the perception of an average audience. Or it is that this poetic little drama of modern life has possibilities which were not explained by the excellent company of actors. The truth is that to the average playgoer the piece falls somewhat flat.

**"Red Indian Drama. 'The God of Gods' at The Everyman." 1931.**[v]

The new management at the Everyman Theatre, Hampstead, opened last night with a novel kind of play. This was "The God of Gods," a Red Indian drama by a Canadian author, Mr. Carroll Aikins. It was given some time ago a Birmingham repertory production, from which it has retained the original costumes designed by Mr. Paul Shelvine [sic], and a setting by Michael Weight, while the dances were arranged by Anton Dolin.

The unusualness of the play and the element of spectacle in it—thought the latter was a little long drawn out—partly, no doubt, account for the favourable reception it received last night, though, it must be added, it is a well-told and well-written story.

Suiva, a daughter of the tribe, has been sold by her mother as a priestess to the god of gods, and consequently renounces her lover, Yellow Snake, for whom she has repulsed the attentions of the chief's son, Mablo. Her lover is killed, shot in the back by Mablo, and is sent in for the "great sacrifice" to the god, the ceremonies of which are conducted by Suiva, all unaware of the identity of the victim. Miss Dorothy Barnes plays Suiva extremely well, contriving to identify herself with the innocent nature of the maid, and Mr. Arnold Riches makes a gallant lover. The piece, at present, besides being too long, lacks cohesion, but this it will no doubt gain when the others in the cast—who include Miss Renée de Vaux, Miss Marie Ault, Mr. Lewin Mannering, and Mr. Martin Walker—settle down in their parts and forget characters in other plays in which they have already appeared.

## PLAYBILLS AND ADVERTISEMENTS

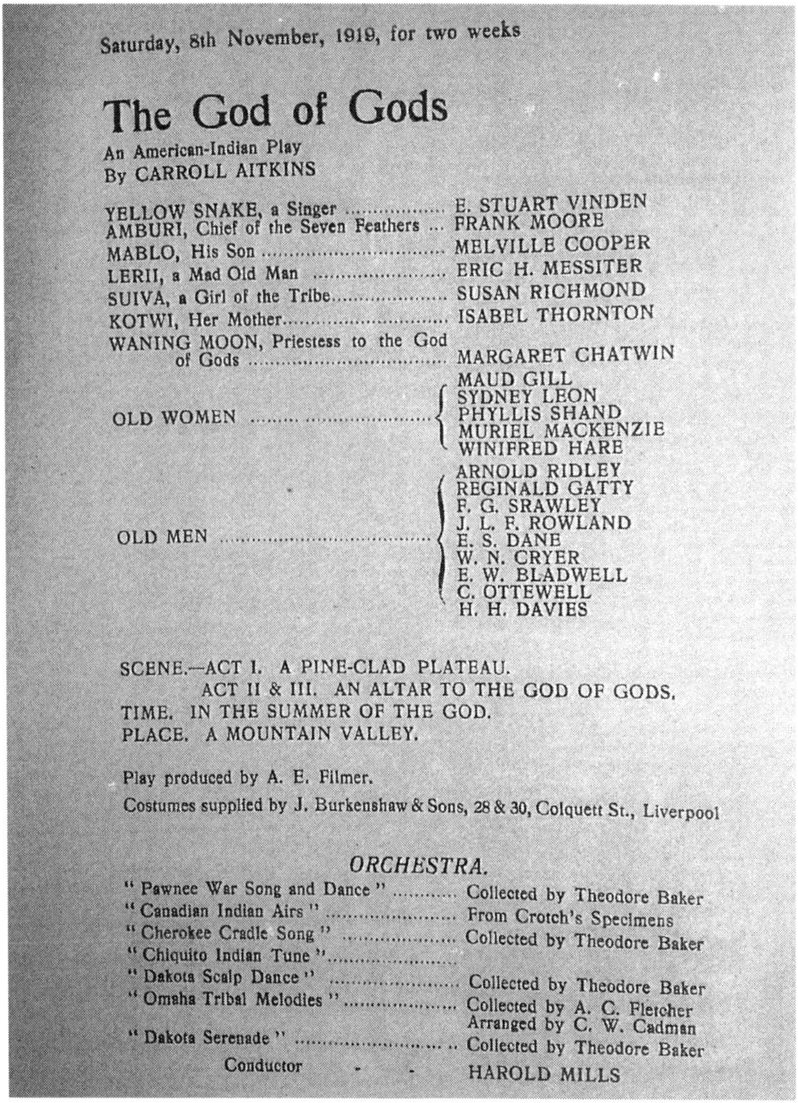

Saturday, 8th November, 1919, for two weeks

# The God of Gods

An American-Indian Play
By CARROLL AITKINS

| | |
|---|---|
| YELLOW SNAKE, a Singer | E. STUART VINDEN |
| AMBURI, Chief of the Seven Feathers | FRANK MOORE |
| MABLO, His Son | MELVILLE COOPER |
| LERII, a Mad Old Man | ERIC H. MESSITER |
| SUIVA, a Girl of the Tribe | SUSAN RICHMOND |
| KOTWI, Her Mother | ISABEL THORNTON |
| WANING MOON, Priestess to the God of Gods | MARGARET CHATWIN |
| OLD WOMEN | MAUD GILL<br>SYDNEY LEON<br>PHYLLIS SHAND<br>MURIEL MACKENZIE<br>WINIFRED HARE |
| OLD MEN | ARNOLD RIDLEY<br>REGINALD GATTY<br>F. G. SRAWLEY<br>J. L. F. ROWLAND<br>E. S. DANE<br>W. N. CRYER<br>E. W. BLADWELL<br>C. OTTEWELL<br>H. H. DAVIES |

SCENE.—ACT I. A PINE-CLAD PLATEAU.
ACT II & III. AN ALTAR TO THE GOD OF GODS.
TIME. IN THE SUMMER OF THE GOD.
PLACE. A MOUNTAIN VALLEY.

Play produced by A. E. Filmer.
Costumes supplied by J. Burkenshaw & Sons, 28 & 30, Colquett St., Liverpool

*ORCHESTRA.*

| | |
|---|---|
| "Pawnee War Song and Dance" | Collected by Theodore Baker |
| "Canadian Indian Airs" | From Crotch's Specimens |
| "Cherokee Cradle Song" | Collected by Theodore Baker |
| "Chiquito Indian Tune" | |
| "Dakota Scalp Dance" | Collected by Theodore Baker |
| "Omaha Tribal Melodies" | Collected by A. C. Fletcher<br>Arranged by C. W. Cadman |
| "Dakota Serenade" | Collected by Theodore Baker |
| Conductor | HAROLD MILLS |

FIGURE 12. THE BIRMINGHAM REPERTORY THEATRE PLAYBILL FOR *THE GOD OF GODS: AN AMERICAN INDIAN PLAY BY CARROLL AITKINS* [SIC]. THE BIRMINGHAM REPERTORY THEATRE 8 NOV. 1919. PLAYBILL, PAGE 1 OF 3. COURTESY OF THE BARRY JACKSON ESTATE.

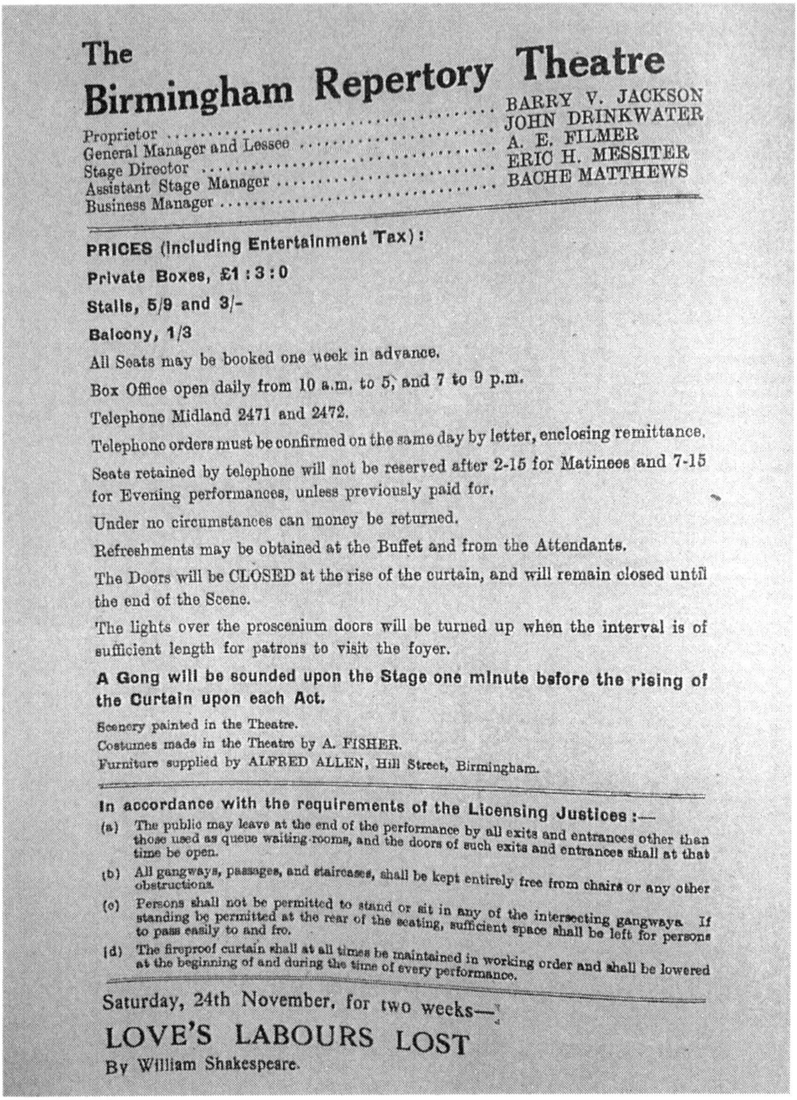

The
Birmingham Repertory Theatre

Proprietor .......... BARRY V. JACKSON
General Manager and Lessee .......... JOHN DRINKWATER
Stage Director .......... A. E. FILMER
Assistant Stage Manager .......... ERIC H. MESSITER
Business Manager .......... BACHE MATTHEWS

**PRICES (including Entertainment Tax):**

**Private Boxes, £1 : 3 : 0**

**Stalls, 5/9 and 3/-**

**Balcony, 1/3**

All Seats may be booked one week in advance.

Box Office open daily from 10 a.m. to 5, and 7 to 9 p.m.

Telephone Midland 2471 and 2472.

Telephone orders must be confirmed on the same day by letter, enclosing remittance.

Seats retained by telephone will not be reserved after 2-15 for Matinees and 7-15 for Evening performances, unless previously paid for.

Under no circumstances can money be returned.

Refreshments may be obtained at the Buffet and from the Attendants.

The Doors will be CLOSED at the rise of the curtain, and will remain closed until the end of the Scene.

The lights over the proscenium doors will be turned up when the interval is of sufficient length for patrons to visit the foyer.

**A Gong will be sounded upon the Stage one minute before the rising of the Curtain upon each Act.**

Scenery painted in the Theatre.
Costumes made in the Theatre by A. FISHER.
Furniture supplied by ALFRED ALLEN, Hill Street, Birmingham.

**In accordance with the requirements of the Licensing Justices:—**

(a) The public may leave at the end of the performance by all exits and entrances other than those used as queue waiting-rooms, and the doors of such exits and entrances shall at that time be open.

(b) All gangways, passages, and staircases, shall be kept entirely free from chairs or any other obstructions.

(c) Persons shall not be permitted to stand or sit in any of the intersecting gangways. If standing be permitted at the rear of the seating, sufficient space shall be left for persons to pass easily to and fro.

(d) The fireproof curtain shall at all times be maintained in working order and shall be lowered at the beginning of and during the time of every performance.

Saturday, 24th November, for two weeks—

LOVE'S LABOURS LOST

By William Shakespeare.

FIGURE 13. THE BIRMINGHAM REPERTORY THEATRE PLAYBILL FOR *THE GOD OF GODS: AN AMERICAN INDIAN PLAY BY CARROLL AITKINS* [SIC]. THE BIRMINGHAM REPERTORY THEATRE 8 NOV. 1919. PLAYBILL, PAGE 2 OF 3. COURTESY OF THE BARRY JACKSON ESTATE.

E. F. HUDSON

*The Dramatic Bookshop,*

116, NEW STREET

(Two doors from Lower Temple St.)

The largest stock in the Midlands of MODERN DRAMA, MODERN POETRY, and Literary Books for Literary Readers.

*—All Repertory Plays kept in Stock.—*

Inspection cordially invited. Telephone, Midland 602

SPECIAL MATINEE—

TUESDAY, 11th NOVEMBER.

JEAN STERLING MACKINLAY

IN——

Old Songs and Ballads

THE BIRMINGHAM & MIDLAND WOMEN'S EMPLOYMENT BUREAU

*Employment Bureau:*

New Street Chambers, 67a, New Street

SECRETARY: MISS MABEL FRANCE.

Hours: 10 to 1. Saturdays, 10 to 1. And by special appointment.

Open to employers and educated women seeking posts. Advice as to training, etc.

*Needlework Department:*

11, Ethel Street, New Street

MANAGERESS: MISS MORTIMER. Tel. Central 3920

Hours: 10 to 5. Saturdays, 10 to 1.

Specially arranged for the sale of ladies' work, and communications can be made there between those who need needlework done, and those who are willing to do it.

THE MAGNETO & SPARE PART Co., Ltd.

227 BROAD STREET, BIRMINGHAM

(2 doors from Granville Street).

ALL MAKES OF MAGNETOS REPAIRED.

Agents for the "Fellows" Magneto. The British Bosch.

FIGURE 14. THE BIRMINGHAM REPERTORY THEATRE PLAYBILL FOR *THE GOD OF GODS: AN AMERICAN INDIAN PLAY BY CARROLL AITKINS* [SIC]. THE BIRMINGHAM REPERTORY THEATRE 8 NOV. 1919. PLAYBILL, PAGE 3 OF 3. COURTESY OF THE BARRY JACKSON ESTATE.

# HART HOUSE THEATRE
## LIST OF PLAYS FOR THE SEASON
### 1921-1922

| | | |
|---|---|---|
| 1. Nov. 1 to 5, - Matinee Nov. 5 | TRIPLE BILL | |
| | A NIGHT AT AN INN | *Lord Dunsany* |
| | PANTALOON | *Sir James Barrie* |
| | WHITE MAGIC | *Algernon Blackwood* and *Bertram Forsyth* |
| 2. Dec. 6 to 10 - Matinee Dec. 10 | CANDIDA | *Bernard Shaw* |
| 3. Dec. 22, 23, 24, | CHESTER MYSTERIES OF THE NATIVITY | |
| 4. Jan. 17 to 21 - Matinee Jan. 21 | MAGIC | *G. K. Chesterton* |
| 5. Feb. 21 to 25 - Matinee Feb. 25 | PLAYBILLS, A Georgian Revue arranged | by *Bertram Forsyth* |
| 6. Mar. 21 to 25 - Matinee Mar. 25 | ROSMERSHOLM | *Henrik Ibsen* |
| 7. April 18 to 22 - Matinee April 22 | THE GOD OF GODS (A Canadian Play) | by *Carroll Aikins* |
| 8. June 6 to 10 - Matinee June 10 | THE TEMPEST | *Shakespeare* |

FIGURE 15. THE HART HOUSE THEATRE 1921–22 SEASON PROGRAMME. COURTESY OF THE HART HOUSE ARCHIVES.

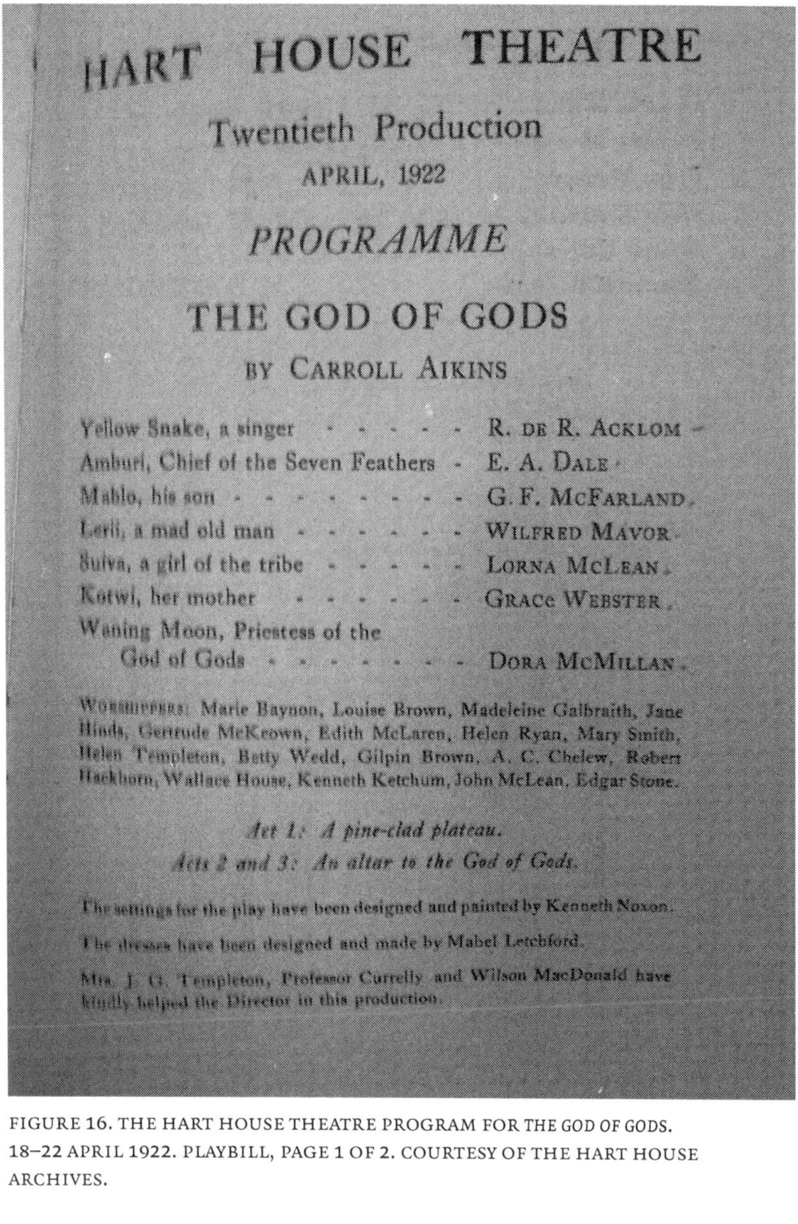
HART HOUSE THEATRE

Twentieth Production

APRIL, 1922

*PROGRAMME*

THE GOD OF GODS

BY CARROLL AIKINS

| | |
|---|---|
| Yellow Snake, a singer - - - - - - | R. DE R. ACKLOM |
| Amburi, Chief of the Seven Feathers - | E. A. DALE |
| Mahlo, his son - - - - - - - - - | G. F. MCFARLAND |
| Lerli, a mad old man - - - - - - - | WILFRED MAVOR |
| Suiva, a girl of the tribe - - - - - | LORNA MCLEAN |
| Kotwi, her mother - - - - - - - | GRACE WEBSTER |
| Waning Moon, Priestess of the God of Gods - - - - - - - - | DORA MCMILLAN |

WORSHIPPERS: Marie Baynon, Louise Brown, Madeleine Galbraith, Jane Hinds, Gertrude McKeown, Edith McLaren, Helen Ryan, Mary Smith, Helen Templeton, Betty Wedd, Gilpin Brown, A. C. Chelew, Robert Hackborn, Wallace House, Kenneth Ketchum, John McLean, Edgar Stone.

*Act 1: A pine-clad plateau.*

*Acts 2 and 3: An altar to the God of Gods.*

The settings for the play have been designed and painted by Kenneth Noxon.

The dresses have been designed and made by Mabel Letchford.

Mrs. J. G. Templeton, Professor Currelly and Wilson MacDonald have kindly helped the Director in this production.

FIGURE 16. THE HART HOUSE THEATRE PROGRAM FOR *THE GOD OF GODS*. 18–22 APRIL 1922. PLAYBILL, PAGE 1 OF 2. COURTESY OF THE HART HOUSE ARCHIVES.

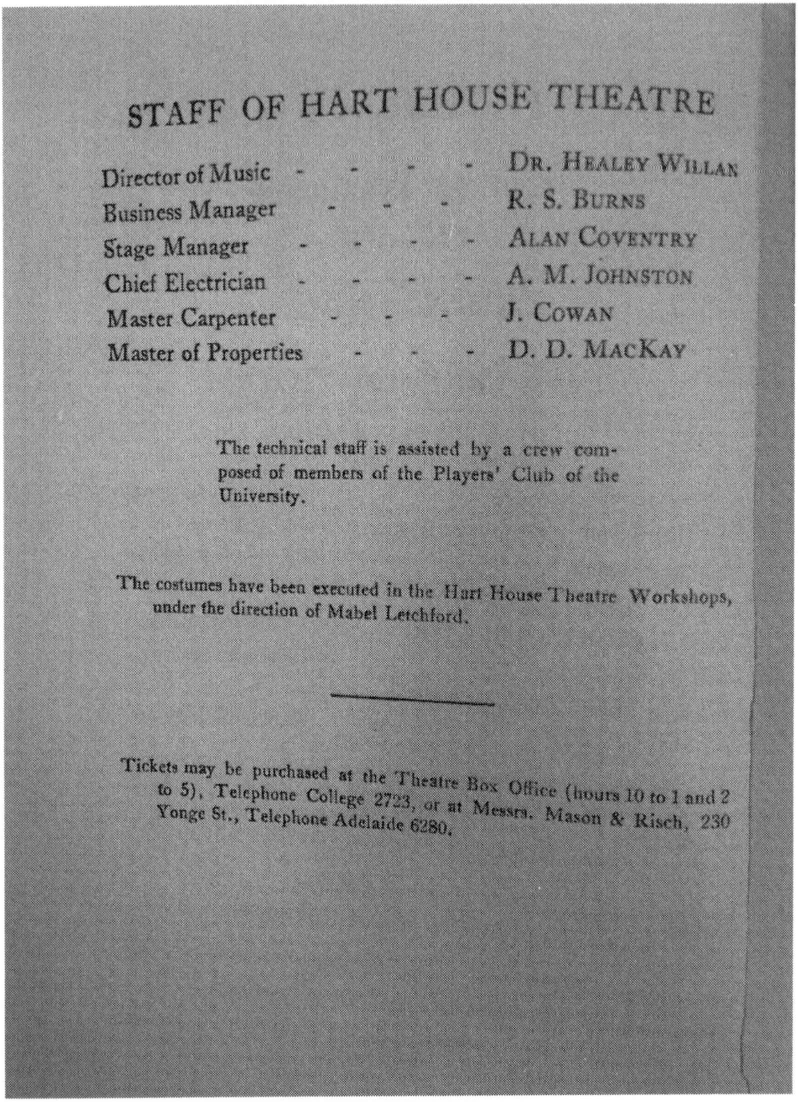

STAFF OF HART HOUSE THEATRE

| | |
|---|---|
| Director of Music - - - - | Dr. Healey Willan |
| Business Manager - - - | R. S. Burns |
| Stage Manager - - - - | Alan Coventry |
| Chief Electrician - - - - | A. M. Johnston |
| Master Carpenter - - - | J. Cowan |
| Master of Properties - - - | D. D. MacKay |

The technical staff is assisted by a crew composed of members of the Players' Club of the University.

The costumes have been executed in the Hart House Theatre Workshops, under the direction of Mabel Letchford.

Tickets may be purchased at the Theatre Box Office (hours 10 to 1 and 2 to 5), Telephone College 2723, or at Messrs. Mason & Risch, 230 Yonge St., Telephone Adelaide 6280.

FIGURE 17. THE HART HOUSE THEATRE PROGRAM FOR *THE GOD OF GODS*. 18–22 APRIL 1922. PLAYBILL, PAGE 2 OF 2. COURTESY OF THE HART HOUSE ARCHIVES.

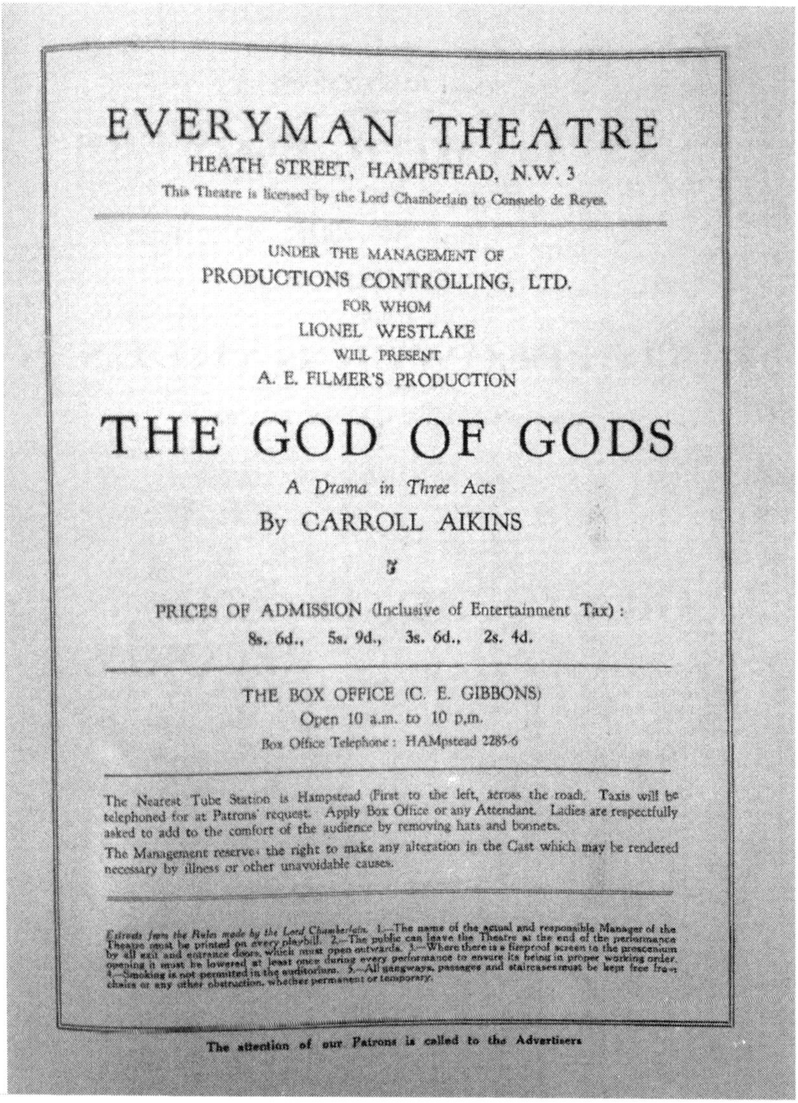

EVERYMAN THEATRE

HEATH STREET, HAMPSTEAD, N.W. 3

This Theatre is licensed by the Lord Chamberlain to Consuelo de Reyes.

UNDER THE MANAGEMENT OF

PRODUCTIONS CONTROLLING, LTD.

FOR WHOM

LIONEL WESTLAKE

WILL PRESENT

A. E. FILMER'S PRODUCTION

THE GOD OF GODS

*A Drama in Three Acts*

By CARROLL AIKINS

PRICES OF ADMISSION (Inclusive of Entertainment Tax):

8s. 6d., 5s. 9d., 3s. 6d., 2s. 4d.

THE BOX OFFICE (C. E. GIBBONS)

Open 10 a.m. to 10 p.m.

Box Office Telephone: HAMpstead 2285-6

The Nearest Tube Station is Hampstead (First to the left, across the road). Taxis will be telephoned for at Patrons' request. Apply Box Office or any Attendant. Ladies are respectfully asked to add to the comfort of the audience by removing hats and bonnets.

The Management reserves the right to make any alteration in the Cast which may be rendered necessary by illness or other unavoidable causes.

*Extracts from the Rules made by the Lord Chamberlain.* 1.—The name of the actual and responsible Manager of the Theatre must be printed on every playbill. 2.—The public can leave the Theatre at the end of the performance by all exit and entrance doors, which must open outwards. 3.—Where there is a fireproof screen to the proscenium opening it must be lowered at least once during every performance to ensure its being in proper working order. 4.—Smoking is not permitted in the auditorium. 5.—All gangways, passages and staircases must be kept free from chairs or any other obstruction, whether permanent or temporary.

The attention of our Patrons is called to the Advertisers

FIGURE 18. THE EVERYMAN THEATRE PLAYBILL FOR *THE GOD OF GODS*. THE EVERYMAN THEATRE AUGUST 1931. PLAYBILL, PAGE 1 OF 3. COURTESY OF THE VICTORIA AND ALBERT MUSEUM, LONDON.

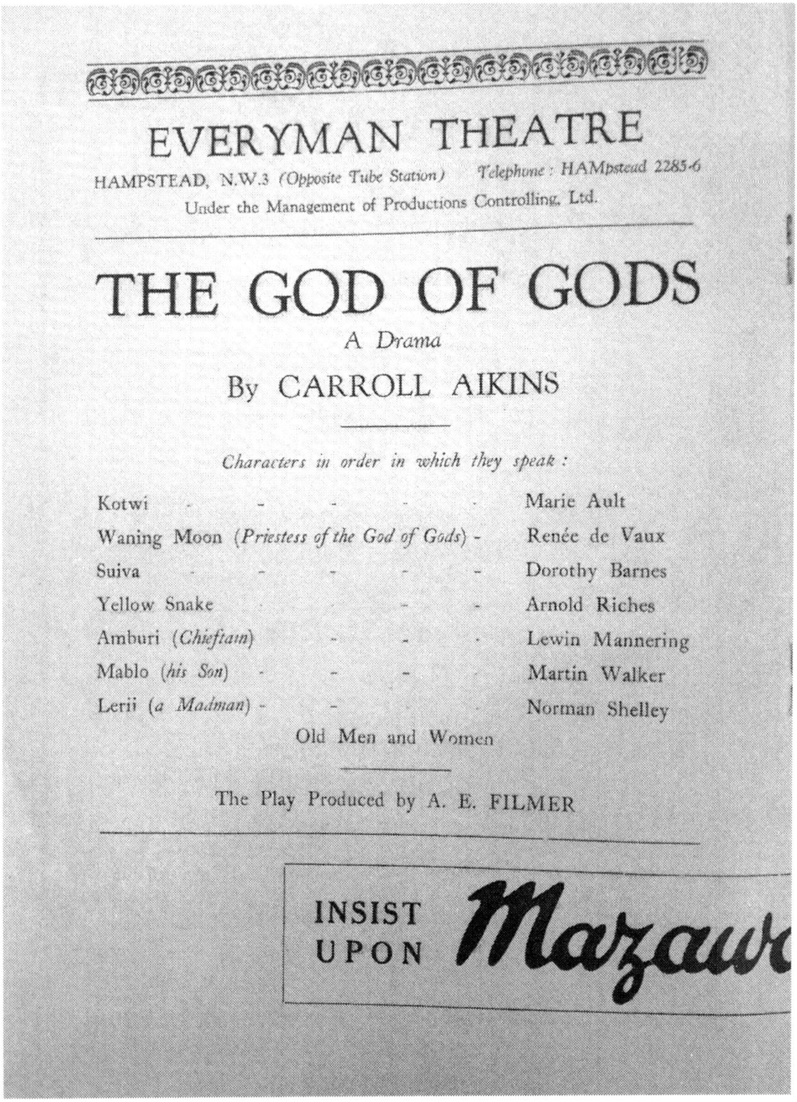

EVERYMAN THEATRE

HAMPSTEAD, N.W.3 *(Opposite Tube Station)* *Telephone:* HAMpstead 2285-6

Under the Management of Productions Controlling, Ltd.

THE GOD OF GODS

*A Drama*

By CARROLL AIKINS

*Characters in order in which they speak:*

| | |
|---|---|
| Kotwi - - - - - | Marie Ault |
| Waning Moon *(Priestess of the God of Gods)* - | Renée de Vaux |
| Suiva - - - - - | Dorothy Barnes |
| Yellow Snake - - - | Arnold Riches |
| Amburi *(Chieftain)* - - - | Lewin Mannering |
| Mablo *(his Son)* - - - - | Martin Walker |
| Lerii *(a Madman)* - - - | Norman Shelley |

Old Men and Women

The Play Produced by A. E. FILMER



FIGURE 19. THE EVERYMAN THEATRE PLAYBILL FOR *THE GOD OF GODS*. THE EVERYMAN THEATRE AUGUST 1931. PLAYBILL, PAGE 2 OF 3. COURTESY OF THE VICTORIA AND ALBERT MUSEUM, LONDON.

*SCENES:*

ACT I. A Plateau

ACTS II. & III. Within the precincts of the God of Gods

PAUL SHELVING has designed the Costumes; MICHAEL WEIGHT the Settings; and the Dances have been arranged by ANTON DOLIN

*PROGRAMME OF MUSIC*

| | | |
|---|---|---|
| Prelude | "Kamennoi-Ostrow" | *Rubinstein* |
| Overture | "A Chorus of Woodland Birds" | |
| Entr'acte 1 | "The Rhinegold" | *Wagner* |
| Entr'acte 1 | "Parsifal" | *Wagner* |
| Entr'acte 2 | "Parsifal" Finale | *Wagner* |
| Entr'acte 2 | "Twilight of the Gods" | *Wagner* |

"*God Save the King*"

The Theatre and Foyer and Club are sprayed with Spraolite, supplied by Messrs. MASLIN BROS., 63, Cowcross Street, E.C.1.

Red Indian Mask. HAMLEY BROS., Ltd., 200, Regent Street, W.1, have supplied the Mask.

VENRECO, Ltd., Electrical Engineers, 55, Neal Street, W.C., have supplied the Electric Light Shades throughout.

Effects by "HIS MASTER'S VOICE" GRAMOPHONE CO., LTD.

The Cheetah Skin worn by "Yellow Snake" by GEORGE AUGUSTUS NICHOLAS, 36, Bruton Street, W.1

| | |
|---|---|
| *General Manager* | Lionel Westlake |
| *Stage Director* | Alick Malcolm |
| *Stage Manager* | Arthur Bradford |
| *Assistant Stage Manager* | Norman Pearn |
| *Press Representative* | Perceval Graves |
| *Secretary* | Anne Hammond |



FIGURE 20. THE EVERYMAN THEATRE PLAYBILL FOR *THE GOD OF GODS*. THE EVERYMAN THEATRE AUGUST 1931. PLAYBILL, PAGE 3 OF 3. COURTESY OF THE VICTORIA AND ALBERT MUSEUM, LONDON.

## BIOGRAPHICAL NOTES AND ARTICLES

**Anonymous. "Life, Letters, and the Arts: A Theatre in the Wilderness." *The Living Age* 3 March 1923: 549.**

The upper story of a fruit-packing house, far away from the crowded pavements of the cities, with miles and miles of fruit-orchard stretching on every hand—what a strange location for a theatre. And yet, you never can tell.

At Naramata, British Columbia, in the middle of the Okanogan fruit-growing country, stands the Home Theatre of the Canadian Players, an experimental theatre and training school for actors, playwrights, and producers, an organization which owes its inception and development wholly to the unflagging enthusiasm and devotion of Mr. Carroll Aikins, founder and director of the company, and of his wife, who assists him in all his productions.

How did a theatre come to be there? The answer to that question is a tale of grim fighting against obstacles, of ingenious improvisation, and of expenditure of money, energy, and enthusiasm quite staggering to think upon. Mr. Aikins is a fruit rancher. He is also a poet. Most of all he is an enthusiast of the theatre, who set himself to do away with the theatrical vacuum in Canada. His own play, *The God of Gods*, has been produced at the Birmingham Repertory Theatre, which has done much for the growth of artistic drama in England. Why not a similar institution fostering the growth of a native school of Canadian dramatists?

But Mr. Aikins also had his fruit ranch to consider—one hundred acres, mostly planted with his own hands. The usual sort of thing quite obviously wouldn't do. He couldn't possibly start the ordinary 'little theatre' in some odd hole in the city. Since the mountains could not go to Mahomet, Mahomet—or rather the drama—must needs [sic] come to the mountains. There are a great many mountains in British Columbia, and now—thanks to the Canadian Players—there is also a great deal of drama.

Though the little theatre occupies the top floor of a fruit-packing house, you mustn't fancy it as a crude, ugly, or ill-equipped makeshift. To the actor, at least, it is the most beautiful theatre in the world, for the windows of the dressing-rooms—instead of giving upon some dingy back alley—open over a glorious expanse of lake, blue as the Mediterranean, and lying between two long chains of rugged mountains; and on the terraced hillsides are orchards and gardens, orchards and gardens, orchards and gardens, with only scattered villas and a few tiled roofs to break the expanse of green.

The theatre is just as beautiful for the audience, who number only a hundred at most, for seating capacity is limited. The stage is at the floor level, and the seats rise steeply about it, achieving the ambition of most modern theatrical architects: there are no 'bad seats' for any of the spectators. The curtains and carpeting are green. One end of the theatre is charmingly furnished with a large Oriental rug, and in the little foyer is quaint old English furniture, where the play can be discussed between the acts.

The stage itself is perfectly equipped. A *Kuppelhorizont*[vi] and as good a color organ as is to be found on this continent of North America produce its admirable lighting. Electricity was at first a stumblingblock [sic]. One does not produce electric current without access to a power house and power houses do not exactly abound in the neighborhood of Naramata; but the ingenious Mr. Aikens [sic] was not to be balked. An abandoned mine possessed a dynamo. He bought it. An ordinary farm-tractor provided power—and now, if a benighted traveler passing the ranch late hears a steady chug-chug-chug in the darkness, he may be quite sure that the ugly inventions of a mechanical age have been harnessed in the service of beauty, and that the drama is flourishing mightily in British Columbia that night.

The little theatre in Naramata is catholic in its tastes. One of Professor Baker's Harvard students has had her play produced there. But then, so had Euripides, whose Trojan Women, with Mrs. Aikins as Hecuba, was given by the women students of the theatre. Yes, students—for the Home Theatre is a training school as well as a theatre. It draws its audiences from the surrounding country. It sometimes goes on tour. And it offers free training in dramatic art to all young Canadians who want it. The season opens in April and lasts until October. Living does not cost very much and the students support themselves by picking fruit—it is a fruit country and pickers are always in demand among the neighboring orchards.

It will be interesting to keep an eye on Mr. Aikins and his fellows. Since the time of the miracle plays the theatre has been as citified as an English sparrow. Can it be taken into the country?

The Canadian Players make it look very much as if it could, for their theatre is a flourishing organization. It is not, of course, a commercial undertaking. All the better!

It is cram-full of promise—a daring experiment, and a fascinating one.

**Anonymous. "Hart House Syndics Name New Director: Carroll Aikins Comes to Theatre From B.C. for 1927–28."** ***Globe*** **24 August 1927: 9.**

Also printed in **"Canadian Director: Hart House Theatre: Carroll Aikins, Naramata, B.C., to Direct Next Year—Walter Sinclair Away."** ***The Toronto Daily Star*** **24 August 1927.**
Hart House Theatre will have a Canadian director. The Syndics of the theatre announce that Carroll Aikins of Naramata, B.C., has been appointed director of the theatre for the season 1927–28. Mr. Aikins will be in charge during the absence of Walter Sinclair, who is acting as director of the Little Theatre in New Orleans for the forthcoming season.

The new director has had considerable experience in dramatic work. He is the founder of the Home Theatre in the Okanagan Valley, which has several successful seasons of dramatic production to its credit. A number of Mr. Aikins's own plays have been produced by his company, and he is one of the very few Canadians whose dramatic work has received professional production abroad, his play, "The God of Gods," having been produced by the Repertory Theatre of Birmingham, England. Mr. Aikins's wife is an accomplished actress.

The Hart House season will commence in October. Among the plays to be produced are: "The Swan," by Ferene Molnar, "The Doctor's Dilemma" by Bernard Shaw, a play founded on Lewis Carroll's "Alice in Wonderland," and Shakespeare's "Romeo and Juliet." One or more Canadian plays will be produced as usual, the policy of the theatre being to give the fullest encouragement to Canadian national drama.

**Photo.** ***Saturday Night*** **3 September 1927.**
Carroll Aikins of Naramata, B.C., who has been appointed director of Hart House Theatre for the seasons of 1927–28. Mr. Aikins is the founder of the Home Theatre in the Okanagan Valley and has had much experience in amateur dramatic work. He has also written plays. Contemplated productions at Hart House include Molnar's "The Swan" Shaw's "The Doctor's Dilemma" and Shakespeare's "Romeo and Juliet."

**Anonymous. "Theatre Forecast for 1927–28: List of Attractions for the New Season as at Present Planned By Our Leading Playhouses."** ***Globe*** **17 September 1927.**
TORONTO is clearly the theatrical as well as the musical capital of Canada, so that not only residents but also visitors from out of town will be interested in the prospects before us for the coming season. Theatregoers will be served by

two first-class houses for visiting companies on tour, the Royal Alexandra and the Princess; one repertory house for better "stock" productions, Vaughan Glaser's Victoria; one pre-eminent Little Theatre at Hart House, with two or three other minor groups in the background; three first-class, first-run, modern picture and vaudeville houses, in Shea's Hippodrome, Loew's Downtown and the Pantages (Shea's having definitely forsaken straight vaudeville for the more popular combination: next week, for instance, a miniature Ned Wayburn revue shares the headlines with a Laura La Plante feature); with the Regent sticking to straight motion-pictures under a new management, and the Uptown really in a class by itself because of Jack Arthur's artistic activities. Dozens of minor "movie" houses and a few enterprises in which Globe readers are not likely to be interested are excluded from this list, but evidently the fare to be presented is very promising in both variety and extent.

This list does not include, furthermore, the activities of our many skilled amateur groups, such as the Dickens Fellowship, Mr. Miller's company, Mr. Middleton's company, the Canadian Operatic Society, the several sets of college players, and others. The Canadian National Opera, moreover, is scheduled to present a season of grand opera in Massey Hall next spring, and the Scottish National Players are considering a season of several weeks here next fall.

[ . . . ][vii]

HART HOUSE THEATRE

The new Canadian director at Hart House, Carroll Aikins of Naramata, B.C., has announced only four of his plays for the coming season namely, Molnar's airy romance. "The Swan"; Bernard Shaw's great as well as sparkling comedy, "The Doctor's Dilemma"; a play founded on "Alice in Wonderland," presumably for the Christmas holidays; and Shakespeare's "Romeo and Juliet." In addition to this quartet, one or more Canadian plays will be given, as usual, for the policy of this theatre has always sought to promote the development of a Canadian national drama.

Mr. Aikins was expected in Toronto yesterday or today, and fuller announcements of his plans may be anticipated shortly.

**"Hart House Theatre Under New Director." *Varsity* 29 September 1927.**

*Carroll Aikins Comes To The University As Guest Director—Mrs. Aikins To Assist Him*

Plans for the coming season at Hart House Theatre are well under way. Mr. Carroll Aikins, director of the Theatre for the 1927–8 season, informed "The Varsity" yesterday.

"My status being merely that of guest director for the next five months, I cannot assume the responsibility of inaugurating any vital changes in the procedure of former years," answered Mr. Aikins in reply to a question on his policy. During the coming season six plays will be produced, which will include "The Swan" by Franc Molnar, "The Doctor's Dilemma" by Bernard Shaw, and for the usual Christmas pantomime, an adaptation of Lewis Carroll's "Alice in Wonderland.["] On the same evening as this pantomime, the Director intends to present an original adaptation of well-known fairy tales, which will be entirely in pantomime in silhouette, against a background of changing colour. The policy of Hart House in giving all encouragement to Canadian Drama, will be carried out by including the usual bill of Canadian Plays in the season's programmes.

Prior to coming to Hart House Theatre, Mr. Aikins was a conspicuous figure of the Little Theatre Movement in the west, having founded "The Home Theatre" in the Okanagan Valley in 1921. He has several plays to his credit, his "The God of Gods," being one of the few plays of Canadian origin to be produced abroad.

In Mr. Aikins opinion Hart House Theatre is almost unique in Canada, its nearest counterpart being the Players Club of the University of British Columbia, an organization which produces three bills annually, taking its spring production on a three or four weeks tour at the end of term.

Mr. Aikins will be assisted in his work by his wife, herself an accomplished actress.

**"Carroll Aikins, New Director at Hart House, Is Interviewed."** ***Globe*** **15 October 1927.**

Hart House Theatre will this coming year fulfill the function that it was originally intended to perform, according to the statement made to The Globe by Mr. Carroll Aikins, guest-director at Hart House for this season. Hitherto the theatre's activities have been restricted almost entirely to a chosen few in theatrical circles in Toronto, whereas in the future every effort will be made to encourage student participation in the plays put on at Hart House.

Mr. Aikins has at present a large number of students at the University of Toronto engaged in pantomime classes under his tuition, and out of these classes will be selected successive groups to take part in the productions that have been planned for the current year. The students are deriving much advantage from these classes, which give a thorough grounding in the fundamentals of stage work, and they are availing themselves of the opportunity offered in large numbers. Mr. Aikins declares himself well pleased with the premise shown by the wide variety of new material that has come into his hands that way.

Speaking of the theatre itself, the guest-director stated that he thought that the arrangement of the theatre was as perfect as he could wish, and added that he believed that Hart House Theatre was "quite unique."

Unfortunately, Mr. Aikins is obliged to return to his own theatre in the Okanagan Valley, B.C., as soon as the six-month schedule at present arranged for has been concluded. No announcement has been made as to the conduct of affairs at our Little Theatre after that date.

**"They Have to Doubly Live up to Their 'Helpmeet' Now."** ***Toronto Telegram*** **26 October 1927.**

Mrs. Carroll Aikins, who delivered a most interesting address at the Heliconian Club luncheon on "Relationship of the little theatre to the professional theatre."

When recently the London press acclaimed that the leaders of both Canada's old parties were bachelors, whole columns were published to prove how helpful was the wife of a modern politician. But since the arrival of the new director of Hart House, Toronto is finding that modern stage producers are also calling on their wives to share their public work. For the second time this month, when Mr. Carroll Aikins has been invited to address a local organization he has replied that Mrs. Aikins would do his speaking for him.

Accordingly it was Mrs. Aikens [sic] who addressed the Heliconian Club on "The Little Theatre" yesterday. Mrs. Aikens [sic] in reviewing the history of the Little Theatre Movement stressed that unless it developed dramatists. Again if the Little Theatre movement was to be different from the old "amateur" dramatic societies, it must provide some training for its people. Mrs. Aikins expressed deep delight of the wonderful awakening of a dramatic feeling in rural Canada.

**Ashley and Crippens. "Mr. Carroll Aikins. New Director of Hart House Theatre."** ***University Monthly*** **Oct 1927. Photo.**

**"Carroll Aikins Will Direct Hart House Theatre."** ***University Monthly*** **October 1927.**

Mr. Carroll Aikins, who for several years has been the head of the Canadian Players in the Okanagan Valley and developed there the best equipped little theatre west of Chicago, will take charge of the Hart House Theatre this year. Mr. Aikins is himself a successful author, having had his Indian play "God of Gods" produced by the Birmingham Repertory Co. in England, and later at Hart House.

For the past seven years Mr. Aikins has been producing plays in the Okanagan and has built up a summer school at his own theatre for all the Arts of the Theatre. Mr. Aikins' viewpoint is peculiarly Canadian, and as a result he is particularly anxious to do what he is able to foster Canadian talent, not only in acting but also in play-writing, so that the usual bill of Canadian plays will be put on this year. The program for the year has been slightly shortened and will consist of the following:

Oct. 24–29. The Swan, Ferenc Molnar.
Nov. 28–Dec. 3. The Doctor's Dilemma, Bernard Shaw.
Dec. 28–31. Alice In Wonderland, Lewis Carroll.
Jan. 30–Feb. 4. Wild Birds, Violet Pearn.
Mar. 1–3. Plays by Canadian Authors.
Mar. 26–31. Romeo and Juliet, Shakespeare.

**"How Canada Will Develop National Theatre."** ***Toronto Telegram*** **16 November 1927.**

One of the most interesting addresses of this autumn was that given at the Women's Press Club yesterday afternoon by Mrs. Carroll Aitkens [sic]. With her husband, the new Hart House director, she was a guest of honor, as was also Miss Kathleen Shackleton, the English artist.

"My husband is the director, I am the directed," smilingly explained Mrs. Aitkens, whom her husband delegates to make the public speeches for the family.

Mrs. Aitkens told of the way their theatre on their British Columbia ranch had developed. They had built it on top of their packing-house, but after the model of the most advanced European play-houses. Its seats are on a sloping surface, sixteen feet from the stage, which they look down upon as a picture of another world. Mrs. Aitkens claims this makes for a fine illusion.

Mrs. Aitkens believes that the constant urge in cities for outside stimulation is one of the modern tragedies and believes that much can be done in the country where people look more to themselves than to stimulation from the outsire [sic]. She believes that through constant work of some years in Little Theatres groups will finally be evolved that will give to Canada what the Moscow Players have done. To-day's stage is suffering from people who rush into it without preparation. They would not think of rendering classical music without years of study, yet so many think they can become stage stars overnight. Miss Shackleton rejoiced to have heard of Canada's work in the Little Theatre and declared she would be so happy to tell of Canada's cultural interests when she returned to England, where so many still picture this country as primitive.

**Brewster, Muriel. "Canadian Players and Plays to Tour World?" *Star Weekly* 3 December 1927.**

*This Is Hope of Carroll Aikens [sic] Guest Director of Hart House Theatre*

Why is it that so many people, particularly debutantes and students, are so keen about "acting?" A rather surprising light was thrown on this question by the guest director of Hart House theatre, who has been carrying on for some years a most interesting experiment in the training of young Canadian would-be actors and actresses in a secluded spot in the Okanagan Valley, in British Columbia.

From the summit of a high, quiet cliff, in the midst of a great orchard, looking across Lake Okanagan toward the peaks of the coast range, to the busy corridors of Toronto University is quite a change, but Carroll Aikins, Canadian poet, playwright, and director who has recently experienced this metamorphosis in order to be at Hart House during the absence of Walter Sinclair, sat at his desk in the director's den and seemed not at all unhappy over it.

"Yes, it is a change," he agreed, "but such an interesting one! I do miss the silence—when you are accustomed to working among huge pine trees, wide waters and high hills, a busy college campus like this is a bit disturbing. But I like it. What do I think of the Toronto students? Oh, I haven't had time to see enough of them to discover their special characteristics. But they are a nice, clean-looking crowd, and I like them very much indeed. And then, you know, I am still a student myself!"

Asked if he had done much professional acting in the course of his study of the theatre, Mr. Aikins laughed. "Oh now, I should be an absolute wash-out as an actor. My job is the selecting of the right person for the right part, and then the producing of the plays as well as can be done with the materials at hand—and a little better, with luck. It's the best fun in the world."

THE RANCH THEATRE

Mr. Aikins has come from his British Columbia eyrie with very high ideals, and I asked him to tell me about the "Canadian Players Theatre" at Rekadom Ranch, Naramata, British Columbia, which is one of the brightest jewels in the ever-growing chain of "little theatres." He told me many interesting things, but almost every sentence contained the words "my wife and I," and it was not until, at his suggestion, I went to visit Mrs. Aikins, that the whole story of Rekadom was revealed.

"You see," she said with a smile, "my husband is a builder; he is only happy when he is at work on the construction of something—something beautiful. When the ranch was more or less established, he looked about for something else to build, and out of his literary and artistic interests in the drama, the idea of the theatre was born. He wanted, as he probably told you, to provide a centre for a Canadian theatre movement, to discover and train Canadian dramatic artists. We hoped that our ranch would support the theatre, as a beginning. We have a big fruit crop every year. And the only place to put the theatre was over the big packing house, so there it was built. The auditorium slopes upward from the stage, and the stage is, as it were, below the audience, so that you get away altogether from the effect of looking up at the actor's feet. It is so much more natural to look directly into the faces. The theatre doesn't look like a theatre from the outside. The inside is what matters, and the inside is very interesting. The situation, of course, is magnificent. The building stands on the edge of a cliff, and looks out over the lake to the mountains. It is very beautiful."

The students, she went on to say, came to Rekadom from all over Canada, and when they first arrive in the quiet and simplicity, they are apt to be a bit superior and scornful. But invariably, before a month of their training has passed, a transformation has taken place, with a complete shift of the point of view. "They learn," she said, "that art is long, and that a stage is not merely a place to show off some gift of mimicry or a pair of pretty ankle, but rather a place in which to create moments of beauty—if they are lucky! It is wonderful to watch the change that takes place in our students at Rekadom."

Mr. and Mrs. Aikins were born just across the border from one another, in home estates almost adjoining; hers in Vermont, and his in Quebec. Mrs. Aikins' father has recently retired from the post of consul-general of the United States to Canada, which he held for thirty years, and the Aikins family has contributed many distinguished figures to Canadian public life. The two families have been friends for four generations, and Carroll Aikens [sic] and Katherine Foster were born within a few days of each other. They were friendly companions as children, but their ways separated during a long period, while Carroll Aikins went through McGill and spent four years abroad, and Katherine Foster graduated from Vassar and took up teaching. They have been married for some years, and their three children love Rekadom as much as their parents do.

## HIS CANADIAN ART IDEA

"Ranching and writing was my idea of a thoroughly satisfactory life," said Mr. Aikins. "We finally settled in the Okanagan valley, bought a ranch, and built a bungalow. But I began to get more and more interested in plays and the theatre, and I wanted to do something about forming the nucleus of a company of real Canadian players. We have had a hundred and seventy students pass through our hands, and I know of at least six of our students who are playing in first-rate productions in the states, with the idea of returning to us some day, brining the benefit of their experience to the work in Canada.

Some day I hope to have a company of players who will tour the world in a repertory of Canadian plays. But there is a lot of hard work to be done first, and much of it will be done here at Hart House, as well as at Rekadom, and probably, as time goes on, in many other centres as well. But I don't think there will ever be another theatre where the wailing of a mountain lion reaches the ears of the company while they rest between rehearsals on the steps of the theatre."

"Do you have electricity?" I asked him.

"Now we have. But at first, although we installed an excellent lighting system when the theatre was built, we had no power, so we got an old world-out dynamo and belted it to a farm tractor, and when we found that it worked, we proceeded to put on the first Canadian performance—and I believe the first performance in America west of the Rockies—of 'The Trojan Women.' We started off very well, but presently the spark plugs began to give out one at a time. My mechanic, who is one of those people who refuse to be down-hearted, performed the miracle of changing the plugs as they died, while the performance was going on and the motor was running full speed. The audience was entranced with the curious lighting effects, for the lights would suddenly lower with a buzz every few minutes, which added considerably to the high moments of tragedy! But now we have a well-behaved lighting plant."

Mr. Aikins went on: "The average student approaches the theatre with a sense of frivolity. But the theatre must be treated entirely as an art."

"Then you think the modern desire to escape from form is wrong?"

"You cannot escape from form," said Carroll Aikins. "There is good form, and there is bad form, but form there must always be!"

"Before you go," he said, "I want to pay a tribute to the memory of one who sat in this very chair not long ago—Bertram Forsyth. I did not know him intimately, but I had a great liking for him, and the warmest admiration for his work. He was a great loss to the art theatre movement."

### Massey, Vincent, ed. *Canadian Plays from Hart House Theatre*. Vol. 2. Toronto: Macmillan of Canada, 1927. 1–67.

CARROLL AIKINS has achieved a wide reputation through his work in the theatre which he built, in 1920, on his ranch in the Okanagan Valley, British Columbia. Mr. Aikins's distinguished work as a producer and author of plays has made a very important contribution to the development of a native Canadian drama. A number of distinguished productions have been achieved by his group of

Canadian players in the Home Theatre, including Mr. Aikins's own Passion Play—Victory in Defeat—in 1922, which marked a notable experiment in dramatic productions in Canada.

**Jacob, Fred. "Monday Nighter at Large." *Mail* 7 April 1928.**

At the end of his first season as director of the Hart House Theatre, Carroll Aikins has departed for his home in British Columbia, leaving the patrons of the little theatre with the feeling that they have had a highly satisfying Winter. Mr. Aikins did fewer plays than any of his predecessors, but all of them, with the exception of "The Swan," turned out to be good shows, and "The Doctor's Dilemma" took rank among the best presentations ever made there. Mr. Aikins had the satisfaction of being the first director to make good in his first season. Roy Mitchell started out with rather a chaotic year, and of course the general public still had to be taught the purposes of the non-professional theatre. There was a good deal of organized prejudice against Bertram Forsyth when he arrived, and he had to build up his group of players, so it took him more than a year to do himself justice. Walter Sinclair's ideal was to establish something like a non-professional stock company, doing conventional plays in a conventional manner. It was not until his second season that he did anything worth remembering, except his Christmas show, "The Rose and the Ring." Then Carroll Aikins walked in, and with the support of the excellent organization of actors built up by the late Bertram Forsyth, made good almost at once.

CREDIT WHERE DUE

Speaking of the strong acting group at the Hart House Theatre, one is reminded of a regrettable mistake that recently appeared in the "Theatre Arts Monthly." In speaking of Walter Sinclair, the editor made the statement that he "was for two seasons director of the Hart House Theatre, where his work attracted wide attention, and where he built up a well-rounded company and an enthusiastic public." During his second season Mr. Sinclair earned a great deal of praise, especially with his final production of "Twelfth Night," but I think that he himself would have been the first to acknowledge how much he owed to Bertram Forsyth for the well-rounded company with which he worked. To Mr. Forsyth must be given the credit for the standard of the non-professional acting that is now being done in Toronto; that was his contribution during the five years that he worked here. He taught many of our best players all that they know; he drew out the best that was in several of our natural actors; and he made known a large number of men and women who had been appearing with such excellent organizations as the Dickens' Fellowship. Mr. Forsyth could teach amateurs to act, and that is why he proved such an invaluable man at that stage of the development of the non-professional movement.

All Mr. Sinclair's best work was done with players who had made their reputation before he came to the city, and I have yet to hear any of the say that they learned anything from him as they acknowledge their indebtedness to Bertram Forsyth. He made good use of the material that was placed in his hands, but added nothing to it. It seems a pity that a well-informed theatrical paper like the "Theatre Arts Monthly" should fail to give credit where credit is due, especially when Mr. Sinclair has enjoyed so much other success. Of course, their informant in Toronto is probably to blame, but anybody who has followed the growth of the amateur movement in Toronto should not have been guilty of such an error. We are building on a strong foundation, for which the late Bertram Forsyth deserves all the honor.

### CARROLL AIKINS' SEASON

The director from Western Canada had everything with him when he came to Hart House Theatre last October. Everybody was pre-disposed to like and support him, and none of those who came before him had that good fortune. He found plenty of well-trained actors and actresses, all of them eager to perform. He was called upon to do only five productions; when poor Walter Sinclair came to Toronto, the Syndics set him the task of staging 15 plays, mostly mediocre London failures, in one season. There was no opposition of any kind, and no petty interference. Altogether, Mr. Aikins was very happily circumstanced.

If one may judge from Carroll Aikins' first season, he has an instinct for putting on a good show. It is not easy to describe why some men do that so much better than others, but the fact remains that when certain directors complete the finishing touches of a production, they have put into those things that appeal to the play-going public, whereas another director with just as much technical skills, leaves them out. All the plays presented at Hart House Theatre this season, no matter how different in character, contained the qualities that make a show. They left me with the impression that Carroll Aikins is an instinctive showman.

A great many of us were delighted also to find him interested in the art theatre. His production of "Romeo and Juliet," a very original experiment, indicated that he has ideas, and is not afraid to try them out. During Walter Sinclair's regime, nothing experimental was done at the Hart House Theatre. He was quite out of sympathy with the art theatre, and looked upon it as an affectation. He was quite ready to support that viewpoint, and as a consequence was rather at a loss in the presentation of a play like "The Toy Cart," which has to be done in an imaginative manner. But Carroll Aikins has returned to the earlier tradition of Hart House. Without showing Roy Mitchell's inclination to give undue importance to the backgrounds of every play, he was not afraid to do "Romeo and Juliet" in a new way.

INDIVIDUAL PERFORMANCES

Of course, his actors have given him splendid assistance, and there have been numerous individual performances that should go on the Hart House honor roll, even though it only exists in the memory of the patrons. "The Swan" was the weakest of the productions, but it contained two excellent impersonations, Miss Agnew Muldrew as the Princess Maria Dominica and Archibald Swan as Father Hyacinth. In "The Doctor's Dilemma," which followed next, Ivor Lewis did one of the most natable [sic] pieces of acting of the season as Sir Patrick Cullen, and he scored again in February as John Rutherford Sr. in "Rutherford and Son." Mr. Lewis was the outstanding figure of the year. In the Shaw play Dixon Wagner was superb as Louis Dubedat, a role in which his unusual talent obviously reveled, and in the same production Monroe Grier did the best work of his career as an actor. There was not a weak performer in that offering.

Several details of "Alice in Wonderland" come back to the memory—H.E. Hitchman reciting "Jaberwocky," the White Queen (Miss Cotter) and the Red Queen (Mrs. MacMillan) badgering Alice, the battle of Tweedledee and Tweedledum, and the trial scene. Clearest of all, one recalls the perfect impersonation of Alice done by Margaret Wilson, who might have been one of Sir John Tenniel's illustrations come to life. Miss Wilson was the find of the season, and she did a lovely Juliet in the closing bill. In Merrill Denison's "The Prize Winner," part of the Canadian week, Edgar Stone played brilliantly as the village half-wit, and one must not forget Mrs. Frances Rostance as the nurse in "Romeo and Juliet."

It has not yet been announced whether Mr. Aikins will return to the Hart House Theatre for a second season. Everybody hopes that he will accept the appointment. All the other directors have done better in their second seasons, so we could hope for some outstanding weeks. It is well known that Mr. Aikins favors the policy of fewer plays and more time spent in preparation for each one.

### "To Again Direct." *Star* 8 October 1928.

TO AGAIN DIRECT

Carroll Aikens [sic] will again be director of Hart House theatre and will arrive from Naramata, B.C., this month. The Hart House season will be short, opening with a Christmas production of "The Bluebird." The other productions listed are "Juno and the Paycock," the program of Canadian plays, and Shakespeare's "Anthony and Cleopatra."

**Star 5 March 1929.**

Mr. Carroll Aikins, director of Hart House theatre, is in Winnipeg attending the funeral of his uncle, the late lieutenant-governor of Manitoba. Mr. Aikins is returning to town to-morrow.

**"Hart House Director Embraces New Work." *Star* 22 September 1929.**

*Carroll Aikins Arrives in Toronto Enthusiastic Over Season's Plans*

Carroll Aikins, appointed director of the Hart House theatre for the coming season, arrived in town yesterday and is already taking charge of activities at the playhouse in Queen's Park. Mr. Aikins is a Canadian by birth and hails from Naramata, British Columbia, where he owns a ranch.

Seen by The Star to-day, Mr. Aikins expressed his delight with the theatre of which he is to be director, and considered it possessed of very fine equipment technically and an excellent stage. He is greatly impressed by the quality of previous Hart House productions, which be believes have been notable for artistic work, both in acting and scene designing. He stated that Hart House theatre was in the very forefront of the experimental theatre movement, and was considered so not only in Canada but also in the United States. It had been a real asset to the cultural life of Canada, Mr. Aikins asserted.

"I am very pleased with the selection of plays to be offered this season, which have been arranged by the theatre syndics in conjunction with myself," said the new director. "I am looking forward to the approaching season with a great deal of pleasure."

The plays to be produced have not all been arranged, but they will include Ferenc Molnar's comedy, "The Swan"; Bernard Shaw's "The Doctor's Dilemma," and Shakespeare's "Romeo and Juliet." Mr. Aikins is greatly interested in the Hart House group of players, and is willing to do his utmost to help any untried aspirants for dramatic honors, not only in the university, but elsewhere.

The new director is not a stranger to Toronto, for he has visited the city every few years. He declared this morning he was more than ever impressed by the growth and prosperity of the city and was looking forward very much to having the next six months here.

Mr. Aikins comes of well-know stock, being a grandson of the late Senator J. C. Aikins of Toronto and a nephew of Sir James Aikins, Winnipeg. He has had considerable experience in theatre work having built and equipped an art theatre on his ranch in the Okanagan valley, British Columbia, where he has produced many plays and given training to a number of young Canadian actors and actresses who are now on the stage in the United States.

Mr. Aikins is also a playwright of no mean ability. He is the author of the Indian play, "The God of Gods," which has been produced in Hart House theatre and also in England. He is also known as a poet. He is accompanied here by his wife, who is an actress of talent and experience, and is associated with her husband in dramatic work.

Greatly interested in the general development of Canadian drama and literature, the new director expressed the opinion that there was undoubted future of much promise in this branch of the national life. He stated that there was already a small body of Canadian drama and this would grow[.][viii]

**Berte Berry. "Carroll Aikins: Poet, playwright & theatre founder put Naramata on the map." *British Columbia History* 39.3 (2006): 4.**

*This article comes from the Naramata Heritage Museum, new members of the B.C. Historical Federation. Carroll Aikins' daughter, Mrs. Arnold Beichman still lives in the community and is involved as one of their historians.*

Carroll Aikins, poet, playwright and drama director, was a romantic, looked liked one and lived like one. He was one of the most distinguished citizens of the Okanagan, and for a while, put Naramata on the map in the minds of people in eastern Canada, England and the United States. Born in 1888 into a distinguished family, Carroll Aikins might have been expected to follow a successful business or political career. His maternal grandfather, the honorable Charles Carroll Colby, represented Stanstead, Quebec, in the House of Commons from 1867 to 1891. Described as one of the ablest debaters ever heard in the house, he was president of the Privy Council under Sir John A. Macdonald and author of *Parliamentary Government in Canada*. Atkins' [sic] uncle, C.W. Colby, was a professor of history at McGill University and author of *Canadian Types of the Old Regime* and *The Founders of New France*. Later, he became a very successful businessman. On his father's side, his grandfather, James Cox Aikins was Secretary of State under Macdonald and became Lieutenant Governor of Manitoba, a position which his uncle, Sir J.A.M. Aikins, held later. Carroll's father, Somerset Aikins, briefly sat in the Manitoba Legislature.

Carroll was educated in Winnipeg at St. John's, a private school run by the Anglican Church. He later spent some time in Europe with a tutor, where possibly he acquired his love of the theatre. For one or two winters, he went to school in Dijon, France, he travelled in Germany with his mother and acquired sufficient knowledge of German to translate into English a German book on Buddhist thought, and he spent one term at McGill University. He may not have liked formal academic studies but his health may also have been a problem. Because of a spot on his lung, he spent several years in Sicily and Tunisia. Then in 1908, when he was 20, his father bought him orchard land at Naramata. He gladly left his Winnipeg environment and came west for adventure. He started to clear and plough the land with the help of Chinese workers. Eventually, he owned 100 acres of orchard. "I took to the whole thing like a duck to the water," he told a neighbour, "It was an adventure." In 1913, he married Katherine Foster, daughter of the American Consul-General in Ottawa and brought his cultivated bride, a graduate of Vassar College, to the raw young community of Naramata, with its lack of electricity and other amenities. Mrs. Aikins later spoke of their honeymoon in Windermere where their car was a novelty to residents who had never seen one and for which they had to have gas brought from Golden, in four gallon cans which cost one dollar each.

During the 1914–1918 war, Carroll tried to enlist in the ambulance corps but was rejected because of his health, so with imagination, ingenuity and enthusiasm, he continued to develop his orchard. For instance, one scorching summer a lot of the young trees were suffering, so he rushed to Vancouver, and not finding a diesel engine to serve as a pump, he quickly bought a fire engine.

Obviously enjoying its dramatic effect, he recalled, "It had a superb lot of brass and a bell which was worked by a foot pedal. It arrived on a flat car at Arawana and was driven down triumphantly, the bell clanging all the way." In the meantime, the Chinese workers had assembled lengths of pipe up the cliff from the lake to provide water, and they busily stoked the fire engine with coal night and day until the weather changed and relieved the distress of the trees. A few years later, in 1920, Aikins again demonstrated his ingenuity when, to provide electricity for his theatre, he attached a generator from an abandoned mine to his tractor.

His little theatre represented his long interest in the literary arts. His poem, "A Prairie Cabin," originally published in 1917 in a book of his poems, was later included in an anthology of Canadian poetry for use in British Columbia Schools. He also wrote plays. In 1919, the Birmingham Repertory Theatre in England produced his play, "The God of Gods" which deals with a romantic subject; a pair of tragic North American Indian lovers caught in a web of superstition. It is doubtful if the customs described ever existed, but the situation is full of drama and colour. A Birmingham reporter described it as "one of those rare artistic delicacies reserved for the favor of the comparatively small band of enthusiastic people who delight in "art for art's sake" [sic]. The play was revived in 1931, playing at the Everyman Theatre in Hampstead, England.

As the following article notes, Aikins hoped to found a Canadian theatre with Canadian playwrights and actors. Aspiring young students would come to Naramata to pick fruit in the daytime and to study and rehearse plays in the evening. In recording the early history of the theatre, Mrs. Aikins recalled how her husband, frustrated because he could not go to England to see the production of "The God of Gods," began to think in terms of having his own theatre to produce plays by himself and other young Canadian authors. He designed the building himself but secured the assistance of "Lee Simonson, dean of New York theatre architecture and lighting to help with all the details" in creating this "first 'Little Theatre' in western Canada or [western] United States to have a cyclorama, or sky dome, that received all the sight lines from the audience, the stage was not raised at all but all the seats were raised and were 20 feet from the proscenium. This gave an unexpected sense of distance and illusion of reality and intimacy." Mrs. Aikins paid particular attention to the lighting system, "a fascinating innovation," that Simonson designed. "The dimmer box with flexible levers for changing and lowering lights, was in a platform in the floor just in front of the seating and was raised or lowered from the packing house below by a jack system. Spotlights and larger banks of lights were used both on the beams, high above the stage, and from the wings on both sides."

Above the stage were dressing rooms and on the side a scenery workshop with a large paint table described by Aikins himself that included "compartments for different colors of calciums, brushes and all painting requirements" as well as "tools for making scenery flats, covered with burlap, beaverboard for silhouettes of mountains or houses and towns, and lumber for simple platforms and steps for interiors." They also had on hand material for costumes. All of the students had to learn about sets and lighting.

After Prime Minister Arthur Meighen formally opened the building, Aikins "had a trial production of 'The Tinkers Wedding' using boys working on the farm and other locals, including Gladys Robinson who was a steady and charming recruit to our group. Dorothy Robinson became a skilled manipulator of the lights and dimmer box." The play, Mrs. Aikins admitted, was a "ridiculous" one "to attempt as a FIRST. We played it just once to a farm audience and friends and there wasn't a smile to encourage us. We knew how terrible it was but learned a lot from it. That was the early fall of 1920. That winter we worked recruiting a group of students and a teacher of dancing from the New York Neighborhood Playhouse, also a brilliant pianist Henrietta Micchelson. Students came from Vancouver, Toronto, London, Ontario, Hamilton and Calgary."

Mrs. Aikins continued: "After a busy winter of organization, including turning the old barn into a communal dining room which continued to have a slight "horsey" odor in spite of much scrubbing and calcimining, we found ourselves with a local group that wanted to help, both with the technical side and acting and proceeded with our first public production of two short plays "Neighbours" by Zona Gale and "Will O the Wisp" by Doris [Halman]. Taking part in the first were Mrs. Ruth Rounds, Miss L Young and Mr. and Mrs. Alex McNicoll of Penticton. Others were Mrs. Gwen Robinson, Miss B. May, Mrs. Miller and behind the scene music was provided by Mr. Keith Whimster on violin and myself on the piano. These two plays went very well and we had a good audience. Harold Mitchell was a tower of strength behind scenes, changing scenery and adjusting lights. I remember "fluffing" some lines in one of the plays, to my horror but the rest of the cast carried on nobly and no one knew that I had skipped some lines." As Mrs. Aikins observed, "The whole Little Theatre was a distinguished achievement. There were write ups in papers and magazines in the east and west and a call went out for students who might like to earn their way picking fruit and the result was astonishing. It appealed strongly to the mood of the 20's."

Alas, the ambitious plans made by the Aikins and their enthusiastic students were not fulfilled. The demise of the little theatre must have disappointed the residents of the valley who had enthusiastically supported it. The company never went on tour and the theatre had to be abandoned. The packing house was later torn down and only the first floor, which was used for storage, can still be seen from Aikins Loop. Who knows if the plans might have been carried out if the fruit industry had not gone into a decline and Carroll had not found himself heavily in debt. Finances had been very difficult for some time even before the decline in the fruit industry. His daughters tell the amusing story of an example of his aristocratic contempt for the mundane matter of money. A representative of the family in Winnipeg had been sent to warn him to stop pouring so much money into the theatre. In fact, that gentleman told him if he continued such extravagance his children would be going without clothes. "In that case" said Carroll magnificently, "they shall grow fur!" He told a neighbour that he never opened bills or letters from the bank but threw them instead into an old top hat (his older-son thinks into a wire basket)[.] When a little money came in he would pick one bill at random and pay it. One day he went into the bank to see about his usual overdraft, but a cheque from Winnipeg had covered it but Carroll had not opened the bank's letter telling him of this. Asked by Charlie Bennett, the bank manager, how he knew when he had an overdraft, he replied, "I get a burning feeling in the seat of my pants!"

To earn a living after the fruit industry declined, Carroll taught drama in Vancouver for a winter or two. Then in 1927 he accepted Vincent Massey's offer to direct the Hart House Theatre in Toronto where his productions were well reviewed but after two seasons a difference with Mr. Massey over programming resulted in his departure for New York where he failed to find employment. He turned next to Hollywood, hoping to have a play he had written about Paul Bunyan filmed. However, he refused to abandon his artistic standards in commercially minded Hollywood and returned home though not before giving their daughter Katherine a chance to go to school with Jackie Cooper and other child actors.

After 1929, Carroll directed his talents and energies into building a new home on the lake. Not having money for the house, he began with the extensive walls, which his elder son, The Honorable Mr. Justice John S. Aikins of the B.C. Court of Appeal remembers working on it in the summers. As money came in from time to time, Aikins planted the stately pyramidalis trees that line the driveway and the large gardens along Arawana Creek. He also built a large, attractive cabin on Beaconsfield Mountain where he could get away from it all on occasion. Not until after the Second World War, when they received an inheritance, did the Aikins complete their beautiful home. They were able to spend their winters in the southern United States, Mexico, or in Europe, where Mrs. Aikins died while on a cruise in the Mediterranean. She is buried in Aden. Carroll died in Vancouver in 1967 and is buried in the Naramata cemetery.

Mrs. Arnold Beichman (Carroll), his younger daughter, who now owns the family home, describes him as very western in sentiment, particularly enjoying the tales of pioneer times told by his rancher friends. He was a cultivated man with a charming manner, who enjoyed living in gracious surroundings with all the luxuries he could afford. Carroll Aikins has left a memory of himself as a man of artistic talent and vision, many years ahead of his time in his attempt to found a national theatre. He is also remembered for his generosity in lending books from his extensive library that a newspaper described as perhaps the most comprehensive collection of books in Canada. His poems, though few in number, deserve to be remembered. Perhaps his romantic spirit can be felt best in his poem "In The Orchard"

I see God in my orchard every hour
And in the downward pulses of the sun
I reel his heart beat
And in the vast unventured hills I see
The awful measure of his majesty.

*The following was originally published in Saturday Night Women's Edition, December 1921. It was written by Gertrude E. S. Pringle.*

## THE HOME THEATRE IN THE OKANAGAN

It is surely unique to find a perfectly appointed little theatre in the midst of a huge orchard, far removed from the din and surging crowds of city life with which theatres are usually associated. A theatre that starts out by being so original must perforce possess strong reasons for existing. In this case, The Home Theatre at Naramata B.C., in the heart of the famed Okanagan fruit producing district, is the outcome of a poet's idealism and far seeing patriotism. The exquisite beauty of the surroundings, the blue Okanagan Lake, the purply blue mountains reflected in its depths, the primeval pines and sloping orchards must be so much more inspiring to the seeker after beauty than the crowded city.

Mr. Carroll Aikins, the founder is the author of a book of poems and a play entitled, "THE GOD OF GODS", which was recently produced with great success in Birmingham, England. In building the Home Theatre he had two aims. One was to enlist talented votaries, both young men and women, and after trying them out to find ten of outstanding ability to form a company of professional Canadian players to tour Canada. The other aim was to produce plays by Canadian writers. Hitherto, all young Canadians who have felt drawn to the stage either as actors or playwrights have been impelled to market their gifts across the border where gradually they were absorbed by the American stage and so lost their identity as Canadians.

By providing opportunities to employ such talent in Canada, this loss could be prevented, Mr. Aikins believes, and our national life strengthened and unified.

To talented young men and women, Mr. Aikins offers free training for the stage in a thorough way, involving an all around knowledge of the working operations of a theatre. They even learn to paint the scenery and operate the lighting effects. Young people from any port of Canada are invited to take the training which is absolutely free of charge. The season of the Home Theatre opens in mid April and lasts until October. Board can be had at neighbouring homes for $8.00 per week, and during the fruit season of about fourteen weeks the students can earn the amount weekly by picking fruit four hours per day. It is planned to produce three complete plays each season. Although a considerable amount of money must have been expended to bring about such a gem of a little theatre, the scheme is not a money making one. No returns are looked for until such time as the Canadian Players are an established fact. The Home Theatre was formally opened in June 1921, by Hon. Arthur Meighen, Premier of Canada. On that occasion, Mr. Aikins gave concrete expression to his aims, stating that in part: "We feel that we have reached a point in our history where we may look for a Canadian literature to record Canadian achievements, and it is in this faith that we have built this theatre for the giving of Canadian plays by Canadian actors. We hope that it will be used by the young actor as a training ground for his abilities, and by the young poet as a testing ground for his work; and we have great pleasure of offering it to them for the service of beauty and for a true expression of the Canadian spirit." The plays given on that occasion by the Canadian player, students were "The Neighbours" by Zona Gale and "Will O the Wisp" by Doris [Halman]. The second series of plays took place in September last, when "The Maker of Dreams" by Oliphant Down, was produced and also in part, "The Trojan Woman" by Euripides, which was impressively beautiful in colour, grouping and the classic spirit. Indicating the spirit underlying the productions is the printed notice on the back of the programs, requesting a candid anonymous criticism of the plays, the settings and the manner of production.

Although this little theatre is on the top floor of a large fruit packing house, it is one of the best appointed in Canada. Indeed its lighting effects are not surpassed in any theatre on this Continent. The colour organ or dimmer box was made specially in New York and by its use, exquisite and beautiful colour effects are produced. The dome sky, the only one of its kind in Canada is the result of much persevering work, the beautiful back curve being established as a result of many experiments. A 10 watt lamp gives brilliant light when needed and when transfused into marvelous colours and thrown on the soft stage curtains made of grey flannelette, they are made to look like richest velvet, or like dim distance on the darkest night or flame in orange hues of a stormy sunset. The 100 seats are stained green in Mission style, each one numbered. The curtains and carpeting are also green. One end of the theatre is furnished charmingly with a large oriental rug and quaint old English furniture as a little foyer where the play can be discussed between acts. A concert grand piano is part of the equipment and in the girl's dressing room, a shower bath has been installed.

Mr. Carroll Aikins, who was a nephew of Sir. J. Aikins, Lieut. Governor of Manitoba, has a beautiful home on this 100 acre orchard, where some years ago he planted nearly all the trees himself. His living room is an inviting place to work in, with its huge log burning on the open hearth, Oriental rugs, antique furniture and a deep chesterfield, and a view of surpassing beauty looking on lake and mountains. One noted also a business-like typewriter, which Mrs. Aikins, who is deeply interested in her husband's work, has learned to operate. She also takes an active part in the production of the plays. Mere description fails to bring about the realization of the beauty of the scenery in that glorious Okanagan country. Talented young aspirants for dramatic fame who journey to Naramata to become students at the Home Theatre are to be envied for a combination of fruit picking and rehearsals, interspersed by study, and music, in such inspiring settings must needs prove a life of great fascination. Then too, Mr. and Mrs. Aikins are both young and enthusiastic and live for the finer things of life. On asking Mr. Aikins if he had any difficulty in finding talented students, he replied that there were plenty of clever girls, but he particularly wanted young men who were not too proud to act.

NOTES

i. The lines are illegible.

ii. James Fenimore Cooper is an American writer best known for his novel *The Last of the Mohicans* (1826) and its romantic depiction of aboriginal peoples.

iii. Ivor Brown's review was likely from *The Observer*—a weekly newspaper published on Sundays—because Brown was a theatre critic for the journal in 1929, and 23 August 1931 was a Sunday.

iv. Line is missing.

v. The author and source are not included on this newspaper clipping from the Victoria and Albert Museum's Theatre and Performance Archives (PN2598.M6754 Pamphlet).

vi. *Kuppelhorizont*: A German term that translates as "dome horizon"; it references set designer Mario Fortuny's "sky-dome," a 1902 antecedent to a cyclorama.

vii. The theatre forecast for the other theatres has been omitted.

viii. Because the newspaper clipping ends here with no final punctuation, it is unclear whether this point marks the end of the article.

# Works Cited


Aikins, Carroll. "The Destroyers: A Drama in Three Acts." N.d. MS. Mount Saint Vincent University Library, Canadian Drama Collection. Print.

——. "The Fullness of Life: A Play in Three Acts." N.d. MS. Mount Saint Vincent University Library, Canadian Drama Collections. Print.

——. "The God of Gods." *Canadian Plays from Hart House Theatre*. Vol. 2. Ed. Vincent Massey. Toronto: Macmillan of Canada, 1927. 1–67. Print.

——. "The God of Gods: A Play in Three Acts." N.d. MS. Mount Saint Vincent University Library, Canadian Drama Collections. Print.

——. "Real Estate: A Comedy in Three Acts." N.d. MS. Mount Saint Vincent University Library, Canadian Drama Collections. Print.

"A New Production at the Repertory Theatre: Magic at the Empire." Rev. of *The God of Gods*, dir. A.E. Filmer. *Birmingham Gazette* Nov. 1919. Print.

"A Reader's Notes: Books Are a Finer World within the World." Rev. of *The God of Gods*, dir. A.E. Filmer. *Winnipeg Free Press* Dec. 1919. Print.

Aronoff, Eric. "Anthropologists, Indians, and New Critics: Culture and/as Poetic Form in Regional Modernism." *Modern Fiction Studies* 55.1 (Spring 2009): 92–118. Print.

Aschheim, Steven E. *The Nietzsche Legacy in Germany, 1890–1990*. Berkeley: U of California P, 1992. Print.

Barbeau, Marius. *The Downfall of Temlaham*. Toronto: The Macmillan Company of Canada, 1928. Print.

Bendell, Ernest A. "Lord Chamberlain's Plays Supplementary Papers: Registers of Licenses for Theatres, 1898–1921." 27 Oct. 1919. MS. British Library Manuscript Collection, Add. 61955. Print.

Berry, Berte. "Carroll Aikins: Poet, Playwright & Theatre Founder Put Naramata on the Map." *British Columbia History* 39.3 (2006): 4–7. Print.

"Birmingham Repertory Theatre Scrapbook." Held by the Central Library, Chamberlain Square, Birmingham, United Kingdom. Print, Photograph.

Blavatsky, Helena Petrovna. *The Key to Philosophy: Ethics, Science, and Philosophy, for the Study of which the Theosophical Society Has Been Founded*. London: Theosophical Publishing Society, 1893. Print.

Bremmer, J. N. "Greek Normative Animal Sacrifice." *A Companion to Greek Religion*. Ed. D. Ogden. Oxford: Blackwell Publishing Ltd, 2007. 132–44. Print.

Brewster, Muriel. "Canadian Players and Plays to Tour World?: This Is Hope of Carroll Aikens Guest Director of Hart House Theatre." *Star Weekly* 3 Dec. 1927. Print. Hart House Theatre Archives A73-0026/003(41).

Brigg, Peter. "The 'God of Gods' Première: Birmingham, 1919." *Canadian Drama* 3 (1977): 23–36. Print.

Brown, Ivor. "'The God of Gods.' By Carroll Aikins." Rev. of *The God of Gods*, dir. A.E. Filmer. [*The Observer*?] 23 Aug. 1931. Print. PN2598.M6754 Pamphlet. Everyman Theatre 1931 "The God of Gods." Theatre and Performance Archives, Victoria and Albert Museum, London.

Bullough, Vern L. "Transvestites in the Middle Ages." *American Journal of Sociology* 79.6 (1974): 1381–94.

"Canadian Director: Hart House Theatre: Carroll Aikins, Naramata, B.C., to Direct Next Year—Walter Sinclair Away." *Toronto Daily Star* 24 Aug. 1927. Print.

"The Canadian Players." *Christian Science Monitor* 18 Aug. 1924: 6.

*Canadian Theosophical Association*. 2008. Web.

"Cannibal." Noun 1. Def. 1a. *OED Online*. Web.

"Carroll Aikins." Photo. *Saturday Night* 3 Sept. 1927. Hart House Theatre Archives A73-0026/003(41).

"Carroll Aikins, New Director at Hart House, Is Interviewed." *Globe and Mail* 15 Oct. 1927. Print. Hart House Theatre Archives A73-0026/003(41).

"Carroll Aikins Will Direct Hart House Theatre." *University of Toronto Monthly* 1 Oct. 1927: xxviii. Article, Photo, Hart House Theatre Programme. Hart House Theatre Archives A73-0026/003(41).

Charlesworth, Hector. Rev. of *The God of Gods*. *Saturday Night* 29 April 1922. Print.

Clifford, James. *The Predicament of Culture: Twentieth-Century Ethnography, Literature, and Art*. Cambridge, Mass.: Harvard UP, 1988. Print.

Clough, Betty. "Carroll Aikins." *42nd Report of the Okanagan Historical Society*. Vernon, B.C.: Okanagan Historical Society, 1978. 121. Print.

"Coming Attractions: What Playhouses and Concert Producers Say of Their Performances." *Globe* 13 Apr. 1922: 14. Print.

Cornelia. "Now Canada Will Develop National Theatre." *Telegraph* 16 Nov. 1927. Print. Hart House Theatre Archives A73-0026/003(41).

Cranston, Sylvia. *H.P.B.: The Extraordinary Life and Influence of Helena Blavatsky, Founder of the Modern Theosophical Movement*. New York: Jeremy P. Tarcher and Putnam Books, 1994. Print.

Crotch, William. *Specimens of Various Styles of Music, Referred to in a Course of Lectures Read at Oxford and London*. 3 vols. London: Robert Birchall, 1808–09. Print.

Duchesne, Scott. "The Impossible Theatre: Roy Mitchell and *The Chester Mysteries*: Experience, Initiation and Brotherhood." *Theatre Research in Canada / Recherches théâtrales au Canada* 27.2 (2006): 227–44. Print.

Eliot, T. S. "Ulysses, Order, and Myth." *Selected Prose of T.S. Eliot*. Ed. Frank Kermode. London: Faber & Faber, 1975. 175–178. Print.

En'owkin Centre. The Okanagan First Peoples. Web.

"Everyman Theatre: Reopening under New Management." *Times* (London) 12 Aug. 1931. Print.

"Feathers and Faith: Red Indian Play at the Repertory." Rev. of *The God of Gods*, dir. A.E. Filmer. *Birmingham Gazette* Nov. 1919. Print.

Feddema, J.P. (Hans). "The 'Lesser' Violence of Animal Sacrifice: A Somewhat Hidden and Overlooked (Ignored?) Reality in Sinhala Buddhism." *Anthropos* 90 (1995): 133–148. Print.

Feldman, George Franklin. *Cannibalism, Headhunting and Human Sacrifice in North America: A History Forgotten*. Chambersburg: Alan C. Hood, 2008. Print.

Filewod, Alan. *Committing Theatre: Theatre Radicalism and Political Intervention in Canada*. Toronto: Between the Lines, 2011. Print.

——. ed. *Eight Men Speak: A Political Play in Six Acts*. Ottawa: U of Ottawa P, 2013. Print.

Frank, Joseph. *The Idea of Spatial Form*. New Brunswick: Rutgers UP, 1991.

"Fresh Start at the Everyman." *Western Morning News and Mercury* 27 August 1931. Print.

"The God of Gods." Rev. of *The God of Gods*, dir. A.E. Filmer. *Birmingham Evening Despatch*. 10 Nov. 1919. Print.

"The God of Gods." Rev. of *The God of Gods*, dir. A.E. Filmer. *Birmingham Post and Journal* 10 Nov. 1919. Print.

"The God of Gods." Rev. of *The God of Gods*, dir. A.E. Filmer. *Stage* 13 Nov. 1919. Print.

*The God of Gods: An American Indian Play by Carroll Aitkins* [sic]. Birmingham Repertory Theatre 8 Nov. 1919. Playbill.

"The God of Gods: American-Indian Play by Carroll Aitkins [sic]. Produced for the First Time on Any Stage at the Birmingham Repertory Theatre on Sunday, Nov. 9." Rev. of *The God of Gods*, dir. A.E. Filmer. *Era* 12 Nov. 1919. Print.

"Grouse." Def. 1a. *OED Online*. Web.

"Grouse." Def. 1b. *OED Online*. Web.

"Hart House Director Embraces New York: Carroll Aikins Arrives in Toronto Enthusiastic over Season's Plans." *Star* 22 Sept. 1929. Print. Hart House Theatre Archives A73-0026/003(41).

"Hart House Syndics Name New Director: Carroll Aikins Comes to Theatre From B.C. for 1927–28." *Globe* 24 August 1927: 9. Print.

"Hart House Theatre: 'God of Gods,' Strange Mixture of Barbaric Mysticism." *Globe* 19 Apr. 1922. Print.

"Hart House Theatre under New Director: Carroll Aikins Comes to the University as Guest Director." *Varsity* 29 Sept. 1927. Print. Hart House Theatre Archives A73-0026/003(41).

Henderson, Craig. Personal Interview. 27 Jul. 2014.

Hoffman, James. "Carroll Aikins and the Home Theatre." *Theatre Research in Canada/ Recherches théâtrales au Canada* 7.1 (Spring 1986): 50–70. Web.

——. "Naramata Pioneers: Katherine and Carroll C. Aikins." Ed. Glenda Emerson. Newsletter of the Okanagan Archive Trust Society 1.5 (Winter 2009): 12–14. Web.

Huhndorf, Shari M. *Going Native: Indians in the American Cultural Imagination.* Ithaca: Cornell UP, 2001. Print.

Innes, Christopher. "Modernism in Drama." *The Cambridge Companion to Modernism.* 2nd ed. Cambridge: Cambridge UP, 2011. 128–54.

Irving, Howard. "Empiricism, Ideology and William Crotch's *Specimens*." *Nineteenth-Century Music Review* 9.2 (2012): 237–53. Print.

Jacob, Fred. "Monday Nighter at Large." *Globe and Mail* 7 Apr. 1928. Print. Hart House Theatre Archives A75-0009.

Johnston, Lukin. "Canadian Playwright Meets with London Stage Success." Rev. of *The God of Gods*, by Everyman Theatre. *Province* 6 Sept. 1931. Print.

Kornhaber, David. "The Philosopher, the Playwright, and the Actor: Friedrich Nietzsche and the Modern Drama's Concept of Performance." *Theatre Journal* 64.1 (2012): 25–40.

Lacombe, Michele. "Theosophy and the Canadian Idealist Tradition: A Preliminary Exploration." *Journal of Canadian Studies* 17.2 (Summer 1998): 100–17. Print.

L., E. "'The God of Gods.' A Drama by Carroll Aikins." Rev. of *The God of Gods*, dir. A. E. Filmer. 18 Aug. 1931. Print. PN2598.M6754 Pamphlet. Everyman Theatre 1931 "The God of Gods." Theatre and Performance Archives, Victoria and Albert Museum, London.

Lester, Gordon. "The God of Gods." *Canadian Adaptations of Shakespeare Project.* University of Guelph, n.d. Web. 16 Feb. 2010.

"Life, Letters, and the Arts: A Theatre in the Wilderness." *The Living Age* 3 Mar. 1923: 549. Print.

Malinowski, Bronislaw. "Kula: The Circulating Exchange of Valuables in Archipelagoes of Eastern New Guinea." *Man* 20 (1920): 97–105. Print.

Maracle, Lee, Jeannette C. Armstrong, Delphine Derickson, and Greg Young-Ing, eds. *We Get Our Living Like Milk from the Land.* Penticton, B. C.: Theytus Books, 1994. Print.

Massey, Vincent, ed. *Canadian Plays from Hart House Theatre.* Vol. 2. Toronto: Macmillan of Canada, 1927. Print.

——. "Prospects of a Canadian Drama." *Queen's Quarterly* 30: 194–212. Print.

Matthews, Bache. *A History of the Birmingham Repertory Theatre.* London: Chatto and Windus, 1924. Print.

Mauss, Marcel. *The Gift: The Form and Reason for Exchange in Archaic Societies.* Trans. W.D. Halls. London: Routledge, 1990. Print.

McCann, Gillian. *Vanguard of the New Age: the Toronto Theosophical Society, 1891–1945.* Montreal: McGill-Queen's UP, 2012. Print.

Mitchell, Roy. *Creative Theatre.* New Jersey: Kindle, 1969. Print.

——. *Theosophy in Action.* Toronto: Blavatsky Institute, 1951. Print.

Mojica, Monique and Ric Knowles, ed. *Staging Coyote's Dream: An Anthology of First Nations Drama in English.* Toronto: Playwrights Canada P, 2003. Print.

Nietzsche, Friedrich. *The Birth of Tragedy.* Ed. Raymond Geuss and Ronald Speirs. Trans. Ronald Speirs. Cambridge: Cambridge UP, 1999. Print.

——. *The Gay Science.* Ed. Bernard Williams. Trans. Josefine Nauckhoff. Cambridge: Cambridge P, 2001. Print.

*Okanagan Nation Alliance.* Web.

O'Neill, Patrick. "Carroll Aikins's Experiments in Playwriting." *B.C. Studies* 137 (Spring 2003): 65–91. Print.

P. P. "The God of Gods." Rev. of *The God of Gods,* dir. A.E. Filmer. *Evening Standard* 19 Aug. 1931. Print. PN2598.M6754 Pamphlet. Everyman Theatre 1931 "The God of Gods." Theatre and Performance Archives, Victoria and Albert Museum, London.

"Ptarmigan." Def. 1. *OED Online.* Web.

"Red Indian Drama. 'The God of Gods' at Everyman." Rev. of *The God of Gods,* dir. A.E. Filmer. 1931. Print. PN2598.M6754 Pamphlet. Everyman Theatre 1931 "The God of Gods." Theatre and Performance Archives, Victoria and Albert Museum, London.

"Repertory Theatre." Rev. of *The God of Gods,* dir. A.E. Filmer. *Midland Counties* 13 Nov. 1919. Print.

Rossetti, Gina M. *Imagining the Primitive in Naturalist and Modernist Literature.* Columbia: U of Missouri P, 2006. Print.

Ryan, Oscar, E. Cecil-Smith, H. Francis, Mildred Goldberg. *Eight Men Speak: A Political Play in Six Acts.* Ed. Alan Filewod. Ottawa: U of Ottawa P, 2013. Print.

Salting, Don. *Smile of Manitou: The History of Naramta.* Ed. Brian Wilson. Naramata, B.C.: Skookum Publications, 1982.

Sheehan, Jonathan. "The Altars of the Idols: Religion, Sacrifice, and the Early Modern Polity." *Journal of the History of Ideas* 67.4 (2006): 649–74. Print.

Smythe, Albert E. S. "A Propos to Nietzsche." *Lamp: A Theosophical Monthly* 4 (Sept. 1900): 220–23. Print.

"Song of Solomon." *The Holy Bible: King James Version.* Michigan: Zondervan, 2002. 432–34. Print.

"Squaw." Def. 1a. *OED Online.* Web.

——. Def. 1b. *OED Online.* Web.

——. Def. 3. *OED Online.* Web.

"Theatre Forecast for 1927–28: List of Attractions for the New Season as at Present Planned by Our Leading Playhouses." *Globe* 17 Sept. 1927. Print.

Canadian Theosophical Association. "The Theosophical Society." *Canadian Theosophical Association*. Web.

"To Again Direct." *Star* 8 Apr. 1928. Print. Hart House Theatre Archives A75-0009.

Usmiani, Renate. "Roy Mitchell: Prophet in Our Past." *Theatre Research in Canada / Recherches théâtrales au Canada* 8.2 (1987): n. pag. Web.

Wagar, Samuel Eldon Charles. *Theosophical Socialists in the 1920s Okanagan: Jack Logie's Social Issues Summer Camps*. MA Thesis. University College of the Fraser Valley, 2002. Print.

Wagner, Anton, ed. *A Vision of Canada: Herman Voaden's Dramatic Works 1928–1945*. Toronto: Simon & Pierre, 1993. Print.

W., H. M. "A Red Indian Theocracy: 'The God of Gods' at Everyman." Rev. of *The God of Gods*, dir. A.E. Filmer. *The Daily Telegraph* 19 Aug. 1931. Print. PN2598. M6754 Pamphlet. Everyman Theatre 1931 "The God of Gods." Theatre and Performance Archives, Victoria and Albert Museum, London.

Willmott, Glenn. *Modernist Goods: Primitivism, the Market, and the Gift*. Toronto: UTP, 2008. Print.

CANADIAN LITERATURE COLLECTION / COLLECTION DE LITTÉRATURE CANADIENNE

Series Editor: Dean Irvine

The Canadian Literature Collection / Collection de la littérature canadienne (CLC) is a series of nineteenth- to mid-twentieth-century literary texts produced in critical editions. All texts selected for the series were either out of print or previously unpublished. Each text appears in a print edition with a basic apparatus (critical introduction, explanatory notes, textual notes, and a statement of editorial principles) together with an expanded web-based apparatus (which may include alternate versions, expanded textual notes, previous editions, correspondence, photographs, source materials, and other related texts by the author).

The Literary Studies sub-series of the CLC features monographs and edited collections that complement the historical focus of these critical editions.

**Previous titles in this collection**

Miguel Mota and Paul Tiessen (editors), Chris Ackerley and David Large (annotations), *The 1940 Under the Volcano* by Malcolm Lowry, 2015

Robert D. Denham (author), *Northrop Frye and Others: Twelve Writers Who Helped Shape His Thinking*, 2015

Emily Robins Sharpe (editor), *Hugh Garner's Best Stories*, 2015

Bart Vautour (editor), *This Time a Better Earth* by Ted Allan, 2015

Patrick A. McCarthy (editor), Chris Ackerley (notes), and Vik Doyen (foreword), *In Ballast to the White Sea* by Malcolm Lowry, 2014

Ruth Panofsky (editor), *The Collected Poems of Miriam Waddington*, 2014

Michael A. Peterman (editor), *Flora Lindsay: or, Passages in an Eventful Life* by Susanna Moodie, 2014

Vik Doyen (editor), Miguel Mota (introduction), and Chris Ackerley (notes), *Swinging the Maelstrom* by Malcolm Lowry, 2013

For a complete list of our titles in this collection, see:
www.press.uottawa.ca/series/french-and-canadian-studies/canadian-literature-collection

MIX
Paper from
responsible sources
FSC® C100212

Printed in April 2016
by Gauvin Press,
Gatineau, Québec